Imagining
Democracy

Reading "The Events of May" in Thailand

CW00495763

The **Institute of Southeast Asian Studies (ISEAS)** was established as an autonomous organization in 1968. It is a regional research centre for scholars and other specialists concerned with modern Southeast Asia, particularly the many-faceted problems of stability and security, economic development, and political and social change.

The Institute's research programmes are the Regional Economic Studies (RES, including ASEAN and APEC), Regional Strategic and Political Studies (RSPS), Regional Social and Cultural Studies (RSCS), and the ASEAN Transitional Economies Programme (ATEP).

The Institute is governed by a twenty-one-member Board of Trustees comprising nominees from the Singapore Government, the National University of Singapore, the various Chambers of Commerce, and professional and civic organizations. A ten-man Executive Committee oversees day-to-day operations; it is chaired by the Director, the Institute's chief academic and administrative officer.

Imagining Democracy

Reading "The Events of May" in Thailand

by

William A. Callahan

INSTITUTE OF SOUTHEAST ASIAN STUDIES

Singapore · London

Published by
Institute of Southeast Asian Studies
Heng Mui Keng Terrace
Pasir Panjang
Singapore 119596

Internet e-mail: publish@iseas.edu.sg
World Wide Web: http://www.iseas.edu.sg/pub.html

All rights reserved. No part of this publication may be reproduced, stored in a retrieval system, or transmitted in any form or by any means, electronic, mechanical, photocopying, recording or other-wise, without the prior permission of the Institute of Southeast Asian Studies.

© 1998 Institute of Southeast Asian Studies, Singapore

The responsibility for facts and opinions expressed in this publication rests exclusively with the author and his interpretations do not necessarily reflect the views or the policy of the Institute or its supporters.

Cataloguing in Publication Data

Callahan, William A.
  Imagining democracy: reading the events of May in Thailand.
  1. Thailand--Politics and government--1976-
  2. Democracy--Thailand.
  3. Non-governmental organizations--Thailand.
  4. Thailand--Armed Forces.
  I. Title.
DS586 C15   1998   sls97-154962

ISBN 981-3055-64-2 (soft cover)

Typeset by International Typesetters Pte Ltd
Printed in Singapore by Seng Lee Press Pte Ltd

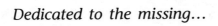

Dedicated to the missing...

CONTENTS

PREFACE

Democracy is a popular topic — especially in the past few years with the momentous events of the disintegration of the Soviet Union and liberation of Eastern Europe. There have been mass democratic movements in Asia as well: the Philippines (1986), Burma (1988), and China (1989). This book looks at differences and commonalities of these political issues through the optic of the 1992 mass movement in Thailand. Indeed, the dynamics of the events of May 1992 are exemplary in that they are explained in terms of the tortuous shift between two very different models of power and governance. The struggle between the military and the middle class demonstrators is seen as the bureaucratic polity *versus* bourgeois polity. But there are other stories....

This book is a collection of stories of "The Events of May" which were told as part of a wide discussion and debate about democracy in Thailand. Retelling these narratives together seems like the logical thing to do since the scattered events strewn over a long period of time suddenly took on a life of their own as an entity called *The Events of May* which could be analysed, dissected, commemorated, understood, criticized, and so on.[1] This crystallization was due in large part to an explosion of media production which included extensive newspaper coverage, dozens of special publications and videos, as well as the inevitable rumours, gossip, and conversations that attend such happenings. A second set of stories, what we might call secondary sources, also sprouted up; they include analytical tales produced in more academic settings to interpret just what the first set of stories meant.

In recounting these tales, I mix them together as a way of writing another interpretation of *The Events of May*. This book is not written as a search for the essential *truth* about the May massacre, so much as to see how these discourses shape our understanding of the workings of politics in May 1992 — and thus produce *truths* about Thai politics, Asian politics, and politics in general. The power of story-telling is that it works quite differently from standard social science's quest for singular truth based on a foundation of hard empirical evidence. The problem of this approach is that the complexities and inevitable contradictions of politics are often silenced by the exclusive use of such a rigorous positivistic theoretical framework: rigour also means stiff.

With story-telling we can (temporarily) suspend questions of truth/falsity to examine how the tales are told: the technologies of discourse. Indeed, as this book argues, much of the meaning of the stories of *The Events of May* comes not from the facts themselves, but from the discursive economies of the text, how the text is produced and exchanged as a social activity: who tells, what is (not) told, where it is (not) told, when it is (not) told, and who is told. Thus while reading the narratives of the May massacre with these particulars in mind, we can guard against taking the stories uncritically as universal meta-narratives of liberation, democracy, humanity, civilization, and so on.

This narrative approach to Thai politics is timely because *The Events of May* was the first popular movement to follow the disintegration of the Soviet Union,[2] which in turn also constituted a crisis for social science which relies so heavily on the bi-polar methodology that attended the bi-polar world view of the Cold War. This narrative research is also particularly appropriate to Thailand where, according to popular images, political space is populated by an assortment of angels and devils, knights on white horses, boys in green, Pied Pipers leading (stupid) buffaloes to their death, and where conflicts are periodically resolved through *deux ex machina*. It would be an understatement to say that these and other images are important. Thailand is a prime example of an economy where one's most important possession is not material, but the symbolic 'face' — which can, of course, provide the material power of capital and arms.

As the title advertises, this book is about imagining democracy. The tales selected for recirculation deal with how concepts of 'people' (Chapter 2) and 'organization' (Chapter 3) are formed, and reformed in Thai political discourse. Thus, though I talk about democracy, I intentionally avoid using the term 'democratization'. This peculiar twisting of words is only possible in an inflected language like English which can take a noun (democracy), make it a verb (democratize), and then turn it back into a noun again (democratization). Such an oblique grammar is used to tell us that "the process of becoming democratic" is straight, singular, (political) scientific, clean, and inevitable. Though the messy blood stains on the streets might call this sterile formulation into question, some labour to chart this democratization on a checklist full of the familiar essentials — free press, civil society, free and fair elections, elected prime minister, mass parties, principles over personality, and so on. Thus I avoid 'democratization' because it sounds too similar to other projects initiated in the 1950s: modernization, development, civilization, and progress which are now increasingly coming into question as the biggest process of becoming: westernization.

So to retell the democratic tales, I recall still other narratives — astrology, national security, Third World feminism, non-violent action, nationalism, poetics — and twist them together into impertinent metaphors which bring out the defining idiosyncrasies of May 1992. What is interesting about *The Events of May* is that it seems to call into question many of the things that are taken for granted in political science and Asian Studies. More and more, scholars are questioning the tradition/modernity binary in comparative analysis (where traditional is past and Oriental, modern is present and Western, and each society is judged to be one or the other). Surprisingly, *The Events of May* was not a battle set in the common spatio-temporal frame of tradition/modernity and East/West. In their political actions people on all sides mixed these metaphors, weaving them together into self/representations: how else can you explain social formations such as the 'Witchdoctors for Democracy' and the 'Sedan Mob'?

The purpose of this project is not so much to understand Thailand, if by understanding we mean taking the status quo for granted, and reduce all happenings to 'essential Thai culture' or 'the modern West'. Sometimes the oblique challenges of misunderstanding are more productive in meaning because they call into question the official stories and thus can leave room for other interpretations. Perhaps I fall into my own trap by simply trading off the binaries for trinities; but I hope that the frames that I use — physical/economic/symbolic power, public/private/ popular sector, and conventional/violent/non-violent politics — end up deconstructing themselves through blurry formulations like 'grass-roots non-violent democracy'.

The familiar narratives are decentred in an effort to look at the things that are often silenced by discourses like bureaucratic polity, political culture, and political-economics, as they have worked themselves out in Thai Studies. Certainly, as the references will attest, I use the insights that such scholars have provided. But I aim to weave them into a different tale. Rather than write another text which aims to describe Thai politics from start to finish, this project utilizes *The Events of May* as a unifying theme from which to explore democratic imaginings in Thailand. This involves a change in the starting point of analysis. Rather than starting with "Thai chiefs and their warrior bands, migrating from Southwest China" into a Thai Buddhist nation-state,[3] or beginning with "The Heritage of Political Values and Symbols",[4] a consideration of the symbolic politics of Thailand begins with an analysis of the mass rallies on the streets. Culture and history are certainly important, but all too often when they are placed at the beginning of a text, and politics is placed at the end, a discursive division between 'tradition' and 'modernity' is built up. However, traditions are rarely so static, but are continually written and rewritten according to historical and social circumstances. Thus this book is involved in two inter-related projects: to use social science methods to analyse cultural artifacts, and to use cultural theory to analyse political events. In this way I labour to place cultural practices in the foreground of politics, rather than using them as a background. Similarly, I use different temporal frames in each chapter, starting out with a tight focus in Chapter 1 on the violence during 17–20 May, then widening the frame in Chapter 2 to April–May 1992, then further in Chapter 3 to 1991–92. Chapter 4 serves as an oblique conclusion, looking specifically at the problems and possibilities of how Thais remembered the events of May between 1992 and 1995.

Hence, this project is not a linear narrative with a definite start and finish. The chapters are written to examine similar issues in different ways, in an effort to appreciate the complexities and contradictions — the multiple readings of *The Events of May* — without having to reduce the analysis to judging between civil or military, tradition or modernity, politics or economics, and so on. Thus there is repetition of arguments and sources, but I hope that this repetition shows how the same events can mean very different things, and relying on one explanation does not always do the text justice. As I argue specifically in Chapter 3, rather than simply reflecting "the truth, the whole truth, and nothing but the truth", this analysis twists new meaning out of the repetition.

Chapter 1 addresses some of the influential theoretical models which are used to explain Thai politics, and argues for a different approach which uses popular culture to examine some of the political and interpretive issues that have been silenced. This chapter highlights the symbolic workings of Thai politics to examine the peculiar economy of silence and noise, censorship and disinformation that was passed on through the popular images of facsimiles and videos.

Chapter 2 addresses the 'people' component of democracy. It questions the dominant interpretation of *The Events of May* which pits middle class against military bureaucrats — civil society against the state — by examining cultural constructions of the people, and thus people power. Through a textual analysis of both military and middle class texts, I argue that the mob is the unifying theme for the discourse of Thai politics on the streets in May 1992. 'Mob' has its own global economy of inclusion and exclusion, rationality and confusion, order and chaos, which simultaneously works in opposite directions; it helped the middle class define itself, while at the same time aiding the military to discursively site demonstrators in its cross hairs.

Chapter 3 addresses the organizational and institutional aspects of democracy. It positions the violent and chaotic mob in front of a mirror to examine its negative image: non-violent action and non-governmental organization. I use theories of 'oppositional consciousness' to imagine unity and meaning not in what people were, but in what they were against. The discursive negativity of the anti-Suchinda protests is examined to trace how they laboured to become a positive pro-democracy movement. I argue that the protests succeeded through a combination of non-violent action and non-governmental organization which radically decentred mass protests, and this strategy can have 'sustainable' effects on the society at large. Using this wider temporal frame, which links the events of May to trends in global political-economics and the February 1991 coup, helps to shift the conception of politics away from parliamentary preoccupations to broader issues of political, social, and economic development. Thus as Chapter 2 deals with the *demos*, part of democracy, Chapter 3 addresses *kratia*, the organizations of power.

Chapter 4 addresses memories of the May events, juxtaposing those of the middle class with those of the missing persons. The three sections switch between subjective and objective, the artistic and the statistic, as well as the emotional and the rational memories. In this way the memories are recalled, but in a critical way: for example, the statistics of the missing, dead, and injured are cited, while the political problems of such evidence are recorded.

The Appendix is a translation of General Issarapong Noon-packdee's written statement to the parliamentary investigative committee. I do a textual analysis of this statement in Chapter 2, and feel that it would be useful for readers to examine "The Soldiers' Story" in full for themselves.

There are many people I would like to thank for their help, comments, advice, and friendship during the course of my nearly five-year stay in Thailand during which this book was written. Firstly, I would like to thank all the people who generously made time for me to interview them; especially those in the police and the army who are missing from the bibliography. As this research began with opinion pieces published in the Bangkok press, and further developed while I was on the editorial staff at *The Nation* in 1992–93, I would like to especially thank Suthichai Yoon, Sonny

Inbaraj, and Kavi Chongkittavorn for their open-minded encouragement. Khien Theeravit and Benedict Anderson also provided much-needed academic advice and comments on this project in its early stages. My colleagues at Rangsit University, where I taught during 1993–96, added considerably to my understanding of Thai politics and society; I would especially like to thank Naruemon Thabchumpon for the lively debates we had over the course of hundreds of lunches. Duncan McCargo gave much academic support and critical friendship in our weekly 'seminars' held at various Italian restaurants around Bangkok. Chaiyan Chaiyaporn, Pitch Pongsawat, Thanes Wongyanawa, and Andrew Russo were kind enough to discuss my research with me over a beer. Other academics and activists who lent their support and made my years in Bangkok enjoyable include Anuwat Wangvanichakorn, Chaiwat Satha-anand, Dej Poomkacha, Gawin Chutima, Gothom Areeya, Kittiporn Chaiboon, Laddawan Tantiwittayaphitak, Pravit Rojan-aphruk, Prudhisan Jumbala, Surachart Bamrungsuk, Sukanya Bumroongsook, Suwanna Satha-anand, Thongchai Winichakul, Wasant Techawongtham, Withaya Sucharithanarugse, and Diana Wong. Last, but not least, I would like to thank my wife, Sumalee Bumroongsook, and her family for their loving kindness.

W.A.C.
Pathumtani, Thailand and
Durham, England

NOTES

1. This is much like how "The French Revolution" and the "Ancien Regime" were created by later politicians and historians. See Ernest P. Young, "Imagining the Ancien Regime in the Deng Era", in *Popular Protest and Political Culture in Modern China*, edited by Jeffrey N. Wasserstrom and Elizabeth J. Perry (Boulder: Westview Press, 1992), pp. 14–27.
2. Indeed, Sulak Sivaraksa was on trial in 1992–93 for a speech in August 1991 which compared the failure of the 1991 Soviet coup with the "success" of the 1991 Thai coup.

3. John L.S. Girling, *Thailand: Society and Politics* (Ithaca: Cornell University Press, 1981), p. 17.

4. David Morell and Chai-Anan Samudavanija, *Political Conflict in Thailand: Reform, Reaction and Revolution* (Cambridge, Mass.: Oelgeschlager, Gunn & Hain Publishers, Inc., 1981).

chapter 1

INTRODUCTION
Astrology, Video, and Symbolic Politics

The middle class has come of age. We feel ashamed at getting rich without true democracy.[1]

The meaning of the blood on the streets of Bangkok that Cable News Network (CNN), Nippon Hoso Kyokai (NHK), and British Broadcasting Corporation (BBC) graphically showed to the world on 17–20 May 1992 is deemed to be very clear. Commentators tell us that it was the middle class, with its new economic power, trying to wrench political power out of the hands of the military.[2] The events themselves are easy to summarize: at first the demonstration in April 1992 was against the unelected Prime Minister General Suchinda Kraprayoon. Suchinda ascended to power on 7 April under a veneer of parliamentary approval after he was invited to form a government by the coalition of pro-military parties that were elected in the March 1992 elections. Even though it was technically constitutional, many people saw this as a continuation of the military rule of the National Peace Keeping Council (NPKC), which led the coup in February 1991 against the elected government of Prime Minister General Chatichai Choonhavan.[3] As the demonstrations against the unelected Prime Minister grew in May, so did Suchinda's resolve not to step down to 'mob rule'.

The coalition parties and the military were intransigent in not compromising in the face of popular demands for an elected Prime Minister, and thus the otherwise peaceful demonstrations led to the 17–20 May massacre, which was seen as a replay of the vicious cycle of modern Thai politics, which is characterized by increasing violence.[4]

Hence after the bloodshed on 17–20 May the protest spread from opposing an unelected Prime Minister to addressing the larger structural issues of the position of the military in Thai society, politics, and economics. After Suchinda resigned on 24 May there was a demand for institutional changes in the armed forces beyond a simple change in the 'top brass'. Many pressed for these changes because they did not want to see the massacre of May 1992 lead to another army backlash; the memories of the political violence of 1973 and the 1976 right wing coup were still fresh.

This is the most convincing interpretation which makes sense of the events in May. Yet the events, and Thai politics in general, are certainly more complex, and often much less coherent. There are many stories being told — it is much more than a struggle between the middle class and the military as many commentators have interpreted.[5] It was also a popular uprising which spread far beyond the middle class and Bangkok to encompass a wide range of people who demonstrated all over Thailand: "Many have talked about the middle-class people and yuppies who joined the protest. They were recognizable with their paraphernalia such as mobile telephones. But it may be more accurate to say that the protestors came from all walks of life."[6]

If the May massacre just concerned the military and the middle class, then the analysis could be limited to official documents, stock market performance, government-generated economic statistics, and interviews with the élites to see the material power relations. But if the events of May were also a popular uprising, then popular culture could also tell us much about the symbolic workings of democracy. In this chapter, I would like to address both these questions using various methods drawn from political science, anthropology, and cultural studies as a start in the analysis of the dynamics of the physical/economic/symbolic power relations of the May uprising in Thailand.

For example, the mass rallies were multi-dimensional events which demonstrated the complexity of Thai politics and culture. Though the blood on the streets of Rajdamnoen has washed the fond memories away, the demonstrations were social events as well as political protests. From the middle of April 1992 former Member of Parliament (MP) Chalard Vorachart's hunger strike in front of Parliament was a festive rally complete with entertainment. Later when Major-General Chamlong Srimuang joined the hunger strike in May, more people came and the protest took on a carnival atmosphere which migrated between Parliament, the Royal Plaza, Sanam Luang (the Royal Parade Grounds), and Rajdamnoen Avenue. This carnival was separate from the rest of the society in the sense that social norms were suspended — people from different classes, ages, and genders mixed together to discuss politics. The demonstrations occupied a special space set off from the normal routine of traffic and pollution that characterizes Bangkok. It was also like a Buddhist temple fair with street theatre, rousing sermon-like speeches, popular music concerts, and vendors snaking their way through the crowd selling dried squid and soft drinks in a parallel economy. People laughed at the jokes the speakers on the podium told while also cursing dictators and cheering for democracy. In addition to being a protest against the Suchinda government, the demonstrations were a social event.[7]

The demonstrations thus were multi-dimensional. They were many things to many people. Indeed, popular representations of the events are diverse and often contradictory: the protests were democratic; the rallies were dramatic; it was students; it was academics; the demonstrations were for the middle class; they were against General Suchinda and Air Chief Marshal Kaset Rojananil; there was a third hand; they were a grass-roots mobilization; they were against the army; they were foreign controlled; it was the whole country rising up; it was a mob; it was just the élite in Bangkok; it was fun; it was horrible.

Interpreting the Events
Just what happened? And where have the events of May led Thailand? The campaign for the September 1992 election showed

how the events of May can be framed in many ways, and how each construction can directly benefit a particular political party. Actually much of the struggle for meaning was not between the 'pro-military' parties and the 'pro-democracy' parties, but between the Democrat Party led by Chuan Leekpai and the Palang Dharma Party led by Chamlong Srimuang. The two stories centred on parliamentary democracy and popular democracy. Chuan highlighted the importance of his struggle in Parliament, while Chamlong maintained that the protests on the streets were instrumental.[8] Actually, both were necessary and aided each other, but that story does not get votes in an election.

Even though the September 1992 election put a 'pro-democratic' government in office, the explanation of the massacre was not settled. Even naming the action is wrapped in the discursive politics: was it a riot, an uprising, or a massacre? There is a similar struggle for meaning over what happened in 1932: historians generally call the changes in 1932 an 'event' rather than a 'coup' or a 'revolution' "to avoid prejudging the issue".[9] In 1992 many commentators settled for calling the May massacre an 'event' or an 'incident', showing how what happened is not only open to interpretation, but also demands interpretation.

Social upheavals often present theoretical challenges to social scientists. The norm for discussing Thai politics since 1966 has been Fred Riggs' 'bureaucratic polity' model where decision-making is dominated by a civil/military bureaucracy which is largely unaccountable to other social groups or even political parties.[10] Some continue to argue that even though there have been many coups to disrupt Thai parliamentary politics, the basic government policy has trudged on largely unaffected under the guidance of the bureaucracy.[11]

The 'democratic period' of 1973–76 challenged this bureaucratic polity model, with the mass uprising of 1973 and the period of open politics that followed effected great changes on the Thai political system. None the less, this came to an end with the brutal right-wing military crack-down on 6 October 1976, which put the civil/military bureaucrats back into power. Still, there was a crisis in scholarship, because even though the bureaucracy was back in power, the bureaucratic polity model which relied on a structural view of Thai society could not explain the conflict and change: structuralism sees meaning in order, and change is a 'problem'.

This theoretical problem was addressed by David Morell and Chai-Anan Samudavanija in *Political Conflict in Thailand: Reform, Reaction and Revolution*, which highlighted the differences between traditional Thai culture and modern democratic politics.[12] At the risk of over-generalizing, one could state that they understand (the failure of) modern Thai democratic politics in terms of three uniquely Thai traditional institutions: the monarchy, the military, and the bureaucracy. This was an important addition to the structural explanations, but this political culture approach tends to ossify élite definitions of Thai culture, leading to problems of cultural determinism. Furthermore, Morell and Chai-Anan still separate the economy from the politics in what amounts to a modified view of the bureaucratic polity which cannot account for the increasing political role of Thai business.[13]

This framework of research, and the bureaucratic polity and political culture models of Thai politics in general, was challenged in the late 1980s and early 1990s by scholars who pointed to the importance of extra-bureaucratic forces, most notably the business classes. Arguing directly against the bureaucratic polity model, Anek Laothamatas writes:

> I view recent Thai politics as a struggle between the military-bureaucratic elite and extra-bureaucratic forces. My major thesis is that organized business, a major societal group, has become strong enough to break the monopoly of the military-bureaucratic elite with regard to the economic policy-making of the state.[14]

Thus many scholars have turned to a political-economic analysis of Thai capitalism.[15] The challenge of the May events greatly strengthened this refocus of Thai politics on the middle class as an extra-bureaucratic force which affected national politics beyond economic policy. This is the powerful optic which is ordering much of the analysis of the May events, but it is blinded to the issues which go beyond class and capital.[16] Like other texts which address Thai politics, these scholars utilize the dualist framework of standard of social science methodology to analyse institutions and events in terms of relations between tradition and modernity, East and West, civilians and the military, élite bureaucrats and the masses, and so on.

But the May 1992 demonstrations and bloodshed pose another theoretical challenge. A close reading of the events demonstrates that too much in Thai politics slips through this dualist grid: what do you do when the anti-military campaign is led by someone who is addressed as 'Major-General'? Where is the middle class in the élite/mass dynamic? Is it in between, or alongside them? Has the aristocracy reinscribed itself as middle class? Is there more than one middle class which occupies various spaces? Or perhaps more to the point, are military officers also part of the middle class, as some claim?[17] A critical reading of the latest 'middle class analysis' shows its limits, for the dualist framework of exclusive binaries where one has to be one or the other (for example, either middle class or military) is still taken for granted.[18] What about the people who are pro-democracy activists, but not in the middle class; where do they fit in?

Rather that using class analysis to name these others as 'working class' or 'peasants', this chapter aims to avoid such a conceptual trap of exclusive binaries to chart a different course through the events of May. To do this, I will look at Thai culture in an international context to show the relationship between the *spirit* of democracy and the power of the military. I hope to examine Thai politics in terms of its hybridity, a curious mixing of narratives which both utilize and call into question the spatio-temporal discourses of East/West and pre/post-modern. This will be done by looking not just at the physical power of the army and the material products of economic development as do most middle class/military frames. There is something else working in Thailand that could be called 'symbolic politics'.

Symbolic Politics

In addition to the material forces of the military and capital there were important symbolic forces that are integral to understanding the events of May and their aftermath. These symbolic forces were not just consequences or 'superstructural' outgrowths of the material forces. As Pierre Bourdieu argues: physical power, economic power, and symbolic power are closely associated and 'mutually convertible' — they produce each other as they contest each other.[19] As so much attention has been given to the military and the economic aspects of Thai politics, this book highlights the heretofore largely ignored symbolic elements of this dynamic.

What is symbolic politics? Since comparisons are increasingly made between Latin American and Southeast Asian politics,[20] it seems appropriate to quote Colombian novelist Gabriel Garcia Marquez. In the following passage Garcia Marquez goes a long way in explaining symbolic politics by cataloguing the 'invisible estate' of one of his recently deceased characters:

> The wealth of the subsoil, the territorial waters, the colors of the flag, national sovereignty, the traditional parties, the rights of man, civil rights, the nation's leadership, the right of appeal, Congressional hearings, letters of recommendation, historical records, free elections, beauty queens, transcendental speeches, huge demonstrations, distinguished young ladies, proper gentlemen, punctilious military men, His Illustrious Eminence, the Supreme Court, goods whose importation was forbidden, setting a good example, the free but responsible press, the Athens of South America, public opinion, the lessons of democracy, Christian morality, the Communist menace, the ship of state, the high cost of living, republican traditions, the underprivileged classes, statements of political support.[21]

Garcia Marquez thus weaves together the cultural and political, the traditional and the modern for a rich symbolic politics in this invisible estate of élites in the military dictatorships of Latin America. Power in this context is diverse, overlapping, and diffuse. This 'framework' highlights the multiplicity of political dynamics: it embraces contradictions for it is not reducible to unity or duality — but it is not chaos either.

How does symbolic politics work in Thailand? Thinking back to the protests in April and May 1992, we can ask not only "What were they?", but also "How were they?", and perhaps more importantly, "How were they different?". The demonstrations were non-violent protests carried out through hunger strikes and mass rallies.

The power was not material. Though some (cynically) characterize the Thai *realpolitik* in terms of military power and bureaucratic corruption, Suchinda was not forced to resign at gunpoint or bribed out of office. Rather, it was a moral and symbolic protest: Major-General Chamlong Srimuang's power did not 'come out of the barrel of a gun' as when he was in the army. It was his speech and his *denial* of material goods in a hunger strike that encouraged many people to join the rallies in May.

With the events of May the dynamic of Thai politics was more symbolic power than material power. The army with its guns and armoured personnel carriers in the end lost to "the bravery and politeness of the protestors"[22] who used non-violent methods. Even though the army's crack-down was deemed 'legal' and 'procedurally correct' the military leaders responsible were transferred out of power because their actions were not moral.[23] Still other questions are better answered through symbolic analysis. What were the demonstrations against? Why did the demonstrators pick on Suchinda? It was not a problem with the very material standard of the law, for Suchinda's government was technically legal. Suchinda continues to justify his premiership on the grounds that his administration was constitutional, since the five coalition parties had selected him as Prime Minister.[24] During the demonstrations Suchinda actually stressed the material standard of the law: "Play by the rules" and work through Parliament, Suchinda kept telling the demonstrators who were protesting on the streets. And as we will see in Chapter 2, once the violence broke out, the military insisted that it was trying to maintain 'law and order'.

Indeed, the legality of Suchinda's government was never an issue. Its legitimacy was the nexus of dispute. The legitimacy of the law — the 1991 Constitution that the NPKC hand-tailored to institutionalize military influence — was at the centre of the dispute. Legitimacy is harder to calculate. It is not rational (*ratios* means 'to count') and measurable like a law or a standard: as Bourdieu said, "symbolic capital is less easily measured than land or livestock".[25] Legitimacy comes out of the context, the time, the symbolic dynamic of a society. For example, when Prime Minister Anand Panyarachun responded to Supreme Commander ACM

Kaset Rojananil's threats of another coup in July 1992, it was not a legal response. Anand talked of the political context: "I don't think that a coup is acceptable in the eyes of the people now."[26] 'Now' is the pivotal word in this sentence. As Craig Reynolds writes: "The legitimacy of the Thai state rests on a web of meanings that are articulated in law, public ceremony and in symbolism."[27] With the events of May we can see how the symbolism in Thailand is important in politics, ranging from the *noise* of 'public ceremonies' of the mass demonstrations to the *silence* of official media censorship.

To demonstrate how symbolic politics works in the material world, an extreme example is useful: the relation between politics, astrology, and magic.

Star Wars, Thai Style

> ...I dreamt of flying by myself over mountains and forests for a long distance and time. That meant I'll fulfill all my wishes and be happy for a long time. And this will apply to my husband. In the dream, I flew for a long distance so his government may last for even ten years.[28]

So said Khunying Wannee Kraprayoon confidently a few weeks before her husband General Suchinda Kraprayoon became Prime Minister of Thailand in April 1992. This quotation shows how influential dreams are in Thailand: people pay attention to the supernatural dimensions and magical signs, for they have power. Although Nancy Reagan was ridiculed in the United States for using the services of her astrologer to influence public policy,[29] such things are not even an issue in Thailand (or many other countries in Asia). For Khunying Wannee the problem is not the dream, but her interpretation of it. As we know, Suchinda's government lasted for only forty-eight days — over 3,600 days short of ten years.

After Suchinda resigned in disgrace on 24 May, Khunying Wannee learned her lesson, and sought professional help to read her fate. Reasoning that Suchinda's problems had nothing to do with his government's legitimacy or the violence of the military response to the protests, Khunying Wannee surmised that it was all 'bad luck'. Soon after Suchinda resigned, Khunying Wannee reportedly went to Wat Bovorniweswiharn, a temple in Bangkok, to see how she could get her husband unjinxed.[30] After consulting Suchinda's astrological charts, a senior monk decided that the problem was simply that 'Suchinda' was an inauspicious name. After some spell-casting, erasing of old names, and writing of new ones, Suchinda was renamed 'Bhumichai — land of victory' to ward off any new bouts of bad luck.

ACM Kaset Rojananil, who was Armed Forces Supreme Commander and Air Force Chief at the time of the May massacre, apparently sought spiritual help as well — this was necessary since he and Suchinda shared the same fate as they were born in the same month and year. Even though his wife Khunying Wathana scoffs at astrological activities, declaring "I will live in reality",[31] Kaset reportedly went to Wat Phrathat Samduang in Chiang Rai province on 6 June where a well-known fortune-teller 'sealed' him from misfortune.[32] This 'young Brahmin' — after a donation of Bt100,000 — reportedly pasted nine squares of gold leaf imprinted with Kaset's astrological sign on his forehead. Then the good luck was sealed by a bath in holy water and reinforced with a talisman of a sacred piece of wood. Though relieved of all guilt and responsibility, Kaset pledged to organize a Bt20 million *krathin* (merit-making) ceremony — just to make sure.

Astrology and magic then are not just for fun and games. They involve the use of symbols that is very powerful in Thai politics. On the one hand it explains why people like Suchinda, Kaset, and Issarapong Noonpackdee persevered in the face of massive democratic sentiments.[33] These military leaders believe in the prophesies which guarantee their power, hence all the 'democratic talk' and military reshuffling is just temporary bad luck. In August 1992 Suchinda flatly stated: "I think what we have done is correct and good. I don't think it was a sin. We regret that many people were killed, but we considered it a matter of karma. ... Things just turned out that way."[34] This bad luck will not be overcome through institutional reform or by the generals' transfer to inactive posts, but through spiritual ceremonies.[35]

It would be a mistake to think that this mix of astrology and politics — since what to the rest of the world was a massacre, to Suchinda and Kaset was karma and 'bad luck' — is limited to the spin control of military dictators who are out of favour. Other visitors to Khunying Wannee's astrologer Phrakru Paritkosol include leading businessmen, senior military officers, politicians, and Field Marshal Thanom Kittikachorn, who was ousted in the pro-democracy student uprising of 1973.[36] Field Marshal Sarit Thanarat also relied heavily on supernatural prophesy,[37] and former Prime Minister Thanin Kraivichian was himself a famous astrologer.[38]

Hence the 'superstitions' of astrology are certainly not limited to traditional village life. The more Thailand modernizes and the economy rationalizes, the more people are displaced — spiritually as well as socially and geographically.

> On the whole, patterns of interest in astrology is highest among the middle class, urban and more educated sections of Thai society. ... This pattern of interest in astrology is probably related to the wider range of options and compara-tively ambitious expectations of — or insecurity regarding — the future among these groups as compared with, say, the less socially mobile farmers and urban poor, who in Thailand generally evince less interest in fortune-telling.[39]

Thus many urban dwellers seek astrological solace to put them into balance with their changing world. The belief in the stars and the reading of horoscopes is widespread, appealing to people regardless of age, socio-economic background, education, religion, or social position: "astrology has at least some following amongst all social groups".[40]

Astrology comes in many forms in Thailand. This occult practice coexists with Buddhism, Brahmanism, and the local religions.[41] The more orthodox official rituals and the Buddhist Law of Karma are criss-crossed with the spiritual services which aim to determine and often circumvent one's fate: astrology, numerology, naming, *fengshui*, horoscopes, palm reading, psychic prediction, and spirit consulting are among the methods used. Indeed almost every temple has a palm reader who will tell you your future, and a monk who will determine auspicious moments for important events in your life: it is a common practice to consult the prophets to determine an auspicious wedding date or to name a child.

Prophesy is also a business. Professional astrologers (*mor doo*) outside the temple also offer their services to the believers. One popular seer treats it as a sort of psychological counselling: "People come and seek advice because they are confused over decisions. The best thing a prediction can do is confirm what's already in their minds."[42] Or perhaps more importantly in economic terms, astrology is crucial to a host of investors on the Stock Exchange of Thailand, and the secular *mor doo* have responded with a new industry of books which apply astrology to stock trading.

Astrology in Thailand is not just a personal concern or an alternative to psychological counselling and portfolio planning. Astrology is a serious discipline with important political conse- quences. One of its main branches is Court Astrology, also some- times called State Astrology.[43] The palace still consults the astro- logical signs before royal activities — especially crucial ones like the ascension to the throne. In the past Thai kings have organized their statesmanship by consulting prophets before making major policy changes such as fighting a war or building a city.[44] Indeed, even the transition from absolute monarchy to a constitutional system was timed according to state astrology: "royal astrologers ... selected December 10 as a most auspicious day for promulga- tion of the [Constitution]...."[45] Now the same applies to planning a coup d'état against a constitutional government: "it is widely thought that military officers are among the most avid followers of astrological advice in political circles, and that some of the recent successors to power by coup have the reputation of being strongly influenced by astrology."[46] In "Supernatural Prophesy in Thai Politics: The Role of a Spiritual Cultural Element in Coup Decisions", Chalidaporn Songsamphan charts out the motivating influence of astrology in the failed coup attempts of 1981 and 1985: actions which had little rational justification. She concludes that the generals use the stars for two general purposes: risk management and damage control.

The military junta which led the coup of February 1991 followed the example of the kings and juntas of Thailand's past. To set the timing of the coup at an auspicious moment, General Sunthorn Kongsompong, the leader of the NPKC, consulted well-known astrologer Kengkard Jongjaiprah who set the time at 11:30 a.m., 23 February 1991.[47] On 23 February Prime Minister General Chatichai Choonhavan was arrested by the NPKC. The irony is that Kengkard was also an astrologer to Chatichai. But Kengkard sees no conflict of interest: "There had to be a coup, otherwise there would have been bloodshed."[48]

As we have seen, stories of the political power of horoscopes are common among the political and military élites. Yet there were new developments in the use of astrology and magic after the May 1992 uprising. In contrast with the lack of spiritual element in the radical student movements of the 1970s,[49] the spirits seemed to have favoured the masses in Thailand's 1992 pro-democracy movement. Part of this is reactive. In early June 1992 the Consti-tutional Tribunal blocked the avenues for social justice through the constitutional system when it upheld Suchinda's hastily drafted 'General Amnesty'. Thus some people struck back and sought justice on the spiritual plane. On 9 June the Slum People for Democracy held a 'Black Magic Rite to Conquer the Tyrants and the Five Devil Parties'. The souls of the dead from the massacres of 14 October 1973, 6 October 1976 as well as those killed during 17–20 May 1992 were democratically called to witness this 700-year old Lanna cursing rite from northern Thailand. Adjacent to the official spir-itual centres of Bangkok and Thailand — the Bangkok City Pillar, Temple of the Emerald Buddha, and Phra Siam Thevathiraat — an elaborate folk ritual summoned the "deities and all the holy spirits of the country [who] are asked to help convict the felons", including both the generals held responsible and the 'Five Devil Parties' of the coalition government.[50]

Though many dismissed this ritual as just a show, the next day, on 10 June, House Speaker Arthit Urairat stunned the country by appointing Anand Panyarachun as the Interim Prime Minister, completely bypassing the leader of the 'devil party' coalition, ACM Somboon Rahong. In other words, according to those who believe in these rites, it took just one day for the curse to work, and in the following months the pro-military parties and the generals of the

NPKC would be swept from power. Such cursing has a definite social effect regardless of its supernatural power. Though the military officers responsible have very thick skins and wide power bases when it comes to challenges from Parliament — Kaset and General Issarapong Noonpackdee refused to attend the Parliamentary Investigative Committee meetings in June 1992 — they do believe in spiritual power.[51]

The ceremony of the Slum People for Democracy was more than just reactive; it was also creative of Thai political culture. The rituals, which were elegantly adapted to the needs of the time, fluently mixed symbolic ceremonies with law — one of the most rational processes in a material society. The black magic rite was held to call 'mass murderers' for the punishment that they deserved. One sorcerer used more specific legal language to describe it: "deities and all the holy spirits of the country are asked to help convict the felons". How are the felons to be convicted? Through magic. Rather than being on opposite sides of some material/ symbolic distinction, here the law and the spirits aid each other for social justice.

The cursing ceremony also added to the Thai political vocabulary. The sign over the Slum People's cursing ceremony read: "Black Magic Rite to Conquer the Tyrants and Five Devil Parties". Soon after, the Thai press switched from calling the Suchinda coalition parties 'pro-military' to *paak maan* — the devil parties. Language is very powerful, and such a simple moral distinction between the political parties was very influential, especially in the provinces where the battles for the September 1992 election were largely fought.

PollWatch — the usually rational election watch-dog organization which was set up to curb vote-buying and encourage participatory democracy[52] — also used this spiritual vocabulary and method in the final days of the September 1992 election campaign. In Nakhon Ratchasima it organized fifty *mor pi* (spirit doctors) to form a National Committee of Local Spirit Doctors which cursed corrupt politicians as 'the devils' in a black magic ceremony.[53] The PollWatch press release states: "In this ceremony spirit doctors and magicians...hurt those who obstruct democracy."[54] Chaisiri

Samudavanija explains that the *mor pi* know the most about the problems of the rural poor. Official channels do not work since the villagers generally cannot trust the local government officials and 'bureaucratic monks' who are more of a problem than a solution.[55] Hence through a new communication network of villages that PollWatch set up with the National Committee of Local Spirit Doctors, the very material problems of the rural poor are made known to the centres of power through symbolic mechanisms. Magic is thus used as a method of resistance to corruption on both a local and a national scale.

To sum up this section addressing 'democratic spirits', a crucial distinction needs to be drawn between the prophesies of the astrologers and the magic of the spirit doctors. Cook has noted that *mor doo* are popular with the urban middle classes, and Chaisiri makes an important observation when he notes that while the middle and upper classes rely on astrologers to read their fate, the urban and rural poor go to spirit doctors to solve their problems.[56] Another PollWatch volunteer interviewed in Sukothai province expressed similar distinctions: he said that astrologers were for "famous people" living in the cities, "not people here".[57] Likewise, the peasants in the PollWatch press release state that "astrology serves dictators and tyrants".

In other words, similar spiritual tools are used in very different ways by the military/middle class and by the rural/urban poor. Selected democratic spirits are utilized with culture and language for a progressive grass-roots politics in the villages, while other spirits work with the urban middle class élites, often against democracy. A reading of spiritual politics then reframes the problematic of the events of May. It is not a question then of a rational middle class in contrast with irrational peasants, the order of the military versus the chaos of the demonstrations. Rather the topic becomes how each group uses its symbolic arsenals in very political ways; ways that serve to efface the analytic distinctions of rational/ irrational, middle class/military, and even spiritual/material. However, most scholars still write off astrology and magic as irrational superstition with little relation to serious politics. Much the same criticism is made of popular culture which is 'fictional', and thus

irrelevant. Academics who are trying to make their work relevant
to society must take this criticism seriously.

One of the problems with astrology is that the data is not firm.
It is mostly anecdotal. It is hard to pin down and quote a spirit.
Much of the information is rumour. And when it is published in
the newspapers, it is often in political gossip columns like the
Bangkok Post's Maew Mong: it is presented as intriguing but not
reliable.[58] Even the newspapers in Bangkok do not take such
rumours seriously. When asked why they print the astrological
references in the regular news pages, the editors reply that they
publish them to show the 'silliness' of astrology.[59]

But when one thinks about what one knows about the events
of May, much of the information is like the astrological data.
Much of it is indeed rumour, reportage, and anecdotes.[60] If we
criticize horoscopes for being unreliable sources, then what was a
reliable source during April and May in Bangkok? It certainly was
not the regular sources of information: television and radio. These
were severely distorted even though Suchinda declared otherwise
in a speech broadcast on 19 May over the official television pool:
"I would like everybody to stay in their place and follow the news
from the radio and television stations, because all the reports will
be the truth and not distorted in any way." Because the official
media were so unreliable, people looked to other sources. The
newspapers are very important, but because of the time lag involved
in the print media many people look to more unofficial media
which are hard to quote, and the personal media that are even
harder to analyse: cellular telephones, videos, t-shirts, buttons,
faxes, leaflets, pamphlets, gossip, and rumours. In other words, it
is not that "truth is the first casualty". Rather, when violence is
done to the official media, rumours and other unofficial information become the truth.[61]

In a symbolic analysis of the events, the *truth* of a source is but
one question asked in seeing how images and information are
managed. Or put another way, the task is to see how the 'truth'
is acted out: if the generals believe that curses placed on them will
work, then they are already effective. To understand both the silence
and the noise of the political situation in May, the focus will be

shifted to more 'economic' issues of how information is transmitted, received, evaluated, and transmitted again.

Electronic Politics

To understand the dynamics of the events, we need to examine the media and how they worked to provide us with 'the facts' of April and May in Bangkok. Certain media worked to motivate the anti-Suchinda protest through the symbolic force of language and images. Again, they did not use material force to mobilize the mass rallies, but the force of ideas to help overcome the armoured personnel carriers. Indeed, the Suchinda government tried to use its force of censorship to silence this dissent. There was a news blackout in April and May about the mass rallies which were drawing tens and hundreds of thousands of people. But this censorship only worked on the electronic media of the television and the radio.[62] This control of the electronic media should not be surprising since two of the five television stations are owned by the army and the other three are under state control; likewise the military owns 128 radio stations, the Public Relations Department owns 127, and the Prime Minister's Office through the Mass Communications Authority of Thailand has sixty-two.

But as the events unfolded in May it was clear that this censorship had backfired: the official silence was attractive and productive. People went to the rallies in May because they wanted to see for themselves what they could not see on the television or hear on the radio. In order to understand what went on we have to look in different places — in symbolic places to see how the spirits of both democracy and death were socially acted out in public space.

The struggle that killed so many very material lives was in many ways held over images: it is noteworthy that the Public Relations Department Building — the headquarters of the caretaker of the government's image — was among the first to be torched. At the height of the protests an army captain told a *Newsweek* photographer: "If I see you again you die, you die, you die. You are hurting the *image* of Thailand." Thailand does not matter; but its image must be defended with lethal force: "We got one of you yesterday," the same army captain yelled at the group of photographers.[63]

The issues of the media then have been switched from silence to noise, from outright censorship to how the media manage and present information. After the violence the army was not concerned about the dead people, but only with its own image and its honour. Likewise, the Tourist Authority of Thailand was not interested in seeing substantive changes made in the Thai military and government. It only wanted to spend Bt40 million on an advertising campaign to brighten Thailand's image overseas. Even the newspapers tried to profit in their own war against the electronic media by painting their image around the sacred word 'truth'. Certainly the newspapers did an outstanding job in reporting the events, but one must remember that newspapers are a business, a business that has been threatened in the past decade by the popularity of television and radio. For example, *The Nation* ran full page advertisements every day of the month following the May violence with the message: "Where can you find the TRUTH when you need it most? The Nation." This sales pitch was printed in huge letters between a large red question mark and the telephone number for subscriptions.[64] But as people in Thailand found out painfully, there is a lot of 'truth' out there. Hence the many alternative sources of information need to be critically examined, because even though they all claim to be 'democratic', many of these media products, upon closer examination, support military intervention in politics.[65]

Videos and Faxes

In the information age images are powerful weapons that pro-democracy forces can use. Indeed, at Tiananmen in China it was facsimiles (faxes) that kept the demonstrators' spirit going once the tanks started rolling. Now with the April-May 1992 demonstrations in Thailand, video was the name of the game as well. These two media are vital because they circumvent the official media to disseminate the truth, not only in Bangkok but more importantly in the provinces as well. They are connected to lower technology unofficial media such as leaflets and photograph exhibits, but have the extra charge of high technology, which adds to their legitimacy.

Yet electricity has no ideology. Faxes and videos are tools just like any other media. What was crucial in May was a democratization of these media tools. Electronic media shifted from the monopoly control of the military government to be used by pro-democratic groups as well. But these same tools were used by pro-military groups in ever more sophisticated ways after the violence in May.

Why are these media so powerful? Video works because it looks so real: it appears to be a true reflection of the events which captures the whole story. But it is not; video, like other media, is a reporting of events through a crafting of available information. This video truth then is not so much a reflection of reality, but one which is produced by organizing/manipulating images through techniques such as editing, layout, language, captioning, camera angles, use of colour, and choice of background music.[66] There are always metres of truth left lying on the cutting room floor. The same politics of production holds for faxes which use the power of desktop publishing for their own reality effect.

With the spread in May and June of popular video and fax representations of the events of May new questions arose about the information: "Whose truth are we watching? Whose interests does it serve?" These questions are necessary because rather than just limiting themselves to censorship, pro-military groups became more skilled at producing information and images, and thus producing their own truths about 'democracy'. Two electronic items illustrate this point: a fax from early June gives a hint of what stories pro-military groups are telling themselves, and the video documentary broadcast nationally on TV Channel 9 shows the story they wanted the rest of Thailand to see as well.

Massacre Videos. One of the fascinating things that happened after the violence ended was that it kept recurring. But after 20 May the violence was removed from the streets to the sidewalks to be played out on the video screen — over and over again. For weeks after the crack-down nearly every corner in Bangkok and many areas in the provinces had a vendor selling pirated tapes of news reports — the famed massacre videos which serve as a collective memory of the tragic events. People gathered around the monitors in front of the infamous Royal Hotel — itself the scene of much of the brutal crack-down — to watch the murders not just for a few days, but for weeks and even months. These videos are powerful because of their pictures. Thais saw reflections of themselves on the television screen — regardless of whether they were on Rajdamnoen Avenue or in the Royal Hotel in May 1992, or not. Video is the best means of information and influence in our post-literate age: since fewer people read, information is transmitted increasingly on the television screen. So we need to look very closely at how these videos are produced, and examine them to detect their politics.

The video televised by Channel 9 on Sunday 24 May right after Suchinda resigned needs to be examined because it is a very sophisticated production of truth. It gains some of its power because it wavers between official and unofficial media: many saw it on television, but many also bought it on the streets from video vendors. Since Channel 9 gained credibility by not being one of the army television channels, the military took advantage of the blur between official and unofficial. The army chiefs were satisfied with Channel 9's videotape, while they were not pleased with other videotapes which were widely sold on the streets. The army produced its own one-hour video from Channel 9 tapes of the 17–20 May crack-down to argue the army's "innocence and tolerance" to people in the provinces.[67]

How was Channel 9's 'truth' produced? The 40-minute documentary went through extensive editing/censoring before it was broadcast.[68] It certainly does graphically show the violence. Although it starts with the demonstrations in early May, it devotes just over half its time to the army crack-down of 17–20 May. But how it constructs the confrontation to present the violence — and thus produce its own truth — is telling. Simply put, the story told is one of the mob harassment and army tolerance. Violence is represented as coming from both sides. It highlights the restraint of the government forces by mixing tolerance in with the violence: in one sequence police are shown beating up a protester, yet a 'good officer' rushes in to stop them. Soldiers are shown aiding demonstrators, tending to their wounds. It is presented as a balanced telling of the story, but the only balance comes from an equalizing of the images of violence which were actually far from equal: while the soldiers had guns, the demonstrators were unarmed.

The video's so-called 'balance' is shown best in a long sequence of a confrontation along Rajdamnoen Avenue in the early hours of 18 May. In a wide angle shot taken from atop a building the whole 'battle scene' is laid out in its full magnitude, with over 100,000 protesters and tens of thousands of police/military personnel lined up against each other. The bird's eye view lends the video a sense of objectivity and truth: on a grand stage it shows the 'rioters' surging towards the police, then the police surging back in an apparently evenly matched battle. All the while we can hear Chamlong Srimuang over the loudspeaker pleading for peace. But in this 'even battle' the police are seemingly compelled to use force, and start shooting.

The video is full of yelling, screaming, and crying in addition to the barrages of automatic gunfire. But its silences are even more crucial. The really brutal footage was left out of the Channel 9 video documentary. Only twice can one see the army shooting into the crowd; and one has to really look for it. Other massacre videos do not bury the army's violence. Many videos have a shot with the camera aiming down the barrel of the rifle while a soldier shoots down a person who is running away.[69] The famous footage of the army's capture of the Royal Hotel where soldiers terrorized protesters and doctors is also not in the 40-minute selection even though it dominated other videos — being replayed again and again. Actually the Channel 9 video only shows soldiers giving first aid to their prisoners outside the Royal Hotel — seemingly erasing the fact that it was these same soldiers who inflicted the wounds. The board is wiped clean, and we must forgive and forget: this is the message of the montage at the end of the video documentary which is played against the utopian background music of John Lennon's "Imagine" (which of course was written in the context of another Southeast Asian conflict), for a new political twist of Music Television (MTV).

What kind of politics are being played out in this music video summation? A simple calculation of images in this music video shows that more pictures are flashed on the screen of injured soldiers and destroyed government property than of dead and injured demonstrators. Again, the only time injured protesters are shown is when the soldiers are tending to their wounds. Thus the conclusion of the video serves to erase any previous political or moral conclusions that viewers might have made. The sense that one can easily get is that the battle was between equals, and that the army had to defend itself against an unruly mob. And even if one is outraged by the images, the music tells one to "imagine all the people living life in peace" rather than to act.[70]

Yet the casualty statistics contradict this story of an 'evenly matched battle' between the army and a violent mob: 132 army/police personnel wounded and none killed,[71] as opposed to the official casualty toll of forty-four dead and 670 wounded among demonstrators and bystanders[72] — not to mention the hundreds who were missing and presumed dead, officially tabulated at forty-two. But the power of Channel 9's 'balanced reporting' serves to erase these statistics even as the other videos sold alongside it highlight them. It is a competition between truths sold on the sidewalk.

To highlight how the Channel 9 video is a production of a forgetful truth, another massacre music video presents the events in a different way. It is set to the biting political commentary of popular Thai rock group Carabao's song "Phuthon — the Endurers", which is taken from the *Phrachathipatai* [Democracy] (1986) album.[73] The images and the music are woven together into a political message in this music video which was shown in the week following the violence. This music video is interesting because it points the finger in two directions at once to criticize both the military and the corrupt politicians. The video graphically focuses on the military's violence from the demonstrator's point of view — not from an 'objective' bird's eye view. The lyrics of the song are about corrupt political parties — some of which were in the pro-democracy opposition — that encourage the military to take a political role. The song title itself is ironic: *phuthon* means 'those who endure', and it is also a pun on *phuthaen*, which means 'Member of Parliament'. With vote-buying and broken promises as widespread as poverty and hunger in the villages, the rural poor have to endure the MPs, the song tells us.

The music ties these literary and visual texts together with the rhythm pushing on the swift succession of scenes in the video: soldiers are shown beating prostrate protesters in the Royal Hotel while Ad Carabao sings of "the government's beautiful policies". The heavy back beat of the song echoes like the gunshots and the police batons beating down on the screen. The last beat of the drum speaks of the official censorship; the video shows a soldier abruptly covering the camera lens with his hand — blinding us to the violence.

This second music video points in a direction for positive change by critically examining the social problems that led to the violence, rather than just trying to forgive and forget the violence as in the Channel 9 production. The symbolic power of images, language, and music are thus used in these MTV texts in very different political ways.

Fax and the Facts. The other medium which I want to consider is the fax. Faxes were important in spreading the word around Bangkok, around the country, and around the world about the killings in May.[74] But faxes are also used in increasingly sophisticated ways not only to spread the word but also to confuse the issues. One example of the twisting of the facts on a fax to produce a partisan truth is a report from the 29 May issue of *EIR International* which was floating around fax machines in Bangkok in June 1992. It is entitled "AFL-CIA leads revolt against Thai government", and appears to be an analysis of the demonstrations and bloodshed. This article reports that the "so-called democracy movement" is "a carefully planned revolution against the Thai government and the king, 100% controlled and directed by assets of the U.S. Central Intelligence Agency and the AFL-CIO [American Federation of Labor–Congress of Industrial Organizations]".

Through a strategy of 'objectively reporting' half-truths, this article aims to discredit the pro-democracy movement. Actually, the article states that it is not a democracy movement at all, but the people are being manipulated by some 'third force' — this time an American-directed third force which is part of President Bush's strategy for controlling the world by annihilating the Thai military in order to destroy the Thai nation-state. But upon examination the arguments and the evidence of this *EIR International* article reveal serious contradictions. There is even a telling error in the title: there is no such thing as the AFL-CIA. It is either the AFL-CIO or it is the CIA. Furthermore, in light of the close relationship between the Thai and the American military, the statement that the U.S. Government is anti-military is unlikely. When the United States wants to control Thailand, it is through the military: "U.S. military aid...served as a symbol of U.S.–Thai relations".[75]

So why lend this article any credence by even discussing it? It is important to recognize faxed articles like this one because the arguments are very familiar. Even though on the surface the article is talking about the overthrow of the military, it uses pro-military logic to discredit the pro-democracy movement. It is full of half-truths like the AFL-CIA. The *EIR International* article paints the grass-roots pro-democracy movement as under the control of a 'third force' aiming to overthrow the Thai monarchy and Government. Leaders of the pro-democracy movement are supposedly discredited in various ways, appealing to the same nationalist and religious fears that Suchinda did in Parliament.[76] Even non-governmental organizations (NGOs) are listed as subversive foreign agents because they receive some outside funding.[77] This logic actually undermines the pro-military argument since the Thai military is partially funded by and often trained in the United States. This argument then is a distortion of the pro-democracy movement that was used by pro-military propagandists to sow seeds of doubt and to reassure themselves of their 'righteousness'.

Where does this 'truth' come from? 'EIR' stands 'Executive Intelligence Review'. *EIR International* is a journal associated with a group led by Lyndon LaRouche, which many describe as 'extremist', 'paramilitary', and like a religious cult.[78] LaRouche is well known in the United States for presidential campaign fund fraud for which he was serving a fifteen-year prison sentence during the Bangkok uprising. In Bangkok LaRouche's organization, headed by Packdee Thanapura, has been involved with various ultra-conservative groups which have close connections to the army.[79] A report by the International Confederation of Free Trade Unions (ICFTU) states: "The group has set up elaborate disinformation methods, based on the exploitation of credulity and lack of information of those it seeks to influence, attract, or manipulate."[80] In short, LaRouche and company are known for their campaigns of misinformation.

Yet even though the arguments do not add up and even come from an unreliable source, the article can become convincing when it is anonymously distributed through the magical power of the fax. The article's layout is very professional, and it appears to be a behind the scenes report of the actual forces behind the 'revolt'. It is published in what appears to be an English/American journal, thus gaining a certain credibility and authenticity from being outside Thai politics. EIR can also be easily mistaken for EIU — the Economist Intelligence Unit (London) — which is a respected source of economic information.[81] Even language is important: English is used here as a language of prestige. Yet it is very simple English — "Easy to understand," notes one Thai commentator — which makes it easier to translate into Thai for further distribution. So it hardly matters that the article is only signed by 'an EIR Investigative Team' and that few people know what EIR stands for. This is actually part of the power of the fax in an unstable situation like that in Bangkok: anonymity lends credibility. Indeed, with desktop publishing and faxes almost anything can be made into the 'truth'.

Ascertaining whose truth it is comes more from the report's distribution than from its production — the fax came from a state enterprise which at the time was chaired by Army Commander General Issarapong Noonpackdee. It was sent to a telecommunications firm which relies on its ties to the military for its profit. Hence this partisan truth is being shuffled back and forth between people who already believe that the army was justified in its bloody crack-down, and more than half believe this article. So with the fax, the truth-value comes not just from 'the facts' but from how they are laid out, and how they are distributed into sympathetic hands.

The moral of this story of electronic politics is not that all videos are lies and all faxes are fabrications. It is not so simple, hence consumers of information must be critical of both official and unofficial reports once the censorship is eased. As Umberto Eco writes of a more hopeful time: "The battle for the survival of man as a responsible being in the Communications Era is not to be won where the communication originates, but where it arrives."[82] The twisting of truth is much more sophisticated than a simple muzzling, for it frames and reframes the meaning of democracy. Some videos point towards an active democracy which will address the problems of people, while the Channel 9 video preaches a forgetful truth and a passive democracy.[83] Likewise, the democracy of *EIR International* is very different from the democracy of many other faxes sent. Hence questions like "Whose interests does this 'truth' serve?" and "What kind of democracy is it?" must be asked. Faxes and videos — however much we rely on them and trust them — are not simply the truth. They are merely efficient modes of distributing information — information which always lies somewhere between fact and fiction.

Conclusion
To repeat the cliché written at the beginning of this chapter, my premise is that the events of May, and Thai politics in general, are very complex and not always coherent. A large part of this complexity involves the symbolic element in the dynamics of power which has received little serious attention. Perhaps this is because symbolic power does not work in the same ways as physical and economic power. An analysis of symbolic power — language, images, and spirits — involves a shift from orthodox sources and establishment media to a consideration of a heterodoxy of representations. Each of these alternative media — astrology, magic, pirated videos, and underground faxes — has its own role in the dynamics of Thai politics which can be highlighted with a combination of the theoretical tools of political science, anthropology, and cultural studies.

Such analysis calls into question familiar conceptual schemes which rely on binary distinctions such as civil/military, élite/mass,

East/West, traditional/modern, rational/irrational, and even symbolic/material — without necessarily having to discard them. We need to read these narratives, without taking them uncritically as metanarratives. Indeed, with this focus on symbolic politics we will return in Chapter 2 to reconsider the role of the middle class and the military to see how they acted out their material politics of money and lethal force in ways that need to be understood in terms of popular participation and popular culture. The multitude of astrologers, spirit doctors, videos, and faxes demonstrate that the May events are not as simple as they might seem. They demand interpretation, and accordingly much of the struggle is not over revealing some 'truth', but with self-consciously constructing the truth and thus defining democracy in various ways.

NOTES

1. Pratumporn Vajarasathira, "Quote, unquote", *Bangkok Post*, 24 May 1992, p. 31.
2. Indeed, to follow current events of the situation, one had to pay close attention to the business pages in the newspapers. It is telling that the business newspapers expanded their coverage of so-called political events in May; for example, *Phuchatkan Raiwan* [The Manager Daily] doubled its space for political stories.
3. This can be seen in many political leaflets distributed at the time. For example, "Answers by Chiang Mai University's Academics for Democracy to Questions Posed by the Public Regarding a Non-Elected Prime Minister" states: "The people do not oppose the work of the coalition government but oppose the dictatorial powers of the NPKC under the leadership of General Suchinda who is trying to carry over the power he attained immorally through a coup d'etat on 23 February 1991 and who is trying to use powers outside the parliamentary system to interfere with the political system which came from the election."
4. For a concise explanation of the vicious cycle model of Thai politics see Chai-Anan Samudavanija, *The Thai Young Turks* (Singapore: Institute of Southeast Asian Studies, 1982), pp. 1–5.
5. Suchit Bunbongkarn uses the subheading "The May Uprising: A Middle Class Revolt" in his article "Thailand in 1992". (Suchit Bunbongkarn, "Thailand in 1992: In Search of a Democratic Order", *Asian Survey* 33,

no. 2 [February 1993]: 220.) The cover of the 21 May 1992 issue of
the *Far Eastern Economic Review* reads: "Middle Class Revolt". The
subtitle of the *Newsweek* article of 1 June 1992 is "A bloody army
crackdown fails to quiet the demands of Thailand's growing middle
class".

6. Gothom Arya, "Has anything changed since last May?", *Sunday Post*
   (Bangkok), 16 May 1993, p. 23.

7. An article which exemplifies this party atmosphere is "A yuppie mob"
   by Wipawee Otaganonta, *Bangkok Post*, 13 May 1992, pp. 28–29.

8. This different figuring of democracy was highlighted in the campaign
   posters for the September 1992 election: Chuan was in Parliament,
   while Chamlong was on the streets.

9. Craig J. Reynolds, "The Plot of Thai History", in *Historical Documents
   and Literary Evidence* (Bangkok: Thai Studies Programme, Chulalongkorn
   University, 1984), p. 13.

10. Fred Riggs, *Thailand: The Modernization of a Bureaucratic Polity* (Honolulu:
    East-West Center Press, 1966).

11. Clark D. Neher, "Political Succession in Thailand", *Asian Survey* 32,
    no. 7 (July 1992): 585–605.

12. David Morell and Chai-Anan Samudavanija, *Political Conflict in Thai-
    land: Reform, Reaction and Revolution* (Cambridge, Mass.: Oelgeschlager,
    Gunn & Hain Publishers, Inc., 1981).

13. For a critical review of *Political Conflict in Thailand: Reform, Reaction
    and Revolution* see Kevin Hewison, *Power and Politics in Thailand* (Manila:
    Journal of Contemporary Asia Publishers, 1989), pp. 21–28. Benedict
    Anderson provides an interesting analysis of the 'democratic period'
    which utilizes both class analysis and political culture in "Withdrawal
    Symptoms: Social and Cultural Aspects of the October 6 Coup", *Bulletin
    of Concerned Asia Scholars* 9, no. 3 (July–September 1977): 13–30.

14. Anek Laothamatas, *Business Associations and the Political Economy of
    Thailand: From Bureaucratic Polity to Liberal Corporatism* (Boulder:
    Westview Press and Singapore: Institute of Southeast Asian Studies,
    1992), p. xi.

15. The political-economic approach is quite diverse. For a useful discussion
    of its history in the 1980s see Hong Lysa, "*Warasan setthasat kanmu'ang*:
    critical scholarship in post-1976 Thailand", in *Thai Constructions of
    Knowledge*, edited by Manas Chitakasem and Andrew Turton (London:
    School of Oriental and African Studies, University of London, 1991),
    pp. 99–117.

16. For example, Hewison's political-economics go too far when they see
    culture as merely superstructure: "I would not suggest that the analysis

of culture and ideology is irrelevant, but I would emphasize that they should be seen for what they are, as reflections, albeit poor and partial, of the real base of society." (Hewison, op. cit., p. 26.)

17. The military officers can be regarded as part of the middle class when applying the standard criteria — family background, education, and income level — to them. (Teeranat Karnjana-uksorn, "Thahan kap thurakit [The military and business]", in *Chonchanklang bonkrasae phrachathipatai* [The middle class and Thai democracy], edited by Sungsidh Piriyarangsan and Pasuk Phongpaichit [Bangkok: Chulalong-korn University and Friedrich Ebert Stiftung, 1993], p. 281.)

18. A text which relies on the middle class democracy argument while recognizing its limits is Sungsidh Piriyarangsan and Pasuk Phong-paichit, eds., *Chonchanklang bonkrasae phrachathipatai* [The middle class and Thai democracy], especially the editors' "Introduction: The Middle Class and Democracy in Thailand" (Bangkok: Chulalongkorn University and Friedrich Ebert Stiftung, 1993), pp. 26–40.

19. Pierre Bourdieu, *Outline of a Theory of Practice* (New York: Cambridge University Press, 1977).

20. For a fascinating example of such comparisons see many of the chapters in Arif Dirlik, ed., *What Is in a Rim? Critical Perspectives on the Pacific Rim Idea* (Boulder: Westview Press, 1993).

21. Gabriel Garcia Marquez, *No One Writes to the Colonel and Other Stories* (New York: Harper and Row Publishers, 1968), p. 161.

22. "Thailand's Unfinished Business" (Editorial), *Asian Wall Street Journal*, 19 May 1993, p. 10.

23. *The Nation*, 6 August 1992, p. A1.

24. "Suchinda breaks silence", *Bangkok Post*, 21 August 1992, p. 3.

25. Bourdieu, op. cit., p. 182.

26. *Bangkok Post*, 17 July 1992, p. 1.

27. Craig J. Reynolds, *Radical Thai Discourse: The Real Face of Thai Feudalism Today* (Ithaca: Cornell University Press, 1987), p. 13.

28. Khunying Wannee Kraprayoon quoted in Sorrayuth Suthassanachinda and Krittia Porasame, "Women behind the strongmen take opposing views on politics", *The Nation*, 18 May 1992, p. A4.

29. Former White House Chief of Staff Donald Regan writes: "Virtually every move and decision the Reagans made during my time as White House Chief of Staff was cleared in advance with a woman in San Francisco who drew up horoscopes to make certain that the planets were in a favorable alignment for the enterprise." (Donald T. Regan, *For the Record* [London: Arrow Books, 1988], p. 3.)

30. "'Big Su' is now 'Big Phu'", *The Nation*, 6 June 1992, p. A3.

31. Sorrayuth and Krittia, op. cit.

32. "Battle lines set for a clash of spirits", *The Nation*, 10 June 1992, p. 1. As it turns out, Kaset was in Chiang Rai that weekend to make sure that the Speaker of the House, Arthit Urairat, would nominate Somboon Rahong, the Chart Thai leader, as Prime Minister. Kaset was unsuccessful; Arthit nominated Anand Panyarachun.

33. Even as late as 14 July 1992 Kaset was threatening a coup if the 13 September election results were not satisfactory to the military. There are many reasons why he would do this, but one of them is that Kaset still did not think that he did anything wrong.

34. "Suchinda breaks silence with new business plans", *Bangkok Post*, 21 August 1992, p. 3. In his first interview after the violence Kaset was even more explicit, and linked together the coup and crack-down in a supernatural fashion: "Kaset blames coup, crackdown on 'fate of the nation'", *Bangkok Post*, 28 January 1993, p. 2.

35. Indeed, when Kaset explained his threatened coup in July 1992 he was giving blood. A newspaper columnist comments: "Long known as a superstitious figure, it could have been that he wanted to shed his blood to eliminate whatever ill omens now staining his stars and stripes after the May bloodshed." (Sopon Onkgara, "Soft landing for Kaset & Co?", *The Nation*, 19 July 1992, p. A9.)

36. *The Nation*, 6 June 1992, p. A3. In the 1 July 1973 issue of *The Nation*, a political cartoon shows Thanom in front of astrological charts "predicting a quick end to student demonstrations" which four months later ousted him from the country.

37. "During Sarit's time, many government officials followed his lead and consulted astrologers at Sarit's temple." (Nerida M. Cook, "Thai Identity in the Astrological Tradition", in *National Identity and Its Defenders: Thailand, 1939–89*, edited by Craig J. Reynolds [Clayton: Monash Papers on Southeast Asia, no. 25, 1991], p. 239.)

38. Morell and Chai-Anan, op. cit., p. 249.

39. Cook, op. cit., p. 236.

40. Ibid., p. 237. Chalidaporn Songsamphan confirmed this in an interview (4 July 1992) and Chalidaporn Songsamphan, "Supernatural Prophesy in Thai Politics: The Role of a Spiritual Cultural Element in Coup Decisions" (Ph.D. dissertation, The Clairemont Graduate School, 1991).

41. Though astrological rituals can be traced to Brahmanism, they are most often performed in Buddhist temples in Thailand. Cook writes that many astrologers point to Buddhist features to get away from "the increasingly discredited Brahamic roots" (Cook, op. cit., p. 241).

42. Saowarop Panyacheewin, "Seeking answers among the stars", *Bangkok Post*, 16 June 1992, p. 31.

43. Cook, op. cit., p. 234.

44. Saowarop, op. cit., p. 31.

45. David Wilson, *Politics in Thailand* (Ithaca: Cornell University Press, 1962), p. 15.

46. Cook, op. cit., p. 251.

47. Saowarop, op. cit., p. 31. Chalidaporn says that many people take credit for naming the auspicious moment for the February coup, thus reinforcing the point of the power of astrology in politics (Chalidaporn, Interview).

48. Quoted in Saowarop, op. cit., p. 31.

49. With the focus on Marxist dialectical materialism, this spiritual power was seen as 'supernatural', or false consciousness. Morell and Chai-Anan write that one of the mistakes of the student movement in the 1970s was that it did not recognize the symbolic power of "nation, religion, monarchy" (Morell and Chai-Anan, op. cit., p. 249). Others point out that they were scripting a different kind of nationalism that did not rely so heavily on this official formula.

50. Pongpet Mekloy, "Curse in a dead man's eye", *Bangkok Post*, 11 June 1992, p. 31.

51. In his first interview since the bloodshed in August 1992, "General Suchinda also denied a report that he had changed his name, adding he did not believe in astrology" (*Bangkok Post*, 21 August 1992, p. 3). Even so, there were numerous reports and rumours about Suchinda's alleged astrological activities. In June and July 1992 reports of other astrological activities filled the newspapers. But the name did not stick; he is still known as Suchinda.

52. For a more comprehensive discussion of PollWatch in Thai politics see William A. Callahan, *PollWatch, Elections and Civil Society* (Aldershot: Ashgate Publishing, 1998).

53. "PollWatch invokes spirits' help", *The Nation*, 10 September 1992, p. 1, and interview with Chaisiri Samudavanija, 18 September 1992. Though *The Nation* and PollWatch translate *mor pi* as 'witch doctor', a more literal and less controversial translation is 'spirit doctor'.

54. "Using 2000-year-old Khmer magic to get rid of devils who obstruct democracy" (in Thai), PollWatch press release, 10 September 1992.

55. Chaisiri, Interview.

56. Ibid.

57. Ratchai Sasiwat, Interview, 28 August 1992.

58. This is where there is an important difference between the Thai language press and the English language press in Bangkok. The popular Thai dailies run many more astrological stories, and the English-language stories quoted in this chapter have largely originated from Thai columns. One could argue that there are different views of

rationality in English and in Thai, and that Thai rational space includes astrology and magic within its boundaries. Although as Nerida Cook points out in her essay, there is also an important debate in the Thai discourse about the worth of astrology and magic.

59. Chalidaporn, Interview.
60. It is telling that one of the chapters of *Catalyst for Change: Uprising in May* is called "Who's to Blame: Rumour Mill Goes into Overdrive" (Post Publishing, *Catalyst for Change: Uprising in May* [Bangkok: Post Publishing, July 1992]).
61. For a critical examination of this phenomenon see Gladys D. Ganley, *The Exploding Political Power of Personal Media* (Norwood: Ablex Publishing Corp., 1992).
62. The Thai Development Support Committee has compiled copies of newspaper articles in English from Thailand and abroad on the freedom of the press issue. ("Special Issue: 47-Day Crisis of the Mass Media under Suchinda's rule", *TDSC [Thai Development Support Committee] Information Sheets*, no. 4, June 1992.)
63. *Bangkok Post*, 24 May 1992, p. 31.
64. The *Bangkok Post* also ran full-page advertisements claiming to be "Thailand's Voice" and saying "In times of crisis, you can rely on Bangkok Post", with subscription information underneath.
65. For example, in June 1992 the ultra-conservative violent forces reorganized themselves with deceptively democratic names; the most important anti-democracy group Apirak Chakri (Defend the Chakri Dynasty), which has close ties to the Air Force, renamed itself Organization of Democracy under the Monarchy. It soon changed its name back again.
66. A classic of social/literary analysis is Roland Barthes, *Image-Music-Text* (New York: Hill and Wang, 1978). For consideration of video texts see Ellen Seiter, "Semiotics and Television", in *Channels of Discourse*, edited by Robert C. Allen (Chapel Hill: University of North Carolina Press, 1987), pp. 17–41. Reynolds, "The Plot of Thai History", also uses such literary theory.
67. "Arthit gets special protection", *The Nation*, 13 June 1992, p. A2. Though then Army Commander General Issarapong Noonpackdee gave a copy to the United States Ambassador, his successor Army Commander General Wimol Wongwanich would not give me a copy one year later. It was produced for public consumption, but only for certain audiences in the village and on the international scene. This was especially effective in the battle of the September 1992 elections. ("The underground war: Groups use massacre videos, leaflets in drive to take the North", *Bangkok Post*, 23 August 1992, p. 9.)

68. The video was delayed for 7½ hours while it was censored; in the end Channel 9's staff still protested its biased production (*Bangkok Post*, 26 May 1992, p. 1).

69. The coroner's report confirmed that many of the dead and wounded were shot while running away (Kritaya Archavanitkul et al., "Political Disharmony in Thai Society: A Lesson from the May 1992 Incident", *Asia Review 1995* 9 [1995]: 49).

70. Actually viewers have to imagine these lyrics since the instrumental version of the song is played.

71. "No members of the security forces received gunshot injuries and none were killed as a result of the crackdown." (Vincent Iacopino and Sidney Jones, *Thailand — Bloody May: Excessive Use of Lethal Force in Bangkok: The Events of May 17–20, 1992*, A Report by Physicians for Human Rights and Asia Watch [New York: Human Rights Watch, October 1992], p. 13.)

72. This is official Ministry of Public Health information which was taken only from hospitals as of 12 June 1992. The number of injured is closer to 1,000. (Kritaya Archavanitkul, Interview, 24 April 1995.)

73. Ad Carabao, the leader of the group, is known for his political activism. The songs and advertisements for the group's then-current album were banned from army radio in April 1992. ("Army radio bans Carabao album songs and ads", *Bangkok Post*, 5 May 1992, p. A3.)

74. One colleague who spent 18 and 19 May sending out faxes complained that her telephone bill was very high for the month of May.

75. Surachart Bamrungsuk, *United States Foreign Policy and Thai Military Rule, 1947–77* (Bangkok: Editions Duang Kamol, 1988). This study provides a general argument about the ties between the U.S. and the Thai military. One sentence tells it all: "Once Kissinger told reporters that they should not pay attention to Thai politicians, but rather to the Thai military." (p. 179).

76. Chamlong Srimuang, the leader of the Palang Dharma Party, is described as "the leader of a renegade Buddhist cult, Santi Asoke, which has ties to the Hare Khrishna drug cult". New Aspiration Party leader General Chavalit Yongchaiyuth, 'slum angel' Pratheep Ungsongtham Hata, and noted critic Sulak Sivaraksa (who was in exile at the time) are listed as subversive foreign agents.

77. This article was used as evidence in a semi-secret report on NGOs as a subversive force, written by right-wing academic Senator Poonsak Wannapong for the Army Defence College in 1992.

78. *The LaRouche Organisation* (Bruxelles: International Confederation of Free Trade Unions, 1987).

79. For more information on Packdee's activities which link the military with labour in Thailand see "Expose on the force that serves the dictators: the revival of the vampire movement", *Phuchatkan Raiwan* [The Manager Daily], 9 June 1992, p. 16. Chin Taplee, head of the National Labour Congress, also criticized pro-democracy protesters, claiming that they were paid Bt40 million by the CIA to rally on 17 May 1992 (*Bangkok Post*, 3 June 1993, p. 1).
80. *The LaRouche Organisation*, p. 4.
81. Ibid., p. 16.
82. Umberto Eco, "Towards a Semiological Guerilla War", in *Travels in Hyper Reality: Essays* (San Diego: Harcourt Brace Jovanovich, 1983), p. 142.
83. General Suchinda exemplified this 'forgetful truth' as a witness at Sulak Sivaraksa's *lèse majesté* trial: his most common answers to simple questions about the February 1991 coup and May 1992 crack-down were "I don't know" and "I don't remember" (1 March 1994, Criminal Court, Bangkok).

chapter 2

MOB DISCOURSE AND THE CULTURAL CONSTRUCTION OF 'THE PEOPLE'*

> ...everyone believes to some degree that wolves howl at the moon, or weigh two hundred pounds, or travel in packs of fifty, or are driven crazy by the smell of blood. None of this is true. The truth is we know little about the wolf. What we know a great deal about is what we imagine the wolf to be.
>
> – Barry Lopez[1]

"The events of May 1992 in Bangkok which overthrew the government of General Suchinda Kraprayoon were a popular uprising." This statement is a common argument, and to support this point numerous investigations, surveys, and essays have been written to determine just who were at the demonstrations. But as Barry Lopez suggests, often we do not know much about the object of our study — the people — but only about what we imagine the people to be.

Thus it is important to ask 'how' we imagine the community of protesters to examine the underlying discourse that not only ordered the events, but also guides our critical understanding of them. While the main question that haunts both the protesters and the soldiers is "Why did protest leader Chamlong Srimuang lead people to their death?",[2] this chapter seeks to question the way this kind of question has been asked. The purpose is not necessarily to rehabilitate élite actors like Chamlong, but more to examine the place of 'the people' and 'public opinion' in Thailand.[3]

Lopez's passage is even more appropriate since many characterized the people involved (*demos*) in the mass protests (demos) as 'mobs' — a term which usually carries the same violent and bloodthirsty imaginings as the wolf. 'Mob' is an oblique entrance into an examination of the political violence of May 1992 because this term is shared by the two opposing forces — the military and the middle class — and can help us re-examine this figuring of the events in terms of identity politics. By tracing this term 'mob' as it has been used in both Thai- and English-language writings about the May events we can chart how it is used to both assemble and dissolve the demonstrations. In other words its meaning, and thus the identity of 'the people' involved in the May events, is open to interpretation and contestation. Mobs were not only imagined communities,[4] but counter-imagined communities as well. And this is not just a question of semantics or borrowings of English terms into the Thai language, for the representations had force: lethal force that killed and injured hundreds of protesters and continues to define scores of missing demonstrators.

The basic argument of this chapter is that even though newspapers and protesters tried to redefine popular political action in May by bringing in new groups — including the middle class — and different methods — including non-violence — there was still the same bloodshed. One reason for this is because they redefined their mode of action by simply modifying old terms, like 'mob', which are also used by the forces of violence in different ways to justify a crack-down. Even though the mass movement in Bangkok and the provinces was characterized by five disciplined weeks of non-violent mass rallies and hunger strikes, the demonstrators were still labelled a 'mob', a chaotic and violent group of people who by definition need to be dispersed. Thus a discursive battle over the definition of 'the people' set the stage for the violence.

Hence this suspicion of political gatherings is not just a military problem; it is embedded in the Thai language and, perhaps more importantly, the Thai political imagination:

> It's a matter of language, and it's not an accident but deliberate. For example, when you talk about gatherings, we usually add the word "protest". I understand that by using the word "mob" or using the word "protest" after the word "gathering" is to create the picture. It is how to use the language to lead the people's opinion in your direction. This reflects the opinion that still influences Thai society which tries to make people understand that the peasants' movement or the ordinary people's movement is not right. Some people may think that only the parliamentary activities are right, and that activity outside parliament is wrong. Therefore they put in the word "mob".[5]

Though many activists are aware of these problems, there does not seem to be a proper and accepted name for a large group of responsible protesters: "As long as we cannot present a new better word, it is very difficult to change the attitude of the people."[6]

Thus there is little room for 'the people' or 'public opinion' as a legitimate force; in May 1992 one well-intentioned person wrote a letter to the editor declaring they "didn't believe that a crowd as big as 100,000 could be engaged in non-violent action".[7] All conflicts are seen as disorder and all differences are seen as violence.[8] In other words, one of the questions asked in this chapter is whether in Thailand there is such a thing as an 'orderly demonstration' or whether the phrase 'non-violent protest' is an oxymoron, a fatal contradiction in terms. Indeed, less than a year after the violence that put both of them into power, Prime Minister Chuan Leekpai and Army Commander General Wimol Wongwanich agreed that grass-roots environmental protests were leading to "mob-rule" and demonstrators "had no respect for the laws and regulations of society". Wimol urged the people to "not be used or manipulated by other people who want to cause rifts and do not want to see peace restored in society".[9]

Peoples, Publics, Crowds

Before looking at mobs in Thailand, it is important to examine how 'the people' is defined in social science. This may seem like an obvious empirical question, but as the *International Encyclopedia of the Social Sciences* points out "there is no generally accepted definition". But that is not to say that the public or "public opinion is in any sense meaningless".[10] The meaning of 'the people' comes through how it is used; in other words, 'the people' is continually defined and created, redefined, and reimagined according to historical and social demands. For example, in 1932 'the people' were limited to a few dozen bureaucrats and military officers in the People's Party which overthrew the absolute monarchy in Siam.[11]

Historically, the public as a responsible force that could have a valid opinion — public opinion — is a relatively recent concept. These notions of the people originated from the development of capitalism and the European Enlightenment. People became a powerful public through education and open conversation, active debate, and "reasoned discourse" in civil society; in coffee-houses, salons, and table societies "the authority of argument supplanted the authority of title".[12] In other words 'the people' are not profitably imagined according to a stable epistemological category of essential identity — who you are: an aristocrat — but more as an ontological discussion of identity defined according to what you do: a witty bourgeois.

The public as a responsible force flowered in eighteenth century France leading up to the French Revolution, which was perhaps the first time that 'the people' rose up in a political movement that displaced a whole social and economic system. Price argues that "With the growth of a politically active public sphere, public opinion emerged as a new form of political authority — one with which the bourgeoisie could challenge absolute rule."[13] Yet 'the people' was not a clear concept then either, for Price also notes that the struggles in France were not simply the public against the monarchy and the aristocracy.

> *The public* was mainly a political or ideological construct without any clear sociological referent; it provided an implicit new system of authority in which the government and its critics had to claim the judgement of public opinion to secure their respective aims.[14]

Both the monarchy and its critics created 'the public' and used its 'opinion' to their advantage. Indeed, though many point to Rousseau's populist notion of 'the public' and the common good, others credit Necker with popularizing the notion of public opinion in the service of the King of France. As Necker said in 1792: "Only fools, pure theorists, or apprentices fail to take public opinion into account."[15] Yet which 'public' was this? This naming of the people signified a shift from aristocratic court politics to bourgeois capitalist political-economics: for Necker public opinion refers to the opinion of the French Government's creditors.

'The people' and 'public opinion' were also used in both democratic and undemocratic ways in 1992. Even though the movement can accurately be called a popular struggle, it was not simply 'the people' *versus* Suchinda or civil society *versus* the state. Rather 'the people' and 'public opinion' as concepts were shaped and used by different groups, including the Suchinda government, the Confederation for Democracy, and later Interior Ministries. Suchinda insisted to the end that he had a popular mandate through Parliament, that the people as voters had indirectly picked him to be Prime Minister through constitutional processes. Others laboured to redefine the Thai people to downplay demonstrations in Bangkok, saying that the silent majority in the provinces supported Suchinda and produced their own popular demonstrations to prove their point — although, as we will see, some of these pro-Suchinda demonstrations backfired.

This discursive practice can be brutal, and it goes beyond the military leadership and its mistakes in 1992 to permeate the Thai political vocabulary. Even though most agreed that the protest was broad-based, the Interior Ministry in November 1992 redefined the category of 'protester' to include only 'those who would likely be there' to lower the number of missing in the service of Thailand's international image.[16] Even when people were shot, their needs were ignored on discursive grounds. For example, although a soft-drink seller was hit in the head by a stray bullet, she could not claim any compensation from the government since she "didn't fit into any of the categories".[17] One way of tracing the discursive violence is to examine the categories used to frame the struggle;

this is a crucial point because new terms were used, terms which are multivalent and open to confusion, imagination, translation, and retranslation: the mob and the mohp.

Mob and Mohp[18]

There are various ways of referring to social groups — the people, the public, the crowd, the mass — and each carries with it its own value judgement. Since 'the public' arose in the Age of Reason as a political force, most of these value judgements concern the rationality of the groups. Rationality was the key to power. Debates about popular action over the last few hundred years have centred on the questions of reason and emotion, organization and spontaneity, and order and chaos. While some championed the devolution of power to 'the people', others feared the tyranny of the majority, rule by the mediocre, and government by the lowest common denominator. Indeed, while supporters of the French Revolution called rule by the people 'democracy', others called it 'mobacracy'.[19] As we have seen, such namings persist today in Thailand: "[Mohp] means a group of people who don't have discipline. People who move crazily.... I prefer to call the gathering of the people a rally."[20]

Collective behaviour became an object of study at the turn of the century because of the increase in spontaneous crowds, strikes, mass demonstrations, and riots.[21] Though 'the public' is seen as a rational actor which discusses issues and can have a valid opinion, 'the crowd' is seen as susceptible to persuasion: emotional and non-rational appeals as well as propaganda. "The puzzle to be solved was how otherwise-civil individuals could be transformed into angry mobs or enthusiastic demonstrators."[22] This puzzle was taken up in 1895 by LeBon in *La Psychologie des Foules* [Mob Psychology] which saw such collective action as destructive and violent, and definitely irrational.[23] In English, as in French, 'mob' is a crucial part of the discursive economy of order and chaos. While theorists were imagining a responsible 'public' in the Age of Reason, others were warning against the irresponsible, uncontrollable flip side of collective action: mobs. Mobs are located on the chaotic side of the order/chaos distinction. Indeed, 'mob' is seen as a bastardization, a popularization of sacred language, as an abbreviation of the Latin term *mobile vulgus*.

There is an important shift here from 'civil individual' to 'violent mass'. Mobs refer to nameless, faceless, and formless groups of people who cannot otherwise be categorized and thus controlled. The first definition for 'mob' is the "disorderly and riotous part of the population...bent on, or liable to be incited to, acts of lawlessness and outrage".[24] Rather than being a responsible political actor that can have a logical opinion, like 'the public', the mob is characterized as emotional, insane, disorderly, unlawful, and violent. In a classic police manual, *Riot Control — Materiel and Techniques*, the word 'mob' appears on nearly every page, along with 'violence', 'riot', and 'terrorist'.[25] While the public can demonstrate and negotiate, mobs can only riot and loot.

Bangkok Rallies: From 'Horse-faced Mohp' to 'Sedan Mohp'

Contrast this riotous assembly with how the *Asian Wall Street Journal* commemorated the first anniversary of the May events: "They were called the mobile-phone mob, the yogurt mob, the fax freedom fighters" who were "brave" and "polite".[26] How did the mob/ mohp enter the editorial pages of the *Asian Wall Street Journal*, and thus the mainstream of middle class capitalist life? To answer this question we must continue to trace the discursive economy of mob images which started with the Latin *mobile vulgus*, was transformed into English 'mob', then Thai 'mohp', which in turn was retranslated back into English 'mob' in the international media.

Even though they are wrapped in the same chain of meaning, the history and usage of Thai 'mohp' differ from those of English 'mob'. It is a relatively recent term in the Thai language and it was debated in two very different contexts: at a Campaign for Popular Democracy (CPD) Roundtable Discussion and in the Sophon Rattanakorn Committee which declared that the crackdown was procedurally correct.[27] Indeed, it has not made it into any dictionaries yet, but both these documents struggle with 'mob' as a borrowed and hybrid term, just as English commentators in the seventeenth century classed 'mob' as a borrowing from Latin *mobile vulgus.* The Thai origin of 'mohp' is not clear; there were few references to 'mohp' in newspapers during the mass demonstrations of the 1970s. It is doubtful that there is one single source; rather it probably appeared at many places in both academic and popular culture in the 1980s, in translations of French and English texts, as well as a borrowed term for newspaper headlines to describe demonstrations.[28]

But out of this murky past, 'mohp' came to dominate both banner headlines and political commentaries in the Thai and English newspapers of April/May 1992.[29] After 4 May 'mohp' was used in the headlines of popular national newspapers like *Matichon* — which translates as *Public Opinion* — nearly every day. Yet even though 'mohp' is a popular term, it is an unstable one. It appeared in reports and commentaries on collective action concerning the appointment of General Suchinda Kraprayoon as Prime Minister of Thailand, but in very different ways over a very short period of time. On 7 April 1992 a "horse-faced mohp" cheered Suchinda's imminent rise to power.[30] On 22 April, after 100,000 people gathered to demonstrate against Suchinda being an unelected Prime Minister, the editor of the same newspaper named this group the *"Mohp Rotkeng* — Sedan mob".[31] This radical change in the short space of two weeks was typical of the discursive mechanisms which would frame the events of May in the following month. Hence in this section I would like to trace the transformation of the 'horse-faced mohp' to 'sedan mohp' — in the next section we would see how it was transformed back again.

'Horse-faced mohp' is the literal translation of a theatrical term used to describe a group of people who have been hired to applaud a public figure. In the 7 April newspaper there is a picture of people energetically congratulating Suchinda. The caption reads: "Horse-faced mohp [*mohp naamaa*]…A group of people came to give a basket of flowers to General Suchinda Kraprayoon to support him to be the new prime minister." Thus *mohp naamaa* here refers to the groups of people that 'spontaneously' came out to support Suchinda's controversial rise to the office of Prime Minister. On page two is an article entitled *"Mohp jatdang* — Organized mohp came to praise Su, and encourage him to be PM".[32] The article goes on to report that most of the people in the Army Auditorium cheering Suchinda were from paramilitary groups such as the National Defence Volunteers and Military Reservists for National Security. "The army provided excellent service, and they are well prepared to greet guests. They had rented out the mobile toilet trucks. The army sent letters to all newspapers announcing that there would be people coming to support Suchinda, and that there would be a lunch for reporters."

An 'organized mohp' then is not taken very seriously as a measure of genuine public opinion. Although organized mohps have been quite violent in the past, there is an obvious joking tone to these articles.

As in the English definition, a people can be organized, *mobilized*, if they are manipulated by another force. The only disorganization in this mohp came when a village leader from Ratburi province told reporters that she wanted "Big Jiew" (General Chavalit Yongchaiyudh, one of Suchinda's rivals), to become Prime Minister. She corrected herself once her colleagues reminded her that they were there to support Suchinda.

The next mass demonstration in Bangkok came on 20 April; but it was quite different, and involved a new configuration of people in a different kind of organization. The demonstrators defied the usual categories of 'protester'. They were neither the regular pro-military protesters — bused in from the villages or the army's mass organizations — nor were they the regular pro-democracy protesters — students, academics, opposition party members. "Just who was there?" was the question that many were asking the next day.

Though the headlines of *The Manager Daily* did not label the second mass rally in April a 'mohp', and this newspaper refrained from using 'mohp' in banner headlines until well into May, the newspaper's editor made an important switch. In his 22 April column, Kamnoon Sittisaman noted the difference in the organization of the 100,000 demonstrators on 20 April that distinguished it from the 6 April gathering. It is common in Thailand for opposition parties to bus in organized mohps from the provinces as a way of destabilizing the government, and many assumed that the 20 April demonstration would be the same. Kamnoon writes that according to sources in the New Aspiration Party, one of the opposition parties that hosted the demonstration, "There were reports that someone was prepared to bring people from the provinces to fill the square."[33] But the turn-out to the demonstration called this horse-faced mohp scripting into question:

> ...the character of the people who came was different, they were a *mohp rotkeng* — sedan mohp. Five to six thousand people [of 100,000 demonstrators] were from non-government organizations or were allies of the four opposition political parties, as well as reporters and intelligence agents. The remaining people wore neckties and drove personal cars or rode motorcycles carrying briefcases and files. They had pagers clipped to their waists, and carried mobile phones when they came after their businesses closed. They were not college students, workers, vocational students or political party members. Imagine who were they?

The article goes on to give a social and financial profile of these new middle class demonstrators who drove up in their cars — thus the term 'sedan mob'.[34] By focusing analysis on this article in *The Manager Daily* I do not mean to say that it originated the mohp argument. There are also many other examples in the more popular press. Rather, I am intentionally citing articles from the business-oriented press — *The Manager Daily* and the *Asian Wall Street Journal* — to show how 'mohp-mania' was important in the imaginings of 'bourgeois democracy' in Thailand and Asia as a whole.[35]

One way that Kamnoon authorizes this new grouping in terms of a 'public' who could have an 'opinion' is to paint them as people who are tied more to principles and policies than to personalities, who are motivated by their individual beliefs and not some horse-faced opposition politician:

> Mohp rotkeng are not a poor people's mohp or a rich people's mohp. All the characteristics of the people that I am talking are those of the middle class. They do not love Gen. Chavalit Yongchaiyudh. Some dislike him. Not all of them love Gen. Chamlong Srimuang. They may prefer Aphisit V. to his Democrat Party....

This new group of people needed a name to distinguish themselves from the bused-in mobs. But rather than creating a new name, they modified an old one. Thus while mob is characteristically "lower class, rabble, uncultured and illiterate",[36] now the mob is middle class: "Attempts to capture the characteristics of this new breed of protesters resulted in such nicknames as: *mob mua thue* (the mobile-phone mob), *mob hi-tec, mob rotkeng* (the sedan mob), *mob picnic,* and *mob nom priew* (yogurt-drink mob)."[37] In English this 'middle-class mob' naming makes even more sense since this upwardly *mob*ile group used *mob*ile phones, auto*mob*iles, not to mention *mob*ile toilet trucks. Such a formulation of the middle-class mohp was common in editorial cartoons. For example, on 15 May in the nation's largest circulation daily *Thai Rath*, Chai Rachawat's "Muban Tungmamung" comic had a cartoon entitled "How to prevent a mob". The advice included requiring people to get official permission to send phonelink messages, making it illegal to sell or have "instruments to create mob" (which the drawing shows as a mobile phone), and punishing the traffic police who let car drivers come to a demonstration.[38] This middle-class mohp characterization of the 1992 demonstrations came to be the norm, and was translated back into English 'mob' when it made its way into the international media in mid-May:

> Last week's demonstrators were not the rent-a-mob crowd characterized by government broadcasting media. There were numerous mobile telephones, briefcases, and neckties — all symbols of Thailand's growing number of salarymen: well-educated and savvy, but hitherto not known for their burning political passions.[39]

After the term mohp was popularized as a new force, the newspapers endeavoured to redefine mohp into a rational, responsible political actor: to define the faceless mob in terms of actual people, who had not only names, but occupations, children, debts, and thus an opinion in what Price calls a "new system of authority". Indeed, Anek Laothamatas' book on the May events confirms how this ironic characterization of mass action became widespread: *Mobile Phone Mob: The Middle Class and Business People with Democratic Development.*[40]

To craft the middle-class mohp into a responsible public actor, two tried and true methods were widely used. Public opinion surveys were used for macro-level tabulation, and 'wo/man on the street' interviews were used for the micro-level elaboration. The following passage is typical of the surveys:[41]

> On the night of May 17, the Social Science Association of Thailand conducted a sample survey of 2,000 people at the demonstration in Sanam Luang. The survey confirmed that the majority of demonstrators were from middle class backgrounds. 52 percent had a B.A. degree, and 14.5 percent had a higher qualification. Students comprised only 8.4 percent, and workers and slum dwellers accounted for only 10.2 percent. The remainder, numbering over four-fifths of the total samples, included salaried workers in the private sector, civil servants and business owners. As for income, 14.1 percent received less than 5,000 baht per month; 28.5 percent between 5,000 and 9,900; 45.5 percent received between 10,000–50,000 baht; and 6.2 percent above 50,000. *The typical member of the 'mob' was a well-off, well-educated, white collar worker.* [emphasis added][42]

It was not just that members of the mohp were well-off; they were also well-educated and thus could not be easily misled. Again, Anek's book links the mob with the middle class and democratic development. The mohp was rational and sober, and not just metaphorically. While horse-faced mohps often consumed liquor, and drunken participants became violent more easily, the middle-class mohp was intentionally non-alcoholic to stay non-violent: thus it was called the 'yogurt-drink mohp'.

Newspapers also went to great lengths to interview different sorts of individual people — both before and after the violence — to get specific stories to flesh out the general conclusions of the public opinion polls. The middle-class mohp first became the focus of the English-language press in an article entitled "A yuppie mob",[43] which explained the peculiarities of the second round of mass demonstrations which lasted from 6 May to 11 May.

> One factor that puzzled and fascinated press and observers alike about the recent anti-Suchinda demonstration was that those who "took a walk on the wild side" this time around

> were, and acted, anything but wild. A large number were
> certified members of the comfortable middle class, the people
> for whom mobile phones and pagers are made. They strolled
> to the rally sites in their polo shirts and jeans. Some sported
> loafers or sneakers, predictably chosen for ease of running if
> push came to shove. A few arrived at the rally in their shiny
> Mercedes, and/or decked-up choppers.[44]

The article goes on to catalogue the 'goodies' sold by 'vendors for democracy' and highlights the extremely non-confrontational, non-violent feeling of the demonstrations which were variously described as a festival, a party, a picnic: all suitable for a Sunday middle-class family outing.[45] Again, this middle class character of the demonstrations was described in terms of food: "Many of the protesters brought their own provisions. Prepared for all situations, they came equipped with, not gas masks or bullet-proof vests, but bags of drinks and snacks."[46]

Other articles focused on the political issues rather than playful ethnographies. People were asked questions such as whether they had been 'organized' or whether they had come 'spontaneously', whether they were there to support a particular person, or whether they were there to support 'democracy'.[47] As one person put it on 10 May when violence seemed imminent: "Joining the rally does not mean that we support any particular person. We are doing it for the future of the country."[48] On 18 May General Chainarong Noonpackdee, the commander of the First Army Region troops which executed the crack-down, asked a man who was being arrested on Rajdamnoen Avenue: "Were you recruited to join the demonstration?" The man answered: "No, I've never voted for Chamlong or his Palang Dharma Party candidates. But I came here to fight for democracy because opposition MPs were prevented from carrying out their parliamentary duty."[49]

So even the middle-class mob member's answers keep leading us back to the army's scripting of the mohp: are you blindly following Chamlong?

Army's Mohp

> An angry mob is attacking the palace.[50]

The military story of April–May 1992 is one of order and chaos. Their statements both before and after the violence made their position quite clear. The mohps did not "play by the rules" and were creating chaos with their mohp rule. As Khien writes: "The government used the barbed wire wall to stop demonstrators but the latter failed to respect the government's rights by destroying the barbed wire."[51] The military thus was forced to step in and restore order as democratic peace-keepers — recall that the junta called itself the National Peace Keeping Council (NPKC). The military was thus imagining the demos at the demos with an Oxford English Dictionary – *Riot Control* notion of a mob. The military government considered that ulterior forces were at work, and hence the people who were demonstrating were not a responsible public, but an organized mohp.[52] The army felt that critics were "simply a bunch of professional agitators, students who should be studying or greedy politicians who just want the same benefits for themselves".[53] Suchinda was suspicious of opposition politicians who had failed to gain power in the March 1992 elections, specifically those who had military training — Major-General Chamlong and General Chavalit. Here Suchinda was taking advantage of common international definition of popular support which looks to voting behaviour: "election outcomes are perhaps the most visible instances of public opinion…".[54]

Yet Suchinda's new-found respect for parliamentary rule seemed rather cynical since he had led a coup against an elected government fourteen months earlier. While the NPKC was in power, he made sure that everyone knew that parliamentary politics was beneath him: "I cannot go begging for votes. I cannot lower myself."[55] The military championed parliamentary rule and constitutional government only once they had hand-crafted the constitution as a means to perpetuate and institutionalize military power. After the March 1992 elections the military controlled the House of Representatives, the appointed Senate, as well as the troops of the three armed services which were united for the first time since 1973. Hence parliamentary rule and military order supported each other. Indeed, according to Suchinda, the orderly way to solve problems was to "play by the rules" and debate the issues in Parliament. Politics on the streets is not a festival, a party, or a picnic, but mob rule which challenges law and public order.[56] The traffic jams that demonstrations created discursively played into this discourse of military order — *jarajon* (traffic) is a homophone for *jalajon* (riot). Hence General Issarapong could state: "If there are demonstrations that cause traffic jams and disrupt people's lives I, in my capacity as commander of the Internal Peace-keeping Command, will order a stop to such activities."[57] People were transformed into a violent mohp, and thus order and peace could only be restored through lethal force: the only way to deal with a mohp is to "dissolve" it.[58]

According to then Supreme Commander ACM Kaset Rojananil in his first interview after the violence, lethal force was not just necessary, it was the civilized way to restore order. When asked why the army used bullets rather than tear gas in crowd control as in 'civilized countries' he answered:

> I don't know how civilized countries deal with the mobs. But I think those countries use more violent measures…[against those who] want to overthrow a government which is democratically legitimate…. When the bloodthirsty mobs came near the soldiers, they had to aim their guns low and fire to intimidate them.[59]

Violence and civilization are thus wed: "War…is the fundamental concept of our civilization."[60] Order and force are allies against chaos. Though many dismiss Kaset's statements as thin excuses and empty rhetoric for military miscalculations, there is an order to the military's discourse of chaos and civilization which goes far beyond May 1992 and Kaset. It is important to look at this notion of order/chaos to see how the military imagined the violence and thus reframed 'the people' into a 'mohp'. For example, the military was sounding the warnings of a violent mohp when there was little evidence of any violence: Kaset first warned of an "explosive mohp" and "riots" on 4 May in response to Chamlong's non-violent hunger strike. In other words, even though the soldiers shot unarmed civilians, the army imagined itself as peace-keepers and agents of law and order while it imagined the people as a mohp instrument of chaos.

This military notion of the mohp persists and is also shared by military officers who did not support the violent crack-down.[61] These 'pro-democracy' officers blame Issarapong, Chavalit, and Chamlong for the violence since as soldiers they should have known better than to bring people out on the streets.[62] This view of the people is shared by many academics. The assumption is that whenever people demonstrate on the streets, there will be violence; there is no such thing as a non-violent protest.[63] According to this view of Thai society, the people are never a public which can have an opinion, for every popular protest is always manipulated by a 'third hand' for less noble aims.

In this section I will explore the presuppositions of military order and how it constructs its Other — the mohp — through a discursive analysis of selected military texts which give an international frame to Thai activities. While I will point out contradictions to the military story, I am more interested here in the discourse of order which often serves to produce chaos. This is not limited to Thailand, but also occurs in other military governments around the world; the official discourse surrounding the 4 June 1989 massacre in Beijing is also littered with references to 'chaos'.[64] Thus analysis will dwell on how the Thai army frames its statements in such a way as to guide the discourse to questions which will legitimize its immediate actions and, perhaps more importantly, guide the discourse away from questions which may present problems to its ideology. Then I will reframe the question to re-examine the military's action to see if it is a mohp by its own definition of violence and chaos, or if the extreme violence was part of the plan.

Military Order

Order is both the strength and weakness of the military. As General Saiyud Kerdphol, a former Supreme Commander, says: "What is good about the military is that they are disciplined. And the weakness of the discipline is that they follow orders."[65] The philosophical concept of Order thus becomes 'orders' for the military. This paradox of military order is not peculiar to Thailand. The narrative of rationality and violence is common to many discourses of the military and democracy throughout the world, and the word 'mob' is central to them. Ever since militaries were made into mass armies and professionalized in the nineteenth century, the military has been the institution that is defined in terms of order. In Thailand the military is often seen as the only well-organized institution.[66] Even though philosophers like to equate rationality with peace, actually the military and its organized violence is another outgrowth of science and rational planning: "To conduct war is to execute a rational plan, in other words to launch an enterprise."[67]

Three writers of the classics of military strategy — Machiavelli, Frederick the Great of Prussia, and Klauswitz — are all noteworthy in their focus on the rational ordering of the military thinking and practice, which was typified by a concentration on mental and physical discipline.[68] Military discipline has its repercussions on the rest of society, and some note that the mix of military and civilian culture through practices like conscription did not serve to civilize the army, but to militarize the civilian sphere.[69] Klein goes one step further: "In traditional military strategy, the disciplining of forces was an essential element of being able to conduct success-ful operations. The idea was rather straightforward: to domesticate one's own people."[70] This domestication of people was not merely conducted through military drills. The discipline permeates social discourses of language and thought. Klein makes the connection between language and society to argue that military strategy has its own discursive forces that go far beyond physical discipline: "...strategy has been predicated on a series of bifurcations: of the Self and the Other, domestic and foreign, order and chaos, univer-sality and particularity, unity and anarchy".[71] The order here is the order of discourse which itself is not natural, but self-reflexively defines the 'natural'. This military ordering is not an either/or choice; these binaries have hierarchical moral judgements attached to them. The military discourse

> does its work through the establishment of dyads, imposing the rule of two onto a field of many, followed immediately by the assignment of hierarchical ordering: there are two forces in the world (e.g. "us" and "them", or safety and

danger) and one is benevolent while the other is suspicious. Never mind all the places and persons that don't fit into either category, or spill into both. Never think of the possibility of difference that is neither oppositional nor hierarchical, of equality that does not collapse into sameness, of proliferation that defies linear rank ordering. ... Let no otherness escape either conquest or conversion.[72]

In other words once the military defines itself as 'order' it produces chaos; once it defines itself as a peace-keeper, the 'other' thus must fill the mirror role as the instrument of violence. "Language does not correspond to an external world of referents; rather, language constitutes, produces, and reproduces its own system of referents. Strategic language as well creates that to which it purports to be responding."[73] The military imagines its enemies in a strict moral system where the instruments of violence are used in 'peace-keeping'.

Klein argues that the images deployed in the military order of discourse set the stage for material conflict: "military strategy is engaged in a construction and circulation of particular visions of political life, and that these visions entail the violent domestication of forces that are presented as external, alien, and in need of taming".[74] Military order thus is the only order. As one Thai academic commented: "The military establishment will not tolerate any disobedience since a soldier considers order as power. Any form of insubordination is immediately regarded as a challenge to this power...."[75]

Military strategy's "effect as a discourse of power is certainly to inscribe a political space with violence".[76] One way that militaries inscribe political space with violence is to set up the peace/violence dyad with themselves on the peaceful end. Mehmed, Ferguson, and Turnbull (with Mulford) point out how national security discourse works this way: The United States military uses the discourse of peace/national security, rather than the discourse of violence/war.[77] War is associated with heroes, military virtues, and victories, but also with destruction, death, and loss. War is more personal — something that "our boys go off to" — and it is something which is won or lost. Actually war is associated with confusion, dislocation, and challenges to military order and virtue. "War carries the risk that we might lose a way of life, and life itself."[78]

National security, on the other hand, is a discourse of order and chaos. The U.S. military changed its institutional name from the War Department to the Defense Department during World War II, and national security entered the strategic vocabulary soon after as a way of explaining the new kind of the discipline needed for the Cold War.[79] The central idea in national security discourse is "we live in a dangerous world", which includes both foreign enemies and domestic agents of chaos. Though war is traditionally organized around territorial borders, national security is organized more around discursive borders. National security brings the military more directly involved with politics, because the soldiers have to work to define their enemy, rather than just firing at the opposite trench. Thus national security is wrapped up in national identity and its own discursive boundaries. In the United States the discourse of national security set the stage for things like the House Un-American Activities Committee, where political activities were criminalized into 'treason'. Laws are easily broken in the name of the law and order of quelling communist hordes waiting at our borders; just ask Oliver North. Mob discourse co-operates well with national security discourse. The dedication to Applegate's *Riot Control — Materiel and Techniques* reads: "Respectfully dedicated to free-world law enforcement agencies, with confidence that they will be able to meet and surmount mob violence and incipient insurrection, whenever and wherever they may occur." Excepting if they occur in communist countries, that is.

The discourse of peace-keeping has intensified since the Soviet bloc collapsed. In a way the collapse of the United States/Soviet Union binary intensified the national security discourse through George Bush's 'New World Order'. After this fundamental binary dissolved, uncertainty and chaos have increased; hence heavily armed international peace-keepers are called in to bring order to the chaos of Rwanda, Somalia, and Bosnia. This order is also very discursive since these complex conflicts, which involve multiple factors, cannot be reduced to simple ideological labels which rely on us/them, self/other. As one of the U.S. army recruiters said while bombs were raining down on Baghdad during the Gulf War: "We're about peace, not war."[80]

Thai Military Order

When it ousted a democratically elected government in 1991, the Thai junta did not call itself a 'War Council', but the 'National Peace Keeping Council' (NPKC). This of course is not the first time that the Thai military defined itself as a saviour and held a coup for the benefit of democracy.[81] The tone of the announcements of the NPKC echoed those of previous coups in 1947, 1957, and 1958.[82] The key words of NPKC came from the conservative vocabulary: literally, the NPKC translates as the "council to preserve the peace and orderliness of the nation". Orderliness here refers to the conservative ideology of nation, king, religion, and military.

Indeed, Suchinda repeated such tropes in his parliamentary response to the no-confidence motion in early May 1992. Suchinda criticized his opponents in terms of the national security of national icons: General Chamlong was figured as a threat to Buddhist religion and General Chavalit was framed as a communist threat to the monarchy. Before the violence in May 1992 many people commented that the army was using the same national security script that it had used before to justify violence.[83]

Unlike national security discourse in the United States, which is focused on nuclear weapons and the Soviet Union, the dance of order and chaos is largely internal in Thailand, especially since the communist insurgency inaugurated its armed struggle in 1965.[84] Thailand thus fit into the global Cold War equation as a hot spot, Kissinger's Unsinkable Aircraft Carrier, for what was foreign in America was domestic in Thailand.

> The discourse of national security is undoubtedly a very effective paranoia put into Thai people's heads by the Thai state. The creation of otherness, the enemy in particular, is necessary to justify the existing political and social control against rivals from without as well as from within. Without this discursive enemy, all the varieties of coercive force, from a paramilitary organization on every border of Thailand to the professional army, would be redundant. In contrast to the general belief, the state and its security apparatus survive

> because of the enemy. Discursively, if not actually, what
> actively creates the enemy and produces most threats to a
> country if not the state's security mechanism? The enemy
> must be presented, produced, or implicated and then discur-
> sively sustained. It is always projected — if not overtly *desired*.[85]

Thus, even though the war was waged on Thai soil, up through
the 1970s communism was figured as an external threat not just
to the government, but to the Thai national identity as defined
through the three sacred institutions: nation, religion, and
monarchy. Actually, this was an old tactic, for when 'Siam' was
renamed 'Thailand' in 1939, the definition of treason connected
national identity with national security. Certain groups and political
activities, most notably communists, were thus defined as "un-
Thai" or even "anti-Thai".[86] For example,

> A reporter said he once teased a Thai about being communist,
> but the Thai did not find the remark funny and quickly
> replied: "I am not a communist. I am a Thai." This is how
> the Thai state officially view communism as well. In a nut-
> shell, the rationality of the anticommunist act (1952), whose
> model was the un-American activities legislation, was that
> communism is un-Thai in its ideas and way of life.[87]

Hence the military's strategy to combat the communist insurgency
was to hunt down and shoot the communists as "traitors under
the direction of foreign powers and undeniably enemies of the
country".[88]

But after over a decade of the army's imaging the enemy in
order to shoot it, history shows that the communist insurgency
was growing in the late 1970s. The more ruthless the army was,
the more people joined the Communist Party of Thailand (CPT)
to resist it. In other words, the army's strategy for stamping out
communist insurgency in Thailand was not only not working, it
was creating and reproducing its enemy far too effectively: "It was
judged that using primarily military means to solve the problem
of communism only resulted in expanding the problem...".[89]

The Thai military expanded the communist insurgency even
further with the violent right-wing crack-down in 1976 and its
discursive ordering of social forces. While the period of Open Politics

was characterized by a multiplicity of groups and ideologies, the society polarized once the army enforced its binary ordering of Thailand. After the 6 October 1976 crack-down students and other progressive groups were forced to choose between two, and only two, options in the right/left political distinction. Once again military order is the only order. Either they supported the right-wing military, or they fled to the jungle to join the CPT.

To better address this growing insurgency, the military had to reimagine its enemy and switch from war-making to peace-keeping. It was reorganized in 1980 with a broader mission of national security that inserted soldiers more directly into the political field.[90] The Thai military had a national security discourse in place that could both produce an enemy and justify violence against it, in the name of peace-keeping and law and order.

Indeed, there are obvious parallels in the ordering imperatives of the national security discourse and the discourse of 'the people'. Suchinda insisted that the demonstrations were part of a new communist insurgency. In his speech to Parliament Suchinda "accused some of the opposition leaders of wanting to set up a communist system", and on television on 19 May Suchinda stated that because communists and ex-military leaders were behind the unrest it "made it hard for the government to maintain law and order". To underline his point, he said: "They want to destroy the system of government, overthrow the constitutional monarchy and bring in a government that will machine gun people in the streets."

The Soldiers' Story[91]

> The government declared a state of emergency.... But the protesters failed to perceive the government's good intention to restore peace.

> We are poor creatures, we have nothing but our teeth; whatever we want to do, good or bad, we can tackle it only with our teeth.[92]

The military had many explanations, some of them conflicting, for the violence. In addition to examining what the military says, it is important to analyse how the military wrote the story as a discourse to create the meaning. At the risk of anaesthetizing the

violence, this section aims to show how the military uses its discursive arsenal to site the enemy where there was none, and then
shoot the demonstrators with very real guns. To reframe a quotation cited above, we will examine how the army transformed
"otherwise-civil individuals...into angry mobs or enthusiastic
demonstrators".[93]

Though there are many quotations from military sources about
the May violence, the order of the military discourse came out
much more in June 1992 when Kaset and Issarapong were asked
to testify before a parliamentary committee investigating the
massacre. Neither of them showed up for the 16 June 1992 session,
but both offered written testimony. It is through this written
testimony that the random quotations from interviews and official
statements can be woven into a narrative with its own logic in
terms of a plot-line, characters, and grammar.[94] In other words, in
writing this short history of the events of April and May 1992, the
military emplots the facts:

> [The historian] makes his story by including some events
> and excluding others, by stressing some and subordinating
> others. This process of exclusion, stress, and subordination is
> carried out in the interest of constituting *a story of a particular
> kind*. That is to say, he 'emplots' his story.[95]

"The Soldiers' Story" is such a history of a particular kind, and it
was not written by a disinterested historian. It is much like the
dynastic histories of China which were written by the conquerors
in a moral tale to justify their expenditure of life and property. Yet
since the army 'lost' the struggle in May, Issarapong was on the
other end when he presented this history to the parliamentary
committee in June 1992. "The Soldiers' Story" is one among many
which try to justify the fatal violence, while at the same time
expressing regret for the losses which were, nevertheless, scripted
as "unavoidable". It relates to the mohp and the brutality in a
moral tale which appeals to reason, law, and national security.

Characters: Peace-keepers vs Rioters
Characters are actually hard to find in this military text. The
grammar is such that many of the sentences lack definite subjects.

People are largely nameless and faceless. Yet even with all these indefinite actors, there are two, and only two, clear[96] sets of characters in "The Soldiers' Story": the military and the mohp.

Issarapong sets the stage of his story in terms of military order by introducing himself and the text in terms of the customary list of official positions: army commander-in-chief, director of the army's internal peace-keeping forces, director of the Capital Security Command, and capital peace-keeping commander. Thus his positions authorize the text, but more importantly, this excessively long list of titles lends Issarapong authority as a peace-keeper who is concerned with security.

People under his command are referred to as the Capital Peace-keeping Force, the authorities, the government, security forces, troops, and soldiers.

Suchinda is mentioned only at the beginning of Issarapong's chronology to weave together the discourses of national security and military democracy: "A royal command appointed Gen. Suchinda Kraprayoon as prime minister, who was recognized by the international community.... Gen. Suchinda resigned from all military positions and was appointed prime minister for the sake of national security and in accordance with the democratic system and the Thai constitution." Although the protests were directed squarely at Suchinda, he disappears in "The Soldiers' Story". All protests against Suchinda are refigured as "anti-government moves". The only other time Suchinda is mentioned is at the end of the story when he had an audience with King Bhumipol. Hence while Issarapong is framed by military authority, Suchinda is framed by the palace. He enters the scene via a royal appointment, and he leaves the text through a royal audience.

The other side is largely nameless, being referred to with mass nouns and plurals such as the masses, the opposition, crowds, mohps, rioters, terrorists, arsonists, demonstrators, protesters, trouble makers, instigators, "obviously aggressive people", "certain groups bent on violent acts", "some groups with malicious intentions", "people who were instigated and were out of their minds", and lastly, "bodies". Thus demonstrators were portrayed as a negative to the army's positive, violence to the army's peace-keeping.

In his conclusion Issarapong notes a difference in the people who came to the rallies at different times: "It should be noted that the 4–11 May rallies were peaceful. But rioters during 17–20 May acted differently. They apparently wanted to create situations which could develop into urban terrorism. The number of rioters was estimated at 500 and they tried to infiltrate the peaceful rallies." As we will see, this contradicts Issarapong's own chronology of the events and narrative of hidden agendas and impending violence.

Proper names are few. Chalard Vorachart is mentioned starting his hunger strike, but his character is domesticated in the same sentence: "[he] received very little attention". Student and non-governmental organizations are also named in the same passage. Major-General Chamlong Srimuang, who is commonly framed as Suchinda's arch-rival, appears by name hunger striking, moving the protests, getting arrested by the army "in a bid to prevent highly possible riots", and having an audience with King Bhumipol.

Otherwise there are no named people or organizations. The Confederation for Democracy, which co-ordinated the 17 May demonstration and was very active after the violence, is conspicuously missing from this account.

The plural naming of characters masks the individuality and thus accountability of both the soldiers and the demonstrators, but this massification works in two very different ways. For the military this domestication brings order, since soldiers will obey, regardless of their personal life and identity. For the civilians, on the other hand, this massification breeds disorder and chaos; demonstrators' differences melt into a homogeneous mohp. But explaining it that way is begging the question, since these characters are not named according to their actions. Rather, Issarapong scripts identities of essence that need not correspond to actions. Thus the mohp is violent before there is any violence because, by definition, mobs are violent. Likewise the army is a peace-keeper and a security force, even though its actions create violence and chaos.

Plot-line of Violence

The literary plot of Issarapong's testimony is a simple linear progression from order to chaos, from peace to violence: "The escalation of rallies into riots had been planned systematically in advance." This linear progression is amplified by the genre in which the bulk of the story is told: the chronology. Although it appears to be a bare-bones listing of the facts without commentary, the chronological form has its own ideology.

> Stories...have a discernible form (even when that form is chaos) which marks off the events contained in them from the other events that might appear in a comprehensive chronicle of the years covered in their unfoldings.[97]

This chronological story is a teleological writing and editing of history: the end determines the beginning, and orders the choice of events to be included in the story, and thus the progression of the chronology. The chronology then is used to trace back the causes that lead to a certain event, while covering its own tracks of production.[98]

Since the army was criticized for the brutality of its crack-down when the demonstrations ended in violence, 'violence' is the topic that orders the choice of events in the chronological listing of "The Soldiers' Story". This of course was not the only choice for a chronology; the story would have been much different if the topic of analysis was the rise and fall of Suchinda, the career of Chamlong, parliamentary politics in Thailand, or non-violent tactics. But for the military, violence regulates the form of this chronological historiography and history, even though the protests were most noteworthy for their non-violent methods. This comes out of military ordering for, as we noted above, military strategy's "effect as a discourse of power is certainly to inscribe a political space with violence".[99] For example, 17 May is named D-Day in Issarapong's chronology.

The first sense of planned violence in "The Soldiers' Story" actually comes with Chalard's non-violent hunger strike: "The Student Federation of Thailand, the Campaign for Popular Democracy and other allies exploited the confusion [on 9 April], sending their members to join Chalard in the hunger protest. They hoped that if something happened to any of the protesters, it could be used as a pretext to extend their campaign."

The next evidence of violence, according to the chronology, comes at the beginning of May with another hunger strike: "Maj.-Gen. Chamlong's vow to fast to death raised the number of protesters, who were soon infiltrated by certain groups bent on violent acts such as throwing stones at the police." The following text reads: "May 6, 1992: Violent trends of the campaign became more obvious.... When the parliamentary meeting ended the demonstrators tried to push their way into the compound and threw missiles at security forces. The situation indicated that riots could break out at any time." The 'missiles' were actually plastic water bottles that about five people threw over the parliament gates. It was the demonstrators themselves who recognized the problem and calmed down these over-zealous protesters. This was the only remotely violent incident before 17 May, yet it was enough to set the Capital Security Command's *Paireepinart* anti-communist plan in motion.

> The authorities decided to implement Operation *Paireepinart*/ 33 because intelligence reports and what had really happened[100] made it clear that without such measures, the loss of lives, damage to public and private properties — as well as damage to the economy and the country's main institutions, particularly the monarchy — might have been beyond all estimate.

Paireepinart, with its linear progression, is the strategic version of the historical chronology. Officially the plan is supposed to start off with lenient measures and progress step-by-step to more forceful action. In this way the plan is written like the teleological chronology which can escalate, but not de-escalate. Yet, the events did not order themselves according to this linear progression; after a week of massive rallies the demonstrators went home on their own accord on 11 May to give the parliamentary process a chance to amend the Constitution. Yet *Paireepinart* continued. Two retired Supreme Commanders stated that it was the wrong plan to use since it was written to combat urban terrorism and armed struggle. General Arthit Kamlang-ek said that it was inappropriate for a non-violent protest, and General Saiyud said that the plan was to fight communists, "But these people weren't communists, so you have to adjust the plan. The plan was not flexible, it is not good if it is not adjustable."[101]

On 17 May the peaceful rally turned violent. In other words, the violence that had captivated the military imagination for weeks exploded on Rajdamnoen Avenue. Issarapong catalogues the ensuing 'riots' in detail: molotov cocktails, motor-cycle gangs, looting, a gun store robbery. Likewise, the Capital Security Command announced that "Maj.-Gen. Chamlong Srimuang and rioters have burned not less than ten government and public vehicles and have injured a number of officials", and thus the army had to use force to end the protest.[102] According to television reports, after Chamlong was arrested a "new group of terrorists" took control of the demonstration, and motor-cycle gangs went wild in the city, destroying traffic lights and other symbols of authority.[103]

What Issarapong's report does not say is that the demonstrators were not charged with these criminal acts, but with the political offence of 'rioting'. Indeed, in testimony that came before this soldiers' story, Deputy Police Chief General Pongamart Amartayakul reported that there were almost no "normal crimes" — robbery and car theft — during 17–20 May.[104] Although the military tried to compare the events of May with the riot that had gripped Los Angeles a few weeks before, the 'riot' in Bangkok was quite different since there was no looting. The protests in Bangkok were not directed at other (racial) groups in the society, but were directed squarely at the Suchinda government.

While reporting the violence of the mohp, "The Soldiers' Story" denies violence against these unarmed protesters. The most extreme case concerned the events at the Royal Hotel — a makeshift field hospital for wounded protesters — where video referred to in Chapter 1 shows soldiers beating prisoners. Issarapong reports: "There were no casualties on either side, nor was there any violence, specifically inside the Royal Hotel. None of the rumors was true. It is not true that troops fired into the hotel." Though the soldiers did not fire directly into the hotel, they did accost medical personnel and journalists there.[105]

Issarapong's story concludes with everything returning to normal. After Suchinda and Chamlong had their audience with the king, "[s]ecurity forces returned to their barracks... and carried out their routine duty by helping out villagers affected by prolonged drought". Moreover, "[t]he government tried its best to help the people affected by the violence" and "[t]he Prime Minister's Office set up a committee to investigate the incident, so did parliament". Once again, the military is there to help, whether the people appreciate it or not.

Grammar: Missing Subjects and Self-defence
The army chronology has established that there was violence, but where did it come from? What moved this plot along? The answer is simple, according to a pamphlet called "How to Answer Questions About the May 17–20 Unrest" that the (anti-communist) Internal Security Operations Command (ISOC) distributed to teachers in the northeastern province of Roi Et.

> Q: What exactly was the cause of the violence?
> A: The violence could have been averted had the demon-strators been peaceful and the protesters unarmed. The riot could also be attributed to a group of opportunists who physically attacked members of the security forces and damaged public property. The riot worsened quickly and necessitated the use of force to put it down. The violence would not have happened if baseless rumors had not been circulated among the protesters.
> Q: Why did the troops have to be so cruel as to shoot demonstrators, killing and injuring many of them?
> A: Soldiers are citizens too. They are not criminals or cruel people. Faced with a great mass of people during the un-rest, the troops were nervous that they would fail to achieve their assignment — to restore peace and order.[106]

The violence that pushed the plot along came from instigators and opportunists, bringing out the other meaning of the word 'plot': conspiracy. Thus, the military, acting as a security force, had to restore peace and order at any cost, even if this peaceful ordering was violently chaotic. Though all the elements of this ISOC catechism are contained in Issarapong's text, he was speaking to a different audience and hence masked many of these accusa-tions in his own peculiar grammar which turned the literary plot-line into a conspiratorial plot.

The social organization of May 1992 comes out in the linguistic grammar of this tale. Thai, like English, is an SVO — subject, verb, object — language. That is how action is ordered. There is a curious grammar involved in this story and other accounts which blame Chamlong for "leading the protesters to their death". The motivation of the extremely violent actions is hidden in the passive voice. Though people were killed, no one pulled any triggers. They "were pulled" as people "were shot". This is a way of saying something, without actually being responsible for what is said — or done. Hence Issarapong's story is a textual version of the army's masking of violence on the video that was analysed in Chapter 1.

In the grammar of Issarapong's story protesters were never the subject of the sentence or the action: only the object. They were the object of the batons and bullets: "Four people were injured and were taken by security forces to the hospital." Soldiers did not shoot people, but security forces cared for them. People also were the object of some mysterious "instigators" and "third hands" who manoeuvred the innocent, naive, and curious into the line of fire. Thus Issarapong concludes that the non-violent methods of hunger strikes led to the violence: "Instigators appealed to the mass by staging hunger protests. When the crowds grew in number, some groups with malicious intentions tried to turn the demonstration into a violent uprising by using abusive language and threatening authorities' safety."

Self-defence. Once these instigators mobilized the crowd, the army was forced to respond. As a senior army officer said: "They forced us to use strong measures to disperse the rally."[107] When the army is the subject of violent actions, it is only because the army is responding to even greater threats. Notice the double passives of the masses and the authorities in this sentence: "The peaceful rally turned violent when the masses were moved to confront authorities." All injuries were inflicted while the soldiers were acting in self-defence: "soldiers fired in air as the next step up, but troublemakers kept on coming; some soldiers stumbled down to avoid molotov cocktails and fired into the crowd injuring four people who were taken to hospital".[108]

Lenience. The passive voice and self-defence assertion serve to bolster the army's claim that it was lenient to the violent mohps. "While the authorities tried to avoid confrontation, the crowds resorted to more violence, setting fire to government buildings and cars and looting government property." There is no discussion of just how the military got onto the streets of Bangkok, or that the heavily armed soldiers might have provoked demonstrators. Issarapong writes: "The government declared a state of emergency before 1:00 am [on 18 May]. But the protesters failed to perceive the government's good intention to restore peace." According to the military, if not for the guns things would have been worse: "All-out riots continued at 10:30 pm [on 18 May] apparently because of soldiers' lenience."

Law and Order. The other force that is producing the action in this story is the law, though in a paradoxical way. The soldiers state that they dissolved the protest to preserve law and order: "We must not let the mohp overwhelm the law." Yet to justify the use of lethal force, law was employed again. None of these arguments mentions if the context justified the use of lethal force. Issarapong writes: "I can stress that the overall mission was entirely based on the legal authority and orders from the relevant superiors."; "Every move of all units in the Capital Peacekeeping was strictly in accordance with particular situations and orders from the chain of command."; and "In his testimony Kaset stated that the use of force was justified by the constitution and the defense law."[109] The government investigating committee decided that the execution of *Paireepinart* was "procedurally correct". Thus the military can be happy that it accomplished its mission of legally restoring order. "Officers take pride in the crackdown which saved lives and public property." In a newsletter distributed to the active troops soon after the crack-down Kaset personally thanked soldiers who "maintained peace and order in the country with restraint and patience".[110]

Reason and Emotion. Issarapong uses other methods to rationalize the use of state violence. He highlights the rational decision-making that was used to disperse the mobs which he at times characterizes as "crazy": "The dispersal of mobs, arrest of protesters, warning gunfire or shooting the tires of buses were all done only after careful judgement in accordance to the circumstances."[111] While the army is rational, the mobs are emotional and chaotic, doing "unimaginable" things such as contesting military order and authority.[112] They contested this authority not just by driving buses at the soldiers' positions when they were surrounded, but mostly through "emotional" means such as "using abusive language". These discursive weapons were apparently very effective on the army. "Rumors were spread to make the demonstrators hate the government." "It was *obvious* that all officers exercised extreme restraint though they were hurt mentally and physically. They were scolded and insulted."

Thus any deaths or injuries which resulted from soldiers firing into the crowd are mistakes, regrettable but understandable under the confusing circumstances. "Shootings were in self-defense," says army spokesman Colonel Banchorn: "It's an accident brought about by confusion. So no one should be held responsible."[113] A close aide to Issarapong, Army Civil Affairs Director General Thongchai Kuasakul, put it bluntly in a report to foreign military attachés: it must have been a mistake since if the army intended to use violence tens of thousands of people would have been killed.[114] The army explanations take the violence for granted, even though the police did not shoot and the navy did not use force at all in crowd control. The navy actually let demonstrators, who were being chased by the army, escape across the Pinklao Bridge.

Lethal Force. While the military was busy defending its honour, others were wondering why there was such an uneven use of force. On the key moment at Paan Faa Bridge on the night of 17 May, both sides actually agree that there were some violent demonstrators. Each side attributes them to some "third hand". But if we look at the statistics, it is clear that there were a small number of 'rioters' and a large number of troops. Issarapong reports: "About 200 people who were obviously aggressive planned to break through police barricades at the bridge." *The Nation* reported that drunken youngsters split from the peaceful crowd and hurled debris at the police and reporters.[115]

Recognizing the problem, Chamlong asked peaceful protesters to keep away from them, and announced to the armed forces that these rioters were not part of the demonstration and advised the police to arrest the unruly ones. But the army's response was to deploy 40,000 troops — who "showed restraint" by firing 150,000 rounds.[116] Still, according to police testimony, the demonstrators were unarmed,[117] so the use of war weapons was unwarranted — even according to the plan for Operation *Paireepinart*/33.

One journalist who witnessed the army attack on the Royal Hotel reported: "the image was one of awesome firepower; M-16s, belt-firing M-60s, M-89 grenade launchers, jeeps mounted with heavy machine guns, armoured personnel carriers.... Neither a truncheon nor a riot shield could be seen. These troops brought to the streets of Bangkok were a fully armed division headed into combat."[118] Autopsy evidence of the bodies shows the result of this deployment. Contrary to the army's claims of lenience, doctors report that the deaths were deliberate — not accidental. "The Forensic Medical Institute has said it found indications that soldiers had deliberately shot to kill."[119] Ballistics tests showed that the angle of the bullets was 15 degrees, hence soldiers aimed directly at people, not into the air to intimidate them, as claimed. Protesters were killed by one or two bullets, some at point-blank range in the forehead. The majority of the casualties were shot in the back while running away (on 18 May) or shot in the head and neck by sharpshooters (on 19 May).[120] Hence the soldiers did not shoot in desperation, as the army maintains; for the soldiers it was "not a confrontation, but a hunt".[121] *Paireepinart* means 'Destroy the Enemy', not control the crowd.

Who Was the Mob?

...pre-meditated, well-orchestrated and unprovoked...[122]

Issarapong's plot does have a seductive order, and it does address the questions that people were asking about the relation between the non-violent demonstration and the brutal crack-down. Unfortunately, Issarapong's story of the lenient shootings has little to do with the stories of those who were brutally shot.[123] The first reports of vandalism and beating — rioting — were not about the protesters, but about the police: a person saw police officers breaking a police car window.[124]

Rather than simply concluding that Issarapong was lying or had bad intelligence, we can turn his story around, and read his accusations of mob violence into confessions of the army's planned suppression. Indeed, little of the (mis)information that Issarapong offered was new when he delivered this report on 16 June. The main point that caught the public eye at the time was that the crack-down operation was approved very early in the protest on 6 May, long before anyone else could even imagine the violence that ensued.

This brings new meaning, and revealing ironies, to Issarapong's statements: "The unrest was planned step-by-step" and "The escalation of rallies into riots had been planned systematically in advance." Following Suchinda, Issarapong is pointing a finger at Chamlong and Chavalit, whom the army scripted as being the "real force" behind the mass demonstrations because of their military background in mass psychological operations: "As a result of the fight against communists generals Chavalit and Chamlong are masters of organizing the masses and propaganda."[125]

But the finger that was pointed at opposition political leaders can be pointed back at Issarapong and the army. It raises the question of whether it was the military that planned the escalation of rallies into riots as a way of opening the door for a violent crack-down — a common practice in Thai military strategy: Why else was the élite Task Force 90 from Lopburi in Bangkok? The Thai army started organizing mass organizations in the 1980s — including the National Defence Volunteers, Volunteer Development and Self-Defence Villages, and Military Reservists for National Security — as a way of countering the communist insurgency. This was seen as 'democratic' because the military was organizing the people, but there were worries that "this 'democratic development' might well be used by the military élites to crush the democratic system itself".[126] Issarapong has experience in mobilizing right-wing groups. He organized the 6 April 'horse-faced mohp' to support Suchinda's bid to be Prime Minister, which included military groups mentioned by Suchit: National Defence Volunteers and Military Reservists for National Security. Newspapers reported after this rally that "Issarapong is well experienced in the culture of creating a mohp" and "Issarapong can't conceal his pleasure, as he smilingly managed the mohp all day".[127]

Throughout the mass demonstrations, Suchinda and the military government also flexed their mass organization muscles. In response to the demonstrations of 100,000 people on 4 May when Chamlong announced his death fast, Suchinda quipped: "I can gather 5 million tomorrow. Want to see that?" after asking if the pro-democracy demonstrators were "ordinary citizens".[128] No one doubted that Suchinda could raise 5 million, and many were afraid that right-wing groups such as the Village Scouts would attack the other demonstrators as in the past.[129] When asked about this possibility on 12 May, Suchinda replied: "I can't stop people from demonstrating."[130] As he was saying this, Interior Minister Anan Kalinta was ordering governors to stop protesters from entering the city for anti-Suchinda rallies, as well as forbidding teachers, civil servants, and state enterprise workers from protesting against the government.

On 15 May — two days before the mass anti-Suchinda protest at Sanam Luang — there were pro-Suchinda rallies in the provinces: Chaiyaphum, Khon Kaen, Lopburi, Nakhorn Phanom, Songkla, Phatthalung, Si Sa Ket, Udon Thani, and Yasothon. Tens of thousands of people rallied in support of the Prime Minister, but as documents later demonstrated, these rallies were mobilized by the government and the military: village headmen and district chiefs organized villagers with "money, food, and transportation". *The Nation* printed a copy of a letter by a provincial governor asking a bus company for its "regular co-operation".[131] The government's organized mohps are further evidenced by a contemporaneous editorial cartoon which has a fat village headman yelling at his assembled villagers to shout "We want Suchinda" louder. When they do not respond, and he asks why, one villager replies, "If you want us to shout louder, then you have to increase the pay to twenty baht".[132]

Even so, there were unreliable mohps: demonstrations in two southern provinces backfired on 15 May. In Songkla province 800 villagers were told they were being bused to the provincial capital to support constitutional amendments, but when they arrived they found out it was a pro-Suchinda demonstration. The villagers were very angry: "One of the councillors criticized Suchinda's supporters as treating the villagers like [stupid] 'buffaloes'." The response was much the same in neighbouring Phatthalung province: "Don't lie to the people," one man shouted at the stage. These mobilization efforts were not effective because "[s]uch mohps work with prior propaganda and the churning up of emotions — not only [the army's] but 'the public' — not by merely pushing buttons on the bureaucratic machine..."[133]

The methods the government used to discourage popular protests bordered on the ludicrous when they commandeered the mobile toilet trucks. Other methods to disrupt the 17 May rally included threatening to extend the Buddhist Week Festival held at Sanam Luang (which had been organized by the military since 6 October 1976), in an effort to portray the protest as anti-Buddhist. When this tactic did not work, the army organized two free concerts to benefit farmers suffering from the drought in the northeast.

By 17 May it was not just the villagers who had been mobilized, but also the troops. Again, one of the army's accusations becomes an interesting, and brutal, confession. Issarapong writes that propaganda was one of the things that fanned the violence: "Rumors were spread to make the demonstrators hate the government." Actually, the military spread rumours among the troops which were brought in from outside Bangkok — from Buriram, Lopburi, Nakhon Ratchasima, and Prachinburi — to make them hate the protesters. Soldiers were told that they were fighting communists, arsonists, vandals, and terrorists, and thus acted accordingly. The soldiers had been isolated from the critical media since mid-April, when certain newspapers were banned from military facilities. Soldiers in the provinces only knew what the army and the official electronic media told them, and as we have seen it fits into the anti-communist mob scenario. Since, as noted above, communists were seen as threats to the three sacred Thai institutions, the demonstrators were treated harshly.

Conclusion

The Thai mohp in May 1992 referred to different images of the people. On the one hand it was a non-violent, rational, middle-class rally complete with food, non-alcoholic drink, facilities,[134] and all-star entertainment. But in the end it relapsed into the classical violent mob of rioters under the direction of the military. The discursive economy of 'the public' in Thailand seems to discredit mass action even before it has begun. Part of this is because the military continues to effectively order the discourse of Thai politics by scripting people as mohps and democratic activists as communists. Indeed, in this last section even I have succumbed to this 'Althusserian interpellation' by responding to the army's misinformation point-by-point, rather than engaging in a critique of the discourse itself. Even when they are thrown out of office and put in disgrace, the military's reading of the events persists because the middle-class imagining of the mob could not resist the peculiar order/chaos logic of mob discourse.

This is not to say that words cannot acquire new meanings — 'mob' actually has more soothing readings in Australia and New Zealand — but only to note that the new Thai scripting 'mohp' did not work for a non-violent mass movement. According to the Thai social/linguistic logic when we use the word 'mohp' to characterize the people in a mass movement, we are left with only two choices: is it an organized mohp or an unorganized mohp. Indeed, the title of a newspaper article reporting on the 20 April rally is telling: "Analyzing the mohp of almost 100,000 who protested against Suchinda at the Royal Plaza: [are they] Organized or Unorganized".[135] The reduction of analysis of demonstrations to two categories is disarming of mass politics. As we saw, to be organized is to be manipulated, so the only genuine demonstration must be spontaneous. But to be effective, a movement must have organization.

Actually mohp worked better in an economy of erasure than in an economy of massing. To put it another way, like in eighteenth century France, the public opinion of the mob was limited to the middle class and upper class, for the sedan mohp's scripting painted over important groups of people, presumably in the interests of bourgeois democracy. In Thailand the range of mob was not merely expanded to include the middle class; this new mob was written to exclude working classes. Part of this erasure comes from the discursive economies of the print media as mirrors of middle class identity. As Benedict Anderson wrote in 1990:

> In the bourgeoisie's successful struggle, the importance of the press should not be underestimated; above all that of the popular newspaper *Thai Rath*, which, with its huge nationwide readership, represents another kind of imagined community, alongside those conjured up by parliamentary institutions or the Nation-Buddhism-Monarchy shibboleth of the old regime.... After all, successful newspapers are large business enterprises, which succeed because they voice, at least to some extent, their readers' aspirations.[136]

Though the over-reporting of the participation of the middle class could be explained away because the 'yuppie mob' was a new phenomenon, this image was also certainly a strategically important way of legitimizing mass demonstrations.[137] In 1992 the slum-dwellers and factory workers were an important part of the demonstration that was largely ignored by the newspapers. The over-reporting of the middle class was most acute in the business press — *The Manager Daily* and the *Asian Wall Street Journal* — as part of a project for bourgeois democracy that did not necessarily meet popular needs:

> the printed information on the struggle for democracy tends to be only accounts biased against the masses. There tends to be only accounts of some groups of people whose social positions are accepted and considered as 'not dangerous to the system'... such as the various kinds of businessmen or big entrepreneurs. ...In this way, their role was much exaggerated. The word "middle class" came into vogue. In the process, the role of workers in general has been much reduced.[138]

While the bourgeois press categorically erased many protesters, the army's scripting of the mob did it literally. The statistics of this random violence are revealing as an alternative accounting to the public opinion polls' random sampling: "Those injured came from all levels within society, and can be sub-classified as labourers

42%, unknown 16%, businesspersons 14%, students 12%, lawyers 8%, government officials 4%, taxi drivers 3%, the police and the military 1%."[139] Thus one report concludes that the

> data indicate that the victims of the May Event were mostly male single labourers in their working age. In other words, they were low-income persons. That is, most victims were not the 'middle-class' whose majority comprised the mass rally, as the papers dubbed them 'mobile-phone mob' or 'yoghurt mob'.[140]

Hence it is best to change the subject and talk about mass movements and the Thai public in a different way, which looks beyond the mobs of the public (army) and private (business) sectors to examine mass action in the popular sector.

An incident at the height of the crack-down is instructive. On an inspection tour of Rajdamnoen Avenue General Chainarong Noonpackdee asked the prisoners: "Were you recruited to join the demonstration?" As we saw above, one man answered this leading question with utmost sincerity. But rather than taking this question seriously, we can consider one woman's answer: "You're disgusting." Though it may seem overly provocative, this person did not take the army's ordering of the discourse for granted, and thus challenges the "state's dangerous monopoly over the symbols of security and danger".[141] Once we have thus discounted the army's discourse, we can consider other readings of the events which highlight such things as non-violence and grass-roots organization — the opposite of the chaotically violent mob.

NOTES

* This chapter is based on an earlier version published in *Alternatives: Social Transformation and Humane Governance*, Vol. 19 (1994), by Lynne Rienner Publishers, Inc. Used with permission of the publisher.
1. Barry Holstun Lopez, *Of Wolves and Men* (New York: Charles Scribner's Sons, 1978), pp. 2–3.
2. For example, Sant Hattirat, a leader of the Confederation for Democracy (CFD), said: "So it's not that the CFD brought the people to their death. They try to smear us with this accusation. Actually when

people came out on the night of 18 May, we were not there at all. At first we planned that if they used any violence we would turn ourselves in so they would stop the violence. But after Chamlong let himself be arrested, the shooting did not stop. So we met each other and decided that it was no use trying to talk to them: they wouldn't talk, just shoot." (Interview, 18 November 1992.)

3. For an in-depth consideration of Chamlong and his role in the May events see Duncan McCargo, *Chamlong Srimuang and the New Thai Politics* (London: Hurst & Company, 1997).

4. Here I am using Benedict Anderson's notion of nations as imagined communities, to consider movements within one 'nation' (Benedict Anderson, *Imagined Communities: Reflections on the Origin and Spread of Nationalism*, rev. ed. [New York: Verso, 1991]).

5. Phra Paisal Visalo in Prinya Thewanarumikul, discussion leader, *"Ruang Mohp"* [Discourse on mob], *Newsletter of the Campaign for Popular Democracy* (Bangkok) 1, no. 6 (April 1993): 6–17.

6. Ibid.

7. Postbag, *Bangkok Post*, 3 June 1992, p. 4.

8. A controversial analysis of the events of May which takes this conservative stance is Khien Theeravit, *Wikritakankanmuang Thai: karani phrutsapha mahawipyok 2535* [Thai politics in crisis: the case of the May 1992 tragedy] (Bangkok: Matichon Publishing, 1993). Phra Paisal's response to such arguments is: "First they should not see conflict as disorder. For example, when people gather, people might say these protesters are mohp-rule. This reflects the attitude that conflict is unusual and creates the disorder in society. This attitude must be changed. The other attitude that must be changed is the way we see people with different ideas as enemies." (Paisal, op. cit.)

9. They were referring to environmental and human rights protests contesting the Pak Mool Dam in the Northeast Region of Thailand. "Chuan tells army top brass he is worried by 'mob-rule'", *Bangkok Post*, 1 April 1993, p. 3. Also see articles such as Wipawee Otaganonta, "The conflict between peace and democracy", *Bangkok Post*, 29 June 1992, p. 23; "Violent protests touch off debate on new freedom", *The Nation*, 20 May 1993, p. A5.

10. Vincent Price, *Communication Concepts 4: Public Opinion* (London: Sage, 1992), p. 4.

11. The announcement of the People's Party is fascinating in how it speaks for 'the people': "The King did not listen to the voice of the people..." (Thak Chaloemtiarana, ed., *Thai Politics 1932–1957* [Bangkok: Social Science Association, 1978], pp. 4–7).

12. Price, op. cit., pp. 8–10.

13. Ibid., p. 10.
14. Ibid., p. 12. Emphasis in the original.
15. Ibid.
16. Chapter 4 considers how the missing were 'erased' through discursive means.
17. *The Nation*, 14 June 1992.
18. Mohp is the official romanization of the Thai term according to "The General System of Phonetic Transcription of Thai Characters into Roman". There is also a diacritical mark underneath the 'o'.
19. Oxford English Dictionary. Similar 'mob-rule' language was used by James Madison and Alexander Hamilton in the *Federalist Papers* to argue for the restriction of popular powers in the constitution of the new united states of America.
20. Witthiakorn Chiangkul in Prinya, op. cit.
21. Price, op. cit., p. 23.
22. Ibid., p. 24.
23. Ibid., p. 25.
24. Oxford English Dictionary.
25. Colonel Rex Applegate (U.S.A. – Ret.), *Riot Control — Materiel and Techniques*, 2nd ed. (London: Arms and Armour Press, 1981).
26. "Thailand's Unfinished Business", *Asian Wall Street Journal*, 18 May 1993, p. 10.
27. I have quoted from the CPD discussion above. The Sophon report is fascinating because it really struggles with the terms 'mob', 'crowd', and 'gathering'. In the end it declares, "The police must try to change the 'mob' back into a 'crowd'. The meaning of the word to disperse the mob [*kansalaimohp*] doesn't mean hit, arrest or kill the people who are in the 'mob'." (Sophon Rattanakorn, "A Report on the Investigation of the Illegal Use of Power and Survey of Disaster According to the People's Demonstration during 17–20 May 1992 submitted to Prime Minister Anand Panyarachun on 5 August 1992", p. 37.)
28. One observer noted that the use of 'mohp' is not political so much as expedient: 'mohp' is convenient for headlines because it is monosyllabic.
29. The term 'mobile phone mob' (*mohp mua thue*) appeared in Thai newspapers to describe the 19 November 1991 demonstration against the National Peace Keeping Council (NPKC)-drafted constitution. But 'mohp' did not catch on; it did not spread to editorials, commentaries, and feature stories as it did in 1992. It certainly did not make it into the English-language newspapers in Thailand or abroad as it did in 1992.
30. *Phuchatkan Raiwan* [The Manager Daily], 7 April 1992, p. 1.

31. Kamnoon Sittisaman, *"Mohp Rotkeng"* [Sedan mob], *The Manager Daily*, 22 April 1992, p. 8.
32. *The Manager Daily*, 7 April 1992, pp. 1–2.
33. Palang Dharma Party leader General Chamlong Srimuang specifically denied that this "rally comprised mainly of organized masses brought in by opposition parties" (*Bangkok Post*, 22 April 1992, p. 1).
34. This is an example of how government tactics can discursively backfire. The 20 April 1992 demonstration was held at the Royal Plaza because the authorities refused to allow organizers to use the usual venue at the Royal Parade Grounds. Because of the space conditions at the Royal Plaza, demonstrators were forced to park their cars immediately adjacent to the demonstration site, thus highlighting the wealth of this new configuration of protesters.
35. Pasuk and Baker argue: "More than any other journal, Phujatkan reflected the new, younger urban generation's demand for a mixture of business information and sophisticated commentary on politics and society" (Pasuk Phongpaichit and Chris Baker, *Thailand: Economy and Politics* [Kuala Lumpur: Oxford University Press, 1995], p. 371). *The Manager Daily* was very active in reporting the May events, and thus was one of three newspapers ordered closed on 20 May 1992 by the Suchinda government on the grounds of 'national security'. This order was rescinded before it took effect.
36. Oxford English Dictionary.
37. Wipawee Otaganonta, "A yuppie mob", *Bangkok Post*, 13 May 1992, pp. 28–29.
38. This and other editorial cartoons are reproduced in Creative Media Foundation, *Langbang* [Cleanse the village] (Bangkok: Ongkan Glom, 1992), no page number.
39. Ammar Siamwalla, "Thai Junta Does All the Wrong Things", *Asian Wall Street Journal*, 15–16 May 1992, p. 10.
40. Anek Laothamatas, *Mohp Mue Tua: Chonchunklang lae nakthurakit kap phattanakan phrachathipatai* [Mobile phone mob: The middle class and business people with democratic development] (Bangkok: Matichon Press, 1993).
41. The use of surveys in defining public opinion is controversial in Thailand since many question their validity on methodological grounds. "Which public?" is a common response of both right- and left-wing groups to survey conclusions. For an example of a survey that was questioned on methodological grounds see Pasuk Phongpaichit and Sungsidh Piriyarangsan, *Corruption and Democracy in Thailand* (Bangkok: The Political Economy Centre, Faculty of Economics, Chulalongkorn University, 1994).

42. Sungsidh Piriyarangsan and Pasuk Phongpaichit, "Introduction: The Middle Class and Democracy in Thailand", in *The Middle Class and Thai Democracy*, edited by Sungsidh Piriyarangsan and Pasuk Phongpaichit (Bangkok: Chulalongkorn University and Friedrich Ebert Stiftung, 1993), p. 28. This survey was reported in *The Manager Daily*. Others have commented that one cannot characterize the mass movement based on a survey carried out in one night since the participation shifted over time. (See McCargo, op. cit., p. 272.)
43. They were reported as "yuppie protesters" but not a mob in *The Nation* on 7 May 1992.
44. Wipawee, op. cit., pp. 28–29.
45. This Sunday outing was also duly recorded on film, with a favourite spot being the razor-wire fence which had gun-toting soldiers in the background.
46. Wipawee, op. cit.
47. Sirin Palasri, "Why were they anti-Suchinda?", *The Nation*, 23 May 1992, p. A6.
48. *The Nation*, 11 May 1992.
49. *The Nation*, 19 May 1992.
50. Sample sentence for 'mob' from *Longman Dictionary of Contemporary English*, new ed. (London: Longman, 1987).
51. Khien, op. cit., p. 77.
52. This organized mob is resonant with the American scripting of the mob in terms of 'organized crime'. Paisal also points this out: "Actually mob has another meaning in the American language. It doesn't refer to people without order, but people who have much order, but with the outlaw order. They are the mafia." (Paisal in Prinya, op. cit.)
53. *The Nation*, 6 May 1992, p. A6.
54. Price, op. cit., p. 37.
55. Quoted in Kevin Hewison, "Of Regimes, State and Pluralities: Thai Politics Enters the 1990s", in *Southeast Asia in the 1990s: Authoritarianism, Democracy & Capitalism*, edited by Kevin Hewison, Richard Robison, and Garry Rodan (Sydney: Allen & Unwin, 1993), p. 163.
56. A headline on 13 May 1992 read: PM won't "bow to mob rule" (*The Nation*).
57. *Bangkok Post*, 21 April 1992, p. 1. Of course the purpose of demonstrations is to disrupt people's lives to call attention to the problem.
58. This vocabulary comes from the 1970s where students agitated the people (*pluk mohp*) and the army dissolved demonstrations (*salai mohp*) (Prudhisan Jumbala, Correspondence, 27 October 1993). It is interesting to see how 'mohp' was present in a different form in the 1970s. In the 1990s 'mohp' is largely a noun, which is modified as 'horse-faced' or 'mobile phone'. In the 1970s it was part of a compound verb, where

'mohp' was not the focus, but the modifier. This is further shown in the English translation — dissolved demonstrations — which erases 'mohp' entirely.

59. *The Nation*, 22 May 1992.
60. Paul Virilio, *Speed and Politics: an Essay on Dromology* (New York: Semiotext[e] Foreign Agents Series, 1986), p. 22.
61. There were many police and military officers who opposed the army crack-down. During the demonstrations, an anonymous group of people collectively known as Ai Laem disrupted police communications by filling up the radio waves with taunts and curses. Most agree that only skilled police officers could sustain such sabotage over a period of weeks as Ai Laem did. On the more serious side, there seemed to be a split in the army between those who supported Suchinda and Class 5 and those who supported General Prem Tinsulanond, who was against the crack-down. This nearly led to a civil war, and Prem, acting as Privy Councillor, was instrumental in setting up the meeting between King Bhumipol, Suchinda, and Chamlong. See Raphael Pura and Cynthia Owens, "King's low profile reflects reluctance to meddle", *Asian Wall Street Journal*, 22–23 May 1992, p. 1.
62. Metropolitan Police Commissioner Police Major-General Narong Rienthong said: "Who is to take responsibility when those who insti-gated the mobs could not control them?"
63. Khien, op. cit., and Khien Theeravit, Interview, 8 April 1993.
64. "Army-civilization reminds us of Schlegel's remark about 'that mysterious aspiring towards chaos that lies behind every ordered creation'" (Virilio, op. cit., p. 29).
65. General Saiyud Kerdphol, Interview, 15 February 1993.
66. For example, when asked under what circumstances the military should run Thailand, a "leading journalist in political affairs" answered: "For our national survival, it does not matter what form of government we have. To me, the military is well-organized and the line of command is clear. The military can make immediate, decisive decision [sic] dealing with a matter of life and death." (Pongsan Puntularp, "Political Stability: The Role of Political Culture in Thailand" [Paper delivered at the Fifth International Conference on Thai Studies — SOAS, London, 1993], p. 11.)
67. Paul Virilio, *Popular Defense and Ecological Struggles* (New York: Semiotext[e] Foreign Agents Series, 1990), p. 20. This passage ties together war and capital, a very interesting relation in Thailand since the Class 5 military junta is known as soldier-businessmen.
68. Bradley S. Klein, "The Textual Strategies of the Military: Or Have You Read Any Good Defense Manuals Lately?", in *International/Intertextual*

Relations: Postmodern Readings of World Politics, edited by James Der Derian and Michael J. Shapiro (Lexington: Lexington Books, 1989), pp. 97–112.

69. Volker R. Berghahn, *Militarism: The History of an International Debate 1961–1979* (New York: Cambridge University Press, 1981), p. 16. French President Valery Giscard d'Estaing echoed this view in April 1976 at the French military academy: "Alongside the supreme means of ensuring our security (the nuclear vectors), we need a presence of security. In other words, we need to have *a social body organized around this need for security.*" (Virilio, *Speed and Politics*, p. 62).

70. Klein, op. cit., p. 102.

71. Ibid., pp. 104–5.

72. Mehmed Ali, Kathy E. Ferguson, and Phyllis Turnbull (with Joelle Mulford), "Gender, Land and Power: Reading the Military in Hawai'i" (Paper presented at the Fifteenth World Congress of the International Political Science Association, Buenos Aires, 21–25 July 1991), pp. 10–11.

73. Klein, op. cit., p. 100.

74. Ibid., p. 99.

75. *The Nation*, 14 June 1992, p. A8.

76. Klein, op. cit., p. 99.

77. Mehmed et al., op. cit., p. 12.

78. Ibid.

79. See Timothy W. Luke, "'What's Wrong with Deterrence?' A Semiotic Interpretation of National Security Policy", in *International/Intertextual Relations: Postmodern Readings of World Politics*, edited by James Der Derian and Michael J. Shapiro (Lexington: Lexington Books, 1989), pp. 207–30.

80. Mehmed et al., op. cit., p. 14.

81. The junta in October 1976 called itself the National Administration Reform Council (NARC). Actually NPKC is more appropriate for the anti-insurgency activities of 1976, while NARC is a better name for the anti-corruption drive of the 1991 coup.

82. Pasuk and Baker, op. cit., p. 355.

83. Tulsathit Taptim, "Same old rhetoric", *The Nation*, 10 May 1992, p. A10.

84. One could argue that since King Chulalongkorn modernized the Thai military in the late nineteenth century, it has always been more of an internal than an external force. There are few external wars in twentieth-century Thailand, and in the nineteenth century the military was a centralizing order. Though the army was established to back up diplomacy, it proved itself by putting down regional rebellions

and consolidating the "loosely held components of the old kingdom into a nation-state" (Sukanya Bumroongsook, "Chulachomklao Royal Military Academy: The Modernization of Military Education in Thailand (1887–1948)" [Ph.D. diss., Northern Illinois University, 1991], p. 57).

85. Thongchai Winichakul, *Siam Mapped: A History of the Geo-Body of a Nation* (Honolulu: University of Hawaii Press, 1994), p. 167.

86. Craig J. Reynolds, "Introduction", in *National Identity and Its Defenders: Thailand, 1939–89*, edited by Craig J. Reynolds (Clayton: Monash Papers on Southeast Asia, no. 25, 1991), pp. 1–40.

87. Thongchai, op. cit., p. 6.

88. Chai-Anan Samudavanija, Kusuma Snitwongse, and Suchit Bunbong-karn, *From Armed Suppression to Political Offensive: Attitudinal Changes of Thai Military Officers since 1976* (Bangkok: Institute of Security and International Studies, Chulalongkorn University, 1990), p. 56.

89. Ibid., p. 68.

90. Suchit Bunbongkarn, *The Military in Thai Politics 1981–86* (Singapore: Institute of Southeast Asian Studies, 1987), p. 59.

91. This is the title of the article in *The Nation* (21 June 1992, p. A8) in which excerpts of General Issarapong Noonpackdee's testimony are translated into English. Passages cited in this chapter are based on this translation. Please see the Appendix for the full text.

92. Franz Kafka, "Jackals and Arabs", in *The Penal Colony* (New York: Schoken Books, 1976), p. 152.

93. Price, op. cit., p. 24.

94. Tepsiri Suksopha, a well-known story-teller, also pointed out the narrative structure of the May events and its similarities to political events of the 1970s: "I look at everything like a play. There are always characters and settings.... And this time, in the incident in May [1992], the powerful side still wore the same uniforms with guns in hand, but on the protestor's side, a great many new characters emerged. There were those with mobile phones, gangs of motorcyclists, vendors, and many more." (Pongpet Mekloy, "The events of May through artists' eyes", *Bangkok Post*, 21 October 1992, p. 23.)

95. Hayden White, *Metahistory: The Historical Imagination in Nineteenth-Century Europe* (Baltimore: Johns Hopkins University Press, 1973), p. 6, footnote 5 (emphasis in original).

96. Issarapong uses the word 'obvious' many times: this is often a sign that what is being argued is far from obvious.

97. White, op. cit., p. 6.

98. The print media also relied heavily on chronology to report the events of May, although they use this form in quite different circumstances.

Chronologies are most common to describe stories in progress, where no clear end is in sight. Still, the chronology has its own problems when the media use it as well.

99. Klein, op. cit., p. 9.

100. Is Issarapong admitting that his intelligence reports were less than reliable? Many familiar with the military blame the brutality of the crack-down on bad military intelligence. The police testified that they had lots of information, but the Capital Security Command did not use it (*Bangkok Post*, 20 June 1992).

101. Saiyud, Interview.

102. *Bangkok Post*, special afternoon edition, 18 May 1992.

103. *Bangkok Post*, special afternoon edition, 19 May 1992. Traffic lights at 83 intersections and 6 crosswalks were destroyed and 5 control boxes were thrashed (*The Nation*, 26 May 1992). This report is a part of the conspiracy as well. The police tried to tie this to Chavalit's New Aspiration Party which had close ties to motor-cycle taxi organizations. Other politicians who were anti-NPKC and had ties with motor-cycle taxis were Veera Musikaphong and Chalerm Yubamrung.

104. *Bangkok Post*, 7 June 1992.

105. Vincent Iacopino and Sidney Jones, *Thailand — Bloody May: Excessive Use of Lethal Force in Bangkok: The Events of May 17–20, 1992*, A Report by Physicians for Human Rights and Asia Watch (New York: Human Rights Watch, October 1992), pp. 19–23.

106. "Military publishes easy reader on unrest", *The Nation*, 2 July 1992, p. A1. I could not confirm this with a copy of the original pamphlet. The army policy under General Wimol Wongwanich was "no comment". They would not distribute any information, past or present, about the May unrest. Their explanation is that army policy changed with the appointment of a new army commander in August 1992.

107. *Bangkok Post*, 19 June 1992, p. 3.

108. Chai's editorial cartoon in *Thai Rath* on 27 May 1992 ridiculed such army explanations: Headman Ma goes to visit his fellow villager Ai Joei in the hospital. Ai Joei explains that he was shot in the rib when he went to join the mohp at Rajdamnoen Avenue. Ma asks, "They said that they just shot to threaten people; they shot at the ground so they would miss the people. How come the bullet hit you?" Ai Joei replies, "They started shooting at the ground once I was on the ground too."

109. The National Peacekeeping Act was later repealed by Parliament.

110. *Bangkok Post*, 28 May 1992.

111. Issarapong does apologize in an oblique way, although still not taking responsibility for the bullets that came out of the army guns: "This use of weapons might have caused losses due to stray bullets. This was the worst incident. The authorities deeply and sadly regretted it. All security forces only wanted to protect important places and stop the rioting with no intention to hurt any of their Thai brothers."

112. As Khien employs the reason/emotion logic to discredit the demonstrators: "… the legitimate objectives are often abused or changed by people's temper rather than reason because there are some radical people in the mass who want a rapid transformation" (Khien, op. cit., p. 73).

113. *The Nation*, 20 May 1992.

114. *The Nation*, 4 June 1992. Others note that the military was using a strategy of 'managed violence' based on the Thai idiom: "Kill the chicken to scare the monkey."

115. *The Nation*, 25 May 1992.

116. *Bangkok Post*, 28 May 1992. Actually, varying statistics for troop numbers and ammunition were reported. The highest numbers were reported by Kaset in July 1992: he said that one million rounds were fired.

117. *Bangkok Post*, 20 June 1992.

118. Scott Donaldson, "On the wrong side of Ratchadamnoen Ave", *The Nation*, 24 May 1992, p. B5.

119. *The Nation*, 16 June 1992. For analysis see Kritaya Archavanitkul, Anuchat Poungsomlee, Suporn Chunvavuttiyanont, and Varaporn Chamsanit, "Political Disharmony in Thai Society: A Lesson from the May 1992 Incident", *Asia Review 1995* 9 (1995): 39–56.

120. *The Nation*, 5 June 1992; Kritaya et al., op. cit., p. 47; also see Withoon Ungpraphan, "A Study of Autopsy Reports from the Dead Occurring Because of the May 1992 Incident", mimeographed (Bangkok, July 1992) (cited in Kritaya et al., op. cit.).

121. Dr Chaiwat Rakrachakarn of Rajvithi Hospital, *The Nation*, 25 May 1992.

122. Kanjana Spindler, "May 1992: When the tide finally turned", *Bangkok Post*, 19 May 1993, p. 5.

123. See Mukdawan Sakboon, "When the troops fired", *The Nation*, 7 June 1992, p. A8; Asia Watch, "Uncontrolled use of lethal force", *The Nation*, 22 May 1992, p. A6; *Crisis in Democracy: Report of an International Fact-Finding Mission to Thailand on the Events of 17th–20th May 1992 in Bangkok* (Hong Kong, November 1992); Kritaya et al., op. cit.; and Iacopino and Jones, op. cit.

124. *The Nation*, 18 May 1992.

125. Donaldson, op. cit., p. B5. For interpretations of the events of May that view Chamlong as forcing the issue, and thus using violence for his own ends, see McCargo, op. cit., pp. 264–69.

126. Suchit, op. cit., p. 53.

127. *Matichon*, 9 April 1992.

128. *The Nation*, 6 May 1992.

129. Benedict Anderson, "Withdrawal Symptoms: Social and Cultural Aspects of the October 6 Coup", *Bulletin of Concerned Asian Scholars* 9, no. 3 (July–September 1977): 13–30.

130. *The Nation*, 13 May 1992, p. A6.

131. *The Nation*, 16 May 1992, p. A1.

132. Creative Media Foundation, *Langban* [Cleanse the village].

133. Prudhisan Jumbala, Correspondence, 27 October 1993.

134. The facilities were actually an issue, since the military government 'stole/rented' the city's toilet trucks as a way of trying to produce a chaotic mob (of super-saturated folk?). The 'pro-democracy' organizers wittily replied by claiming that the military government was denying the people their human right to piss.

135. *Matichon*, 22 April 1992.

136. Benedict Anderson, "Murder and Progress in Modern Siam", *New Left Review*, no. 181 (May/June 1990), p. 41.

137. And this is nothing new, as Anderson writes of the 14 October 1973 mass demonstrations: "There is no doubt that the new bourgeois strata contributed decisively to the huge crowds that came out in support of the students' and intellectuals' demands for a constitution and respect for civil liberties. Indeed, it can be argued that these strata ensured the *success* of the demonstrations — had the crowds been composed of slum-dwellers rather than generally well-dressed urbanites, the dictators might have won fuller support for the repression." (Anderson, "Withdrawal Symptoms", p. 18.)

138. Suthy Prasartset, "Preface", in Somsak Kosaisuk, *Labour Against Dictatorship* (Bangkok: Friedrich Ebert Stiftung, Labour Museum Project, Arom Pongpangan Foundation, 1993), p. 19.

139. *Crisis in Democracy*, p. 29. Another accounting of the socio-economic characteristics of the victims: "As for occupation, 55 percent of the missing, 43 percent of the wounded and 25 percent of the dead were blue collar workers, such as wage labourers, petty traders and street vendors. Eighteen percent of the wounded had their own business; and 16 percent of the missing were unemployed. For those who were not working but studying, the highest proportion was found among the dead (16 percent) whereas it accounted for only 8 and 5 percent of the injured and the missing respectively." (Kritaya et

al., op. cit., p. 52.) Chamlong did his own informal survey after he was arrested and confined in the Bangkhen Police School with the other political prisoners. He found them to come from all walks of life — farmers, traders, employees, labourers, shop owners, students, and bureaucrats — who came from every region and every province. (Chamlong Srimuang, *Ruam Kan Su* [Unite to fight] [Bangkok: Khlet Thai, 1992], p. 180.)

140. Kritaya et al., op. cit., pp. 52–53.
141. William Connally in Mehmed, Ferguson, and Turnbull, p. 47.

ALTERNATIVE ORGANIZATION
Non-governmental Organizations and Non-violent Action as Political Forces

> Survival...is learning how to take our differences and make
> them strengths. For the master's tools will never dismantle
> the master's house. They may allow us temporarily to beat
> him at his own game, but they will never enable us to bring
> about genuine change.
>
> – Audre Lorde[1]

A strange thing happened on 18 May 1992 at the height of the
brutal military crack-down of the Bangkok uprising. After the army
took control of Rajdamnoen Avenue and arrested Major-General
Chamlong Srimuang, the leader of the pro-democracy movement,
they figured their job was done. The army, Chamlong, and the
media all assumed that the demonstration would be over once its
leader was taken into custody: chop off the head to solve the
problem.[2] This reasoning perhaps stems from the 6 October 1976
experience of both the military and the student movement. As one
former student activist states: "In 1976 the mass power was crushed
because it was too centralized around the student organizations."[3]
Once the students were massacred at Thammasat University the
democratic movement died as well, and when students fled to

the jungle they were transformed into "communist insurgents". Chamlong, on the other hand, wagered that once the army had arrested him, they would lose credibility, and thus would have to resign.[4] But in 1992 both Chamlong and the military were left behind by the demonstrators who not only kept on demonstrating, but protested in new and different ways. Six months later Chamlong admitted not understanding what happened: "When I was arrested I thought that the demonstration was supposed to end. I thought that everyone would go home."[5]

Actually, the mass protest blossomed after Chamlong (along with thousands of others) was arrested and Rajdamnoen Avenue was cleared by the army on 19 May. The configuration of protest in 1992 was much different from that in 1973 and 1976: it did not fragment after Chamlong was arrested — it multiplied. In 1992 the demonstration was not dependent on students, but had many centres, including professionals, health-care workers, business people, slum dwellers, workers, and farmers in Bangkok and the provinces. The complexity of these multiple events is shown most clearly by the spatial organization of the demonstration. There was no single centre of protest. The conservative reasoning which blames the victims relies on the logic of a centralized protest — modelled after the military — with definite leaders and clear battle lines; such authors rely on maps of Rajdamnoen Avenue to represent the conflict at Paan Faa Bridge.[6] But the May protest was multi-centred where various groups — aided by technology such as the telephone, the fax, and the cellular phone which facilitated communications all around the country — continued the protest after their so-called leader was arrested. Whenever the army dispersed a crowd in one spot, another would appear elsewhere. At the provincial level the non-violent mass rallies were not suppressed, though they were conducted under the watchful eye of the police. In Bangkok people still came to Sanam Luang and the Pinklao Bridge to gather just out of range of the soldiers on Rajdamnoen Avenue. There were motor-cycle 'gangs' who fought the police in the streets and smashed symbols of public control like traffic lights and police booths. Most notably, once a curfew was declared on 19 May, over 50,000 protesters regrouped at Ramkhamheang University where they set up barricades to form a non-violent 'commune' separate from the military control of the rest of the city.

In short, the 1992 protest had no single head that could be cut off; in the more democratic environment of the 1990s each person had his own head. Perhaps that is why the military stopped shooting and started talking on 20 May — they did not want to shoot off everyone's head. The understanding of the May movement has to respond to this new mushrooming factor in the protest. Though it is common to explain it as "middle class democracy revolution", a multi-centred approach can make more sense of the different roles played by different people during the demonstrations. A decentred approach to the May events can also help explain why after the demonstrations were over, groups that struggled together later struggled against each other.[7]

In this chapter I would like to follow Audre Lorde's lead to examine the alternative organizations active in May 1992 which challenged not just the soldiers, but the whole military-directed discourse of political organization in Thailand. Indeed, as we saw in Chapter 2, 'organization' itself was a stumbling block: the predominant discourse of organized mobs (*mohp jatdang*) characterized mass action as either "chaotic" or "manipulated", but always violent. My argument is that the two most interesting aspects of the May events — non-violent tactics and non-governmental organizations — represent an alternative form of organization and action which can dismantle the master's house for genuine change.

I will argue that organizational strategies and modes of action that are attentive to differences and diversity can build an alternative society which is more attentive to social justice. To do this I will trace the development of non-violent tactics and non-governmental organizations in recent Thai history and draw parallels between them and feminist theory's "oppositional consciousness" and Michel Foucault's "revolutionary action". Then I will use these popular tools to analyse the April-May 1992 demonstrations as an exemplary case of decentred mass action which uses oppositional consciousness: until mid-May the rallies were characterized more as 'anti-Suchinda' than 'pro-democracy'.

Popular Tools: Seismic Shifts in Participation and Tactics

To understand the events of May 1992 it is necessary to understand recent social history in Thailand. In his insightful analysis of the period of open politics which followed the 14 October 1973 uprising, Benedict Anderson focuses on the dynamics of class formation and ideological upheaval.[8] In 1992 we could say that the main issues had shifted to different modes of participation (non-governmental organizations) and tactics (non-violent action). The following general history uses exemplary stories to highlight how political participation has shifted through the 1960s, 1970s, 1980s, and up into the 1990s as a way to demonstrate the decentred dynamic of non-governmental organizations.

Participation: Classes, Mobs, and Non-governmental Organizations

It is popular in Bangkok to scold college students for not living up to their political mission in 1992, but as Thai society becomes more complex, people organize themselves differently and missions change. In the 1970s activists could be categorized into definite stable social groups. During the period of open politics that started on 14 October 1973, protesters were never called 'mobs', but were named according to socio-economic class analysis as 'students', 'workers', or 'peasants'.[9]

In the 1990s such a clarity of participants is missing: the only class struggle in May 1992 was between Chulachomklao Royal Military Academy Class 5 and Class 7. The newspapers tried to use familiar categories to identify the demonstrators in April 1992 as "students, academics, and opposition party members", but as we saw in Chapter 2 the popular uprising of May 1992 overwhelmed these simple categories. The only word left was 'mob', which means that commentators needed to find new ways to talk about 'the people' that could adequately account for the blurring of participants' multiple identities. Chapter 2 showed how the demonstrators were often called a "middle class mob" so everyone knew that it was a 'good mob', but this paradoxical naming only further obscured matters and encouraged state violence.

How did Thai politics shift from obvious socio-economic classes to indistinct mobs? This gradual shift started in the 1970s with the struggle between left- and right-wing groups. The military saw the power of the mass organizations of students, workers, and peasants and encouraged its own mobs to counter them. Though ultra-right wing movements of the 1970s such as Nawaphol, Red Gaur, and Village Scouts had financial and logistical support from high-ranking military and police officers, they were actually "ad hoc groups with no enduring organization".[10] For example, though many describe the Red Gaur as being 'vocational students' who were involved in a class conflict with 'middle class' university students, on closer examination the Red Gaur were led by "mercenaries and men discharged from the army for disciplinary infractions", who were then "hired by various cliques within the ISOC (Internal Security Operations Command)... the Red Gaurs were not recruited primarily on the basis of ideological commitment, but rather by promises of high pay, abundant free liquor and brothel privileges, and the lure of public notoriety".[11]

This changed with the 6 October 1976 crack-down and coup which came at the end of a time when not only politics was more public, but perhaps more importantly, violence was more public. The years 1978 and 1980 are defining due to significant shifts in policy which ushered in what many call the transition period of "demi-democracy" or "Premocracy" because the unelected Prime Minister from 1980 to 1988 was General Prem Tinsulanond.[12] But this era might better be named the bureaucratic/business alliance of the 1980s, for "the 1978 constitution symbolized a compromise between two elites, military-bureaucratic and extra-bureaucratic". Businessmen and bureaucrats had to strike a deal because "both elites feared worker and peasant upsurges that would endanger their respective interests".[13] But due to the 1973 mass movement, the popular sector could no longer be ignored, and "both sides would respectively attempt to mobilize the masses to their side and to their advantage.... As such [the 1978 constitution] should not be understood as necessarily a transition to democracy, but as a mere ground rule within which bureaucratic-extrabureaucratic political interactions may take place".[14]

Public Sector: Military Mobs. After suppressing student, worker, and peasant groups in 1976, the military moved to fill this social void with its own mass movements. This mass mobilization policy was clarified in 1980 and applied to the whole nation with the famous Prime Minister's Order 66/23 which more explicitly gave the military a role in mass politics.[15] An important part of this was the expansion of the military's role in rural development projects, which was also guaranteed in the 1978 Constitution. The military has a close association with the state's notion of top-down development and welfare projects. And this has always been political. Thai development policy and national security concerns became more closely linked from the late 1970s, and the Fifth National Economic and Social Development Board (NESDB) plan (1982–86) specifically targeted infrastructure to villages in communist areas.

> Aid and development programs were initiated primarily for political and military reasons and only secondarily with altruistic and humanitarian considerations in mind. This explains why the plight of the villages was ignored for so long by the government. Only after the threat of communist subversion fully materialized did the government move on the poverty issues.[16]

Even a decade after the insurgency was over, the communist threat still motivates army resources in rural areas under the theme of "development for stability", and the army continues to justify its role by pointing to the 1991 Constitution which again defines the military's role in alleviating rural poverty. According to an army briefing booklet distributed in 1993, the "majority of H.M. the King's and H.M. the Queen's development projects were planned, carried out, and/or supervised by the Army's units or personnel".[17]

The groups mentioned in Chapter 2 as making up the 'horse-faced mohp' which supported Suchinda's premiership — National Defence Volunteers and Military Reservists for National Security —

were products of this military mass mobilization. These mass movements were more like "state directed organizations charac- teristic of authoritarian regimes than voluntary organizations common in liberal democracies. ...The Army has also quietly established relations with leaders of labour unions, student and business organizations."[18] In Thai political parlance, this is how the organized mobs — *mohp jatdang* — discussed in Chapter 2, were born. *Jatdang* (organize) was probably borrowed by both left-wing students and the military from the Communist Party of Thailand (CPT) in the 1970s.[19] Indeed, this is not surprising for although the CPT and the military were ideological opposites, they used many of the same tactics and discourses in their common quest for state power (this can be seen most clearly in how the Thai army has co-operated so well with the most radical Marxist movement of them all, the Khmer Rouge). Hence, contrary to popular belief, mobs are not necessarily anti-government in Thai- land, but can also serve the interests of the military wherever they are needed.

These military mass organizations became a powerful force in the 1980s, first to signify popular support for military élites such as Army Commander Arthit Kamlang-ek and Prime Minister Prem Tinsulanond. They also provided the military with a mass base that could be used for overtly political purposes such as "rallying votes for a military-backed party in an election or in influencing villagers *not* to vote for a particular party".[20] Military mass organi- zations peaked under the tenure of Army Commander General Chavalit Yongchaiyudh, whose army faction, the Democratic Soldiers, was highly skilled in rural mobilization.[21] These military mass organizations later declined due to neglect once General Suchinda Kraprayoon, the leader of the Class 5 army faction, replaced Chavalit in 1990. Suchinda did not have any political officers in his 1992 government either, and seemed not to appreciate the value of popular support.[22] When the Suchinda government finally tried to use the mass organizations to mobilize popular support in May 1992, the response was quite hollow. This was because the organization was a purely bureaucratic exercise, rather than an ideological manoeuvre.

The army mobs have not been a policy of army commanders after the May events, but the mechanisms are still in place, and army mobs could start moving again if the generals find them useful.[23] The master of military mass organizations, General Chavalit, combined military and political power when he became Thailand's Prime Minister and Defence Minister concurrently in 1996. Indeed, such government-inspired mobs have been used recently to end popular demonstrations in Thailand's neighbouring states of Indonesia, Burma (Myanmar), and Malaysia as well.

Private Sector: Business Associations. There were two other important forces of political participation developing in the 1980s parallel to the army mob: business associations and non-governmental organizations. These three phenomena are integrally related. As noted above, business and military-bureaucracy cut a deal with the 1978 Constitution as a way of controlling the "excesses of democracy". And it turns out that the army often turned to local businessmen to help build their mass organizations in the 1970s and early 1980s.[24] But there were also struggles between the military and business. The 1978 Constitution addressed the excesses of authoritarian government that were exemplified by the Thanin regime that came into power with the 1976 coup.

> This new government first appeared to be pro-business in that it harshly repressed the left-leaning student and labor movement. Later it proved to be suspicious of, or at best indifferent to, all kinds of independent organized groups, including the middle class and business groups.[25]

Because of this harshness, the Thanin regime lasted only one year. Hence in the 1980s power began shifting from the bureaucracy to other more extra-bureaucratic organizations. Anek Laothamatas argues that in the 1980s business groups supplanted students as the major extra-bureaucratic force, "becom[ing] strong enough to break the monopoly of the military-bureaucratic elite with regard to the economic policy-making of the state".[26] Bureaucracy and business thus worked together to make plans and address problems through organizations at the national level such as the Joint Public and Private Sector Consultative Committee (JPPCC), which has been quite active in government/business relations since 1981.[27] This movement was powerful because it was not restricted to Bangkok. Business organizations and chambers of commerce formed at provincial levels as well: provincial JPPCCs started organizing in 1984, and by 1990 there were organizations in each of the provinces.[28]

The key to the success of business in Thailand lies in *how* it was organized; similar to business associations in South Korea, Taiwan, and Singapore, these Thai organizations were fostered by the government. Yet Anek argues that unlike these other countries, business organizations in Thailand are largely independent and can exert their influence as an extra-bureaucratic force in the policy-making arena. Hence Anek characterizes this as a successfully paradoxical "fostered independence". This enables the government and organized business to work together to help each other, rather than being at odds. Instead of being merely a front for government policy as they are in most East and Southeast Asian countries, Thai independent business groups have pushed the bureaucracy to become more of a positive force instead of a hindrance known only for red tape. This is a powerful extra-bureaucratic movement that works at both the provincial and national levels.

Anek quite convincingly demonstrates that these business organizations have been effective in guiding economic policy for industrialization and the export economy. But what about the rest of Thailand? According to political theories of middle class democracy, the key to political development is civil society, and the key to the growth of civil society is an independent business class. But Anek notes that Thai business associations play a minimal role in electoral politics, and actually feel that the role of Parliament is to scrutinize the bills that business associations and departments have formulated.[29] In more local level 'grass-roots spaces' they are not interested in participatory democracy either:

> Businessmen in general prefer a centralized, hierarchical system with strong peak organizations, not a decentralized system. Far from deterring government intervention, business actively seeks official status, assistance and — often — leadership.[30]

Thus, rather than opposing the army, business organizations actually work well with the military. For example, the courses at the National Defence College bring together senior military officers, civilian bureaucrats, and businessmen to build up an élite network of the public and private sectors; candidates from the private sector are nominated by business associations.

In this way Anek seems to undermine his own argument about a change in the character of Thai politics away from the bureaucratic polity model. The bourgeois polity reproduces many of the same corrupt business–bureaucrat relations, but with a new twist that Anek calls "reversed clientelism".[31] Rather than the government officials being the patrons and the (Sino-Thai) traders being the clients, now the businesspeople are the patrons and the bureaucrats are the clients in the same economy of influence and corruption. Some go as far as to say that the vicious circle of Thai politics has been replaced by a "vicious triangle" where veteran politicians, local bureaucrats, and provincial business co-operate in order to divide up the spoils.[32]

This changed briefly after the May events, with the three key metropolitan business organizations opposing an extension of military dictatorship past Suchinda. But this was certainly not an example of business associations leading political reform: "The ready support of many middle-class people for the demonstrations contrasts strarkly with the position of organized capitalists, who were slow in throwing their support behind the demonstrators."[33] The support by business institutions was not necessarily a democratic movement either, since they cheered the selection of another non-elected Prime Minister — Anand Panyarachun, who is known as a businessman and a technocrat. The two progressive business clubs, Business Management Systems (BMS) and the Business Club for Democracy, made ambitious plans to support 'good candidates' in the September 1992 election. But once former Prime Minister Chatichai Choonhavan looked like he might win the election with his new party, they backed off because they feared reprisals.[34] Organized business's interest in parliamentary politics was short-lived. Or more to the point, in the 1980s provincial businessmen as individuals and small groups became heavily involved in a national politics of a more unsavoury kind in the vicious triangle. This mafia-style (or what we might call the 'business mob') politics, which has been described at length in many books and articles, is for personal enrichment rather than for structural or ideological change.[35]

Popular Sector: Non-governmental Organizations. Parallel to the military mobs and business associations, in the 1980s another people's movement was taking shape through the rapidly expanding network of non-governmental organizations. Like the business organizations, non-governmental organizations have developed as a significant extra-bureaucratic force since the early 1980s, at times with the "fostered independence" of government encouragement. There is also a parallel between the growth in number and influence of business organizations and non-governmental organization networks; but it would be a mistake to overplay their similarities. Indeed, their similarity often comes from their being on different sides of the same social and environmental issues.

The emergence of non-governmental organizations was a response to the state-initiated 'development business' that began in earnest after Field Marshal Sarit Thanarat's coup in 1958. This revolution signalled the beginning of an era of political-economic history which vigorously inserted Thailand into the world economy. With the aid of the World Bank, the Sarit regime set up the National Economic and Social Development Board (NESDB) which launched the first national economic development plan in 1961 to court international capital based on an export-promotion strategy.[36] This new 'authoritarian capitalism' certainly gave rise to an independent Thai (as opposed to Chinese) capitalist class which formed the business associations referred to above. But it also further centralized and bureaucratized government policy while extending state intervention for the first time into the daily life of each village in Thailand.[37]

The NESDB's national development plans prioritized commercial, financial, industrial, and urban interests over rural interests in its centrally planned, top-down, government-controlled national development programmes. This "transnationalized model of accumulation" has an ideology of developmentalism, consumerism, and militarism which leads to a concentration of economic and political power in certain social groups, thus marginalizing and disempowering other groups.[38]

> Quite instructively, in Thai official vocabulary, "private sector" simply means those tiny and prosperous minorities in the modern enclave: namely, industry, commerce, and banking, all of which revolving around the concept and sole objective of unlimited industrial growth....Translated into democratic jargon, if there is to be any development at all, it would read something like development of the "private sector," by the "private sector," and for the "private sector."[39]

While business and the bureaucracy benefited from the economic boom of the 1980s, the development was uneven, resulting in increasing economic disparities and an environmental crisis.[40] The turning point occurred during 1984–85, when manufacturing outstripped agriculture in the gross domestic product (GDP); although 70 per cent of the people still work the land, more wealth is now created through industry.[41] Thus, the public/private sector schema does not include the 70 per cent of Thais who are agricultural and industrial workers. This sets non-governmental organizations off as a third sector — the popular sector — of activity as opposed to the public sector, which is defined by the state, and the private sector, which is defined by capital.[42]

There is an important difference in how these three sectors are organized. The army, business associations, and the CPT all use the same model of hierarchical organization. Non-governmental organizations, on the other hand, have developed more egalitarian networks which funnel information and action. This different style of organization comes from how they were originally formed: business associations and military mobs were initiated from the top town, starting out at the national level and working their way down to provincial and local levels. Non-governmental organizations, on the other hand, were not directed by the state, but came more from the grass roots: they worked with scattered village projects, and then built themselves up into regional, national, and international networks. Thus the non-governmental organizations'

vision of development can be more people-centred and participatory. At first non-governmental organizations worked mostly
in alternative development strategies — calling themselves non-
governmental development organizations (NGDOs) — but by the
1990s the movement took a political turn. Because of their grass-
roots organization a politicized network of non-governmental
organizations became the most powerful in the resistance to the
Suchinda military government in 1992.

Though non-governmental organizations did not become a
major force in Thai politics until the 1990s, they have been present
as an alternative force since the 1960s.[43] Before then there was
a general absence of organized groups,[44] and from the 1950s
development work done outside the public sector was seen as
communist.[45] Against this 'national security' backdrop it was
difficult to organize alternatives.[46] Much of the early history of
non-governmental organizations centres around the activities of
people like Puey Ungphakorn. As a former technocrat Puey was
well known to the state, and hence was able to found the first
rural development non-governmental organization, the Thai Rural
Reconstruction Movement (TRRM) in 1967 without arousing anti-
communist suspicions. The principles of the TRRM — livelihood,
education, health, self-government, and non-violence — placed it
squarely against the developmentalism which was impoverishing
the peasants.[47] Though Puey was certainly a Bangkok-based technocrat, he deliberately placed the headquarters of TRRM in the
provincial town of Chainat, away from the urban centres of power
and influence. With the period of open politics from 1973 to 1976,
non-governmental organizations were formed to respond to newly
highlighted social and political problems. For example, soon after
October 1973 the Union for Civil Liberties (UCL) was founded to
serve as an advocate for labour and farmers' groups.[48]

But as Thai politics was increasingly polarized between the
extreme left and right, non-governmental organizations were
marginalized. Many non-governmental organizations, including
the UCL and the Co-ordinating Group for Religion and Society
(CGRS), tried to form a third way between capitalism and the CPT
for "social transformation without armed struggle".[49] But this third

way was attacked from both sides, particularly by the right-wing's systematic propaganda. The violent polarization finally led to the bloody crack-down and coup on 6 October 1976. In the following reign of terror, non-governmental organizations — especially those working in the villages — were forced to disband since most of them were labelled as communist, and many non-governmental organization workers fled into the jungle to join the CPT's armed struggle.

Soon after the coup, activists reorganized along less overtly political lines, focusing on development problems and specific issues of technical assistance and religious matters:

> People set up other organizations that were still working for social justice, but in an indirect way. It could not be directly political, we couldn't advocate for the peasants. So the same activists set up specialized groups on children's issues, drug issues, public health issues, technology issues. I was involved in the Alternative Technology Group.[50]

Still, because of the harsh government of the time and the massive communist insurgency in the late 1970s, these groups were still not a major social force.

1980s: Mushrooming of Non-governmental Organizations. There are many factors that led to the mushrooming of non-governmental organization networks into a social movement in the 1980s. Strangely enough, the shifts can be traced to regional affairs over which Thais had little influence or participation. The Vietnamese invasion of Cambodia in 1978 is a central point which indirectly provided both human and financial/technical resources to non-governmental organizations. International non-governmental organizations came to the Thai/Cambodian border to address the Cambodian refugee problem. After they witnessed the poverty in rural Thailand, they also provided financial resources to Thai projects. Another spin-off of the Vietnamese invasion was an ideological struggle within the CPT which caused many activists to return to the towns. This migration provided valuable human resources to form the social movement of non-governmental organizations.

After activists started returning from the jungles and the political repression cooled off in the early 1980s, people started reorganizing for social justice. But activists did not use the same model of organization. Rather than forming class-based mass movements, they were forced by the political situation to work in a different way from the CPT. Indeed, the CPT mirrored the army's organization, which used linear models of domination. After the bloody struggles of the 1970s there was a crisis of vanguardist models of social change directed by underground parties like the CPT: there was a "shakening of 'conventional' paradigms of revolution, and more attention and interest towards a commitment to social transformation and development by non-military means".[51] Surichai also notes that in the 1980s there was a shift from developmentalist plans which relied on Western economics and technology to see "development as liberation, [which] cannot come from any kind of 'one right answer'" whether that one right answer is from the World Bank, the army, or the CPT.[52]

To understand the novelty of the non-governmental organizations' social movement, it is helpful to utilize the concepts of "oppositional consciousness" and "revolutionary action". The shift from government to non-governmental organizations and from institutionalized violence to popular non-violence in Thailand echoes many of the decentralizing tendencies of political and social theory in Europe and North America for the past few decades. Rather than the class formation of the 1970s that Anderson describes, I argue that Thai social movements are part of a shift in identity formation. This can lead to the new forms of organizing, unity, and 'political massing' which stress difference rather than sameness. This strand of postmodern theorizing has been strongest in feminist theory as it addresses the multiple identities of gender/race/sexuality in what is known as "women of colour" in the United States. Since African-American women are oppressed according to gender and race,[53] organizing along the lines of "women of colour" is used as a strategy for a multiple identity which would be attentive to the multiple oppression that gets effaced in binary oppositions of black/white, male/female.

This is an important shift because identity is no longer organized according to essential categories of race, class, and gender which are positive in the sense that one declares that one is 'black', 'working class', or 'woman' in order to be a member of the group. Rather, "women of colour" is oppositional because people participate by being 'non-male', 'non-white': thus unity is not formed according to positive essential categories — like a liberal feminist woman who is taken to be defined biologically at birth — but according to a common object of resistance: "a viable oppositional alliance is a *common context of struggle* rather than color or racial identifications".[54]

By focusing on the political rather than the biological or cultural aspects, organizers are able to make linkages with many other groups which fall outside the essential constituency of feminism. Thus oppositional consciousness is open-ended and works outside any dialectic of thesis — anti-thesis which demands a totalizing synthesis. This multiple identity leads us away from vanguard parties to a united front politics which is organized on the basis of "conscious coalition, of affinity, of political kinship".[55] Thus with oppositional consciousness there can be the 'political massing' that unity brings, while still being attentive to differences: organization without *mobilization*.

The relevance of oppositional consciousness to non-governmental organizations and non-violent action may not seem obvious, since both these movements have now been 'entified' into stable things — even acronyms like NGO and NVA.[56] (To problematize this entification, I do not abbreviate these phrases.) But if you take these terms literally, their oppositional nature becomes clear. They are not things, but non-things: non-governmental organization, non-violent action. Non-governmental organizations are often described in terms of another oppositional marker: non-profit. *Ahimsa*, the Pali word that Thais use for 'non-violence', also refers to a non-thing: *a* is negative, *himsa* is 'harming'. In this way both non-governmental organizations and non-violent action resist the essentialization. Like oppositional consciousness, they can provide "a chance to build an effective unity that does not replicate the imperializing, totalizing revolutionary subjects of previous Marxisms and feminisms which had not faced the consequences of the disorderly polyphony emerging from decolonization".[57]

Actually, most of the criticisms of non-governmental organizations do not see totalization as a serious issue. It is only the army and its few intellectuals who use the language of "communist threat" to denounce non-governmental organizations.[58] On the other hand, many criticize non-governmental organizations as a negative movement, or a 'residual category'.[59] Still, we need to be careful in how we figure non-governmental organizations and non-violent action as social movements since they both have essentialist tendencies: in the 1980s both were hailed as cure-alls in popular formulations of the politics of social justice. Now in the 1990s many scholars (and activists) caution us not to be sucked up into a 'populist fallacy' or 'utopian analysis',[60] which are seen as just as misguided as state-driven hierarchical activities.[61]

One of the problems with both non-violence and non-governmental organizations, as I have described them above, is that they risk being fundamentalist groups which rely on essential definitions of peace, development, and community. But if we turn the scripting of the social formation around to write it in terms of oppositional consciousness, new space is created for a diversity of groups and difference of opinion. Imagining social movements this way follows Lorde's advice in the epigraph to take the weakness of fragmentation and turn it into the strength of diversity.

In politics this means that non-governmental organizations are not trying to seize state power to set up a new and better state government, but are working for grass-roots participation of more people: empowerment. This is a different kind of politics from parliamentary struggle: "We're different (from political parties). Political parties want to have state power, but the NGOs do not. NGOs don't have a definite position as to support or oppose the government like political parties. We do that on an issue by issue basis."[62] Non-governmental organizations thus guard against re-creating the monster of centralized repression that they are contesting. In this way a decentralized network of non-governmental organizations emerged where people can still be active while not "following government structure".[63]

This is an important point to make because even though the master's house — the state — is the focus of repression, and thus resistance, new strategies must guard against reproducing the politics of dominance that characterize the state. Michel Foucault addresses these concerns to assess both the achievements and the problems of France's 'Events of May 1968':

> If you wish to replace an official institution by another institution that fulfills the same function — better and differently — then you are already being reabsorbed by the dominant structure....
>
> We readily believe that the least we can expect of experiences, actions, and strategies is that they take into account the 'whole of society'. This seems absolutely essential for their existence. But I believe that this is asking a great deal, that it means imposing impossible conditions on our actions because this notion functions in a manner that prohibits the actualization, success, and perpetuation of these projects. The 'whole of society' is precisely that which should not be considered except as something to be destroyed.[64]

By questioning the discourse of the "whole of society", Foucault is working to imagine resistance in different, decentralized ways. Rather than trying to change the "whole of society" and risk reproducing the politics of dominance, Foucault stresses that resistance must be multiple. Foucault thus rewrites the question of social change from how to overthrow governments to "what can be done to disrupt the system's cycle of social reproduction".[65] Foucault's answer appeals to what we now call "oppositional consciousness":

> ...we can't defeat the system through isolated actions; we must engage it on all fronts — the university, the prisons, the domain of psychiatry — one after another since our forces are not strong enough for a simultaneous attack. We strike and knock against the most solid obstacles; the system cracks at another point; we persist. It seems that we're winning, but then the institution is rebuilt; we must start again. But the system it opposes, as well as the power exercised through the system, supplies its unity.[66]

In another interview Gilles Deleuze asks Foucault how such a decentred struggle can be organized: "how are we to define these networks, the transversal links between these active and discontinuous points, from one country to another or within one country?" Foucault answers:

> ...if the fight is directed against power, then all those on whom power is exercised to their detriment, all who find it intolerable, can begin the struggle on their own terrain and on the basis of their proper activity (or passivity). In engaging in a struggle that concerns their own interests, whose objectives they clearly understand and whose methods only they can determine, they enter into a revolutionary process.[67]

This characterization of the struggle leads us back to non-governmental organizations and non-violent action in Asia, where the non-governmental organizations in the 1980s began "the struggle on their own terrain and on the basis of their proper activity" rather than trying to overthrow the whole of society. Since the circumstances and problems were multiple, the organization of campaigns for social justice also had to be multiple, hence people looked to open-ended nature of non-governmental organizations rather than some monolithic party or association.[68]

Non-governmental organizations, as 'non-entities', are, of course, hard to define. As one non-governmental organization worker comments: "I think when you draw a boundary around NGOs, you create the impression that they are an institution which can formulate a common policy. They are not."[69] That they resist singular definition and categorization is one of their strengths, and speaks to the diversity and multiplicity in the movement: "The NGOs are a movement of wide diversity. They should not be one big institute holding on to a single ideal."[70] Thus, as activists pushed for a decentralization of bureaucratic power, the non-governmental organization movement itself decentralized into small-scale affinity groups that worked on issue-based problem-solving rather than class-based state politics. This took advantage of the non-governmental organization experiments of the 1970s and applied them on a much wider scale.

So both out of the necessity of dealing with a military-dominated government and strategy of sustainable social change, activists decentralized into non-governmental organizations. In 1987 the

Thai Volunteer Service counted 135 non-profit organizations, most of which had less than ten staff members and few of which were registered; by 1990 there were over 350 organizations.[71] These non-governmental organizations multiplied because, like in many other countries, the state-run programmes were not successful, and it was seen that "development funds are more effectively used by the voluntary sector...because they tend to be small, efficient, flexible, innovative, non-political and relatively unburdened by bureaucracy".[72] The one key to this success was that non-governmental organizations were not part of the 'development business', but were voluntary organizations which were more people-centred.[73] The slogan in the early 1980s was: "The answers are in the villages".[74] Thus the non-governmental organizations and the villagers worked to carve out separate economic and political space by using integrated farming and holistic development approaches to delink from the market economy, while they linked up across village lines.

This attention to micro issues was successful for a time, but by the mid-1980s the drawbacks of this strategy were clear: while it helped at the village level, the overall approach was fragmentary and unco-ordinated; projects often had limited sustainability, limited technical analysis, and lack of broad programming context. Even if the villages were delinking from the capitalist economy, the capitalist economy was still working on not just a national scale, but an international scale which overwhelmed the small-scale efforts. The non-governmental organizations had to make a more co-ordinated effort in order to push for sustainable development, so they changed the focus from village-based projects to organize themselves into networks to have a larger voice for national public policy advocacy, while still maintaining their independence. Networks act as spaces where small non-governmental organizations can link with other bodies, including other Thai non-governmental organizations, international non-governmental organizations, government agencies, the middle class (including intellectuals, the media, and politicians), and people's organizations.[75]

The primary responsibilities of the network are quite different from those of small-scale non-governmental organizations: communication, consultation, facilitation, and outreach to government organizations, international organizations, and the private sector. These different tasks cast non-governmental organizations as catalytic or strategic organizations.[76] There have been non-governmental organization networks in Thailand since the early 1980s, but the big shift to networking as a strategy occurred in December 1985 with the formation of the NGO Co-ordinating Committee on Rural Development (NGO-CORD). This organization is similar to the business associations in that NGO-CORD was set up with the aid of the NESDB with funding from the Canadian International Development Agency; on the other hand, NGO-CORD actually served to formalize already existing informal contacts between urban and rural non-governmental organizations.[77] Though its name implies that the focus is on rural development, NGO-CORD has come to represent more social and political non-governmental organizations as well, addressing issues of human rights, women's rights, children's rights, public health, and hill tribes' rights.

Oppositional consciousness against state-directed developmentalism is one way to describe how non-governmental organizations have been able to turn fragmentation into a decentred unity through networking. At the macro level these small and specialized non-governmental organizations banded together in networks — much like the social formation "women of colour" — which gives them a voice while preserving the independence of small-scale organization. But soon non-governmental organizations found that their policy advocacy was not very successful because they were attempting to address the "whole of society" rather than specific groups of people. NGO-CORD signified a shift from micro to macro, which separated it from the grass-roots base necessary for political influence. To be effective, non-governmental organizations had to work in both urban and rural spaces at the same time; they needed to go back to the roots and combine micro activities with macro campaigns. As Suthy Prasartset states,

> any policy advocacy and campaign will not carry much weight in the decision-making process at the national level if this is not backed up by solid and wide social bases of

support.... Together with the advocacy work, the organizing
and networking activities must be progressively strengthened.[78]

Networking is now the focus of most non-governmental organizations which work more as catalysts for people's organizations
than as service-providers themselves. "Networking helps to develop
collective strength and mobilize resources; it strengthens linkages
among non-governmental organizations and, at the regional level,
it strengthens Asian perspectives on crucial issues such as people's
participation."[79] The dual focus on local projects and national
networks in Thailand formed what Suthy calls "socio-political
infrastructure". Hence non-governmental organizations form an
alternative form of organization which uses oppositional consciousness to be attentive to both local, national, and transnational
issues and audiences. Since it is active in many spaces, this "socio-
political infrastructure" can be used for village projects, policy
advocacy, and, as the world saw in April-May 1992, for mass
rallies.

Tactics: Mass Action, Armed Struggle, and Non-violence

Non-governmental organizations and non-violent action are closely
related. The shift in participation went hand in hand with the
change in tactics — both of which were the result of a combination of necessity and strategy. Anderson argues that the second
crisis in the 1970s was an ideological upheaval.[80] Though Anderson
is concerned with the ideologies of socialism and capitalism, it is
useful to consider violence as an ideology which was shared by
both extreme right and left movements.

Non-violent action was one of the non-governmental organization tactics in the 1970s; recall that non-violence was one of the
principles of the TRRM. Throughout the period of open politics
groups like the UCL and later the CGRS promoted non-violent
action as an alternative — a third way — between the social
transformation through violence as practised by both the left and
the right. Yet like the non-governmental organizations, this was
overwhelmed by the violent methods in the 1970s and early 1980s.
Most memories of the period of open politics are images of violent
struggles. The students, workers, and peasants were involved in

mass action which was violently opposed by right-wing groups, and after the 6 October 1976 crack-down many of these activists fled to join the CPT's armed struggle in the jungles.

Violence thus developed as a popular ideology on both the left and the right in the 1970s. Political violence has been common throughout the intra-élite struggles for leadership of the Thai state since 1932. But up to the early 1970s, the torture and murders "were typically 'administrative' in character, carried out by the formal instrumentalities of the state, very often in secret. The public knew little of what had occurred, and certainly did not participate in any significant way".[81] This changed during the 'Democratic Period' of Thai history, when democracy also came to mean open public participation in political violence in the two years preceding the brutal crack-down in 1976. Examples of this popular ideology of right-wing violence are familiar: an Interior Minister broadcasting "Right Kills Left" over the airwaves before the April 1976 election, and a prominent monk saying that to kill communists is not a sin. Anderson argues that this was an important shift from earlier political violence:

> The mass media in the 1960s had always warned that the *government* would deal severely with communists and subversives. In 1976, however, the frame-up [of the students in Thammasat University] was staged out in the open, and the *public* was invited to exact vengeance for subversion....And the gruesome lynchings of October 6 took place in the most public place in all Siam — Sanam Luang, the great downtown square before the old royal palace.[82]

Students, workers, and peasants responded to this campaign of mob violence — which included assassinations of labour and peasant leaders and bombings of public demonstrations — with their own violent struggle. The CPT had declared that its revolution was in the stage of armed struggle as early as 1965, and the violence came to the cities in the 1970s. Like Mao instructed, for the CPT power came out of the barrel of a gun: the socialist ideology which included political violence and armed struggle was seen as a persuasive social analysis of Thai politics.[83] In the 1970s, one activist notes, theories of violent struggle were very sophisticated and armed struggle was quite successful in the provinces.[84] After witnessing the assassinations of peasant and labour leaders, the ideology of violence seemed to be the only way to social justice and "political violence forced left into revolutionary struggle".[85]

In the 1990s things have changed radically from the 1970s with non-violent action offering a serious alternative because "[t]he belief of earlier decades that violent struggle would sweep away oppression has given way in many circles to a more sober appraisal of its limited possibilities. In contrast, the power of struggle without weapons of violence has been shown often in our times."[86] Many of the non-governmental organizations of the 1970s were set up in opposition to the violent struggle. Even though they were not successful then, they became more popular after 1980. As a Thai non-governmental organization 'manifesto' said in 1987:

> Thai NGDOs reject the use of power conflicts or violence as a way of solving problems. They associate such models with dictatorship and feel that their use can only lead to further misery, conflict, and violence....The unhappy experiences of many Thai intellectuals with constitutional and rapid popular mobilization efforts, right-wing violence, and an ideologically-backward Communist Party during the 1970s have also played a part in producing a reaction against much radical social theory and the confrontational political activism practiced in other Asian countries.[87]

The violent methods of the CPT seemed to have failed,[88] and in the absence of an armed insurgency alternative visions of social justice which included non-violent action became much easier to promote.[89] "At the present time non-violence is more effective in the democratic atmosphere. It gets both moral and popular support. When we are not under a dictatorial regime it is not reasonable to use violence." Though *ahimsa* might seem like a radical idea in Thailand, one activist argues: "Thai people prefer non-violence, and already use it in their everyday life. In the political area they lack experience. This is the problem."[90]

Non-violent action is also similar to non-governmental organizations in its logic. As a tactic, it does not aim to mirror the army's practices, and thus use the master's tools to destroy the master's house,[91] but leaves the door open for a diverse set of tactics. For example, in the seminal work *The Politics of Nonviolent Action*, Gene Sharp catalogues 198 non-violent tactics. Like the discourse on non-governmental organizations, discussions on non-violent action appeal to oppositional consciousness where they often begin with what non-violent action is not, rather than what it is:

> ...instead of beginning with an arbitrary, a priori definition of nonviolent action, it would be preferable to consider the concept as referring to many different modes of struggle, but all of which arise out of the search by common people for means to carry on conflicts....Rather than being viewed as one-half of a rigid violent-nonviolent dichotomy,[92] nonviolent action then would be understood as a set of options with special characteristics that set it apart from either normal politics or violence.[93]

McCarthy's stress on non-violent action as an alternative tactic is shared by Ralph Summy, who divides political action into three spheres: (1) the conventional sphere of state politics which may include parliament, but also includes structural violence; (2) the violent sphere which includes the military, police, and other groups which use direct violence; and (3) the non-violent sphere which revives participatory democracy in bypassing conventional politics but not through the vertical command structures of the violent sphere.[94]

The links between non-governmental organizations and non-violent action are clear because both jam the discourse of normal politics by opening up a third sector and a third sphere of popular action. Both are part of a world-wide trend towards non-violent tactic that was graphically shown in the Philippines' People Power Movement of 1986, in Burma (Myanmar) in 1988, Tian'anmen Square in 1989, and throughout Eastern Europe in that same year.[95] More and more activists see the relationship between non-violence and democracy, because non-violent action includes public participation at the grass-roots level. As Chaiwat Satha-anand, a leading Thai non-violent activist, explains: "I see non-violent action as a good vehicle to build democracy. This principle contributes to democracy for several reasons because it encourages political

consciousness and participation."[96] Non-violence is good strategically as well, for as Ralph Summy writes, when people resort to
violence "they not only play strategically into the hands of the
ruling elite — since it usually enjoys a superior edge in firepower
— but they undermine the prospects of a reconstituted civil society
with democratic mechanisms of decision-making". Non-violence
thus is not a Utopian dream, but a tactic to produce a more
democratic society for "the opportunity to control their political
environment is not anchored in wishful thinking but rather in
wilful decision-making".[97]

Technologies of Protest

The dynamic of non-governmental organization networks and non-
violent action was graphically shown during the anti-military
protests of 1992. This was certainly not spontaneous, and goes
way beyond the actual struggle in May 1992. Indeed, this narrative
uses quite a different spatial and temporal arrangement of the
conflict from the soldiers' story. Rather than focusing on the violence
and Rajdamnoen Avenue during 17–20 May 1992, political parties,
or public figures like Chamlong Srimuang, this alternative telling
of the story consistently started out with the military coup of 23
February 1991.[98] Indeed, many of the lessons drawn by the popular
sector about the May events were about how to oppose coups in
the future.[99]

This retelling of Thai history goes against the grain of the military stories which typically start on 4 May 1992 when Chamlong
announced his 'death fast', and the 'middle-class mob' tales which
look back to the student movements of the 1970s for meaning.
Though these alternative scriptings are diverse, admittedly incomplete, and sometimes contradictory, they have their own internal
logic which is consistent with the dynamics of the mass movement of May 1992. These dynamics brought together diverse and
sometimes contradictory groups of people from non-governmental
organizations, people's organizations (POs), professional organizations, labour, slum dwellers, businesspeople, students, and
political parties. Indeed, the threat of a long-lasting National Peace
Keeping Council (NPKC) dictatorship spawned an oppositional

consciousness which drew these diverse groups together into both familiar umbrella groups such as the Campaign for Popular Democracy (CPD) and a new sort of organization such as the Confederation for Democracy (CFD).

This complex process of 'massing' also shows how the struggle was not just spontaneous. The mass rallies of May 1992 were part of a long-term process of resistance which was organized by non-governmental organizations as a powerful example of formal and informal networking. In the course of this process non-governmental organizations expanded from working primarily on alternative rural development strategies to become more of a social movement. The non-governmental organization network took a political turn because "[i]t increasingly appeared that the NGO network was providing a channel of representation for the rural and urban disadvantaged as an alternative to the generally ineffectual political parties and parliament".[100] Unlike Thailand's élite-focused political parties,[101] non-governmental organizations were able to become a social movement as demonstrated in the previous section because they had developed a grass-roots base which could be co-ordinated through the socio-political infrastructure. In other words, while political parties by and large only came out for high-profile demonstrations starting in April 1992, non-governmental organizations had been actively working for months on the issues that sparked the confrontation in May.[102] Indeed, Chamlong himself found that working through Parliament and political parties hindered more than helped his role in the struggle. In a very controversial move, Chamlong resigned from the leadership of Palang Dharma Party to act as an 'ordinary citizen' in the demonstrations.

In this section I will recount the activists' narrative to outline the non-governmental organizations/non-violent action dynamic: I argue that non-governmental organizations used the socio-political infrastructure that they had been building over the previous decade in more overtly political ways starting in February 1991, and it was non-violent action that provided the spark in April/May 1992 to transform this infrastructure into broad-based mass demonstrations.

Coup d'état

The February 1991 military coup d'état is an important starting point because it throws the different methods of rapid social change into sharp contrast. In February 1991, as in May 1992, many Thais were unhappy with the government. Yet very different solutions were found to this problem: in 1991 an élite junta staged an armed coup d'état; in 1992 a non-violent mass demonstration forced an unelected Prime Minister to resign. So it is useful to look at these two methods of political organization in a comparative perspective to examine the power dynamics involved in each.

The coup represents the élite aspects of Thai politics which exclude the common people and the popular sector from power and influence. Though the NPKC listed five reasons for the February coup — royal assassination plots, corruption, parliamentary dictatorship, politicians harassing government officials, and disrespect for the military — two years later in January 1993 ACM Kaset Rojananil told the press that the real reason for the coup was that Class 5 officers were protecting their boss.[103] The five points cited to justify the coup are interesting because they demonstrate, along the lines of Lorde's epigram, how the coup reproduced the power that it was seeking to contest, and reproduced it with much more violent consequences. Point by point — in terms of corrupt ministers, parliamentary dictatorship, and politicians harassing government officials[104] — the Suchinda government not only reproduced the politics of dominance of the Chatichai administration, but aggravated them. This explains why many Thais from very different, social, economic, and political positions joined together to oppose the Suchinda government. For this pattern of military interference is not new:

> what are usually listed as democratic pathologies: corruption, nepotism, and administrative incompetence, did exist too in the authoritarian regimes of the past, especially under Field Marshals Sarit, Thanom, and Prapat. Connected to this is the point that, as our history bears witness too, military intervention that seeks to address democratic problems has never produced a better democracy. Virtually all putsches end up with a government which is worse than the regime it replaced.[105]

The centralized élite revolution of February 1991 produced the power and led to the brutal violence of May 1992. The abuse of power expanded dramatically from rampant corruption in the economic sphere to the brutal massacre in the military sphere. The scandals also parallel, with missing money becoming missing persons. When accused of taking bribes in 1990, then Prime Minister Chatichai responded: "Show me the receipts." When asked about killed and missing people during the May violence, then Interior Minister ACM Anan Kalinta replied: "Line up the bodies."

Response to the February 1991 Coup

News reports and academic analyses tell us that the February coup was welcomed by the Thai people.[106] Indeed, many showed their gratitude for being rid of the notorious Chatichai government by presenting the NPKC leaders with flowers.[107] The NPKC further bolstered its legitimacy by appointing Anand Panyarachun, a respected diplomat-turned-business executive, as the interim Prime Minister.[108] After Anand appointed his Cabinet, there were even more cheers: one regional business magazine called it a "coup de technocrat" because the Cabinet list read like a "World Bank dream list".[109]

Yet not everyone welcomed the coup. Two groups of people are noteworthy for their immediate opposition to the February 1991 coup: non-governmental umbrella organizations like the CPD and POs like the Students' Federation of Thailand (SFT), labour unions, and slum dwellers' groups. The reasoning of the POs was quite direct: "no coup has ever been carried out on behalf of workers or on behalf of the majority of the people".[110] Labour activists resisted the coup of 1991 because "whenever dictators seize power the first thing they seek to destroy is the labor movement. This is because unions are basic organizing units in a democratic society."[111] (The brutality of the NPKC in 1992 was foreshadowed by the disappearance of labour leader Thanon Pho-an in June 1991.) Slum leader Prateep Ungsongtham Hata likewise states that though times were bad for slum dwellers under an elected government, they were much worse for slum people with the NPKC.[112] This mirrored the experience of many other non-governmental organizations and

POs, which rallied against the NPKC even though they considered themselves non-political.[113] Indeed, high-profile organizations like NGO-CORD were not officially involved, but the various members used unofficial contacts to co-ordinate action.[114]

Campaign for Popular Democracy. On 19 April 1991 nineteen organizations representing labour, academics, slum dwellers, women, teachers, human rights groups, non-governmental organizations, and the SFT organized themselves into the CPD to co-ordinate activities to both oppose the coup and push for a democratic constitution. Gothom Arya and Somchai Homla-or reactivated the CPD "so the army could not claim that they had the full support of the country".[115] It is noteworthy that no one was asking for the elected Chatichai government back, as is common with anti-coup groups in other countries like Burma (Myanmar) and Haiti. It seems that only non-governmental organizations could be against both corruption and the coup.[116]

There is a distinct pattern of CPD activity which also serves as a guide to how the struggle developed. First, the CPD functioned as a base to keep democratic issues alive, when other methods of criticizing the military NPKC were severely restricted. Second, the CPD organized public forums to criticize the 1991 Constitution as it was being written. Third, the CPD served a mediating role between political parties, POs, and non-governmental organizations. Fourth, the CPD served as a base for nation-wide co-ordinating activities. Fifth, the CPD advocated peaceful struggle and organized non-violent rallies to avoid violence-prone confrontation.[117]

The struggle against the military dictatorship involved many groups beyond the CPD, the SFT, and the unions, including: "academics, teachers, students, workers, poets, slum activists, businessmen, lawyers, musicians, monks, human rights activists, theologians, non-government organizations, politicians, etc".[118] It is important to remember that the mass rallies were not composed of any stable or homogeneous group — middle class or otherwise. Rather, the participation in the long-term struggle for democracy involved shifting groups, with different organizations coming in and out of focus. Sometimes non-governmental organizations were in the spotlight, while at other times the palace, labour, middle class, business groups, and slum groups were the focus of attention. In this way the anti-military struggle was an example of ironic organizing through oppositional consciousness: again, until mid-May the rallies were characterized more as 'anti-Suchinda' than 'pro-democracy'.

These groups all came together in May 1992, even though some had been at odds before Suchinda became Prime Minister, and were again working against each other after the September 1992 elections. The most obvious example of this is the dynamic between labour and business. One way the NPKC appealed to business was by repressing organized labour soon after the coup: "Anand met with many business leaders, but never with labor during his first term...".[119] Yet the activities of the NPKC and its cronies increasingly affected both the international business climate and Thai business community. When the favouritism of Class 5 towards selected business families such as the CP Group became clear, the new middle class was increasingly critical of the NPKC. The junta's repression also quickly spread from labour to the mainstream political realm as well:

> Following the suppression of the labor movement, the NPKC sought to consolidate its power by wiping out other democratically oriented organizations such as political parties...[by] deceiv[ing] the people into believing that politicians were inevitably corrupt, untrustworthy and self-interested.[120]

It soon became clear that the coup was not simply an attack on Chatichai or corrupt politicians, but an attack on the civilian-dominated parliamentary regime that had been asserting itself over the traditional military-bureaucratic state. For example, Hewison notes that the military targeted specific institutions of this democratic system: the Constitution, Parliament, and Members of Parliament, hence "the 1991 coup attempted to maintain the conservative capitalist state by ridding itself of the civilian government and parliamentary regime".[121]

As the NPKC's long-term political ambitions became clearer, other groups became involved in the struggle against it. Two events served as rallying points for opposition forces: the critique of the

1991 Constitution, and the formation of PollWatch to monitor the March 1992 election.

The 1991 Constitution. These three events — coup, constitution, and election — are actually all linked together. A coup d'état is a violation of the constitutional mechanisms of government. Hence after each coup in Thailand the existing constitution is abrogated, and it is customary for the junta to write another document and call an election. Thus seventeen coup attempts have resulted in fifteen constitutions and seventeen elections between the 1932 revolution and 1992. The February 1991 coup followed this well-travelled path, and soon after the coup the NPKC promised a new constitution which would lead to quick elections. The committee to write the constitution was appointed by the NPKC, and it soon became apparent that this document was being written to per-petuate the power of the military. Rather than being more demo-cratic, the 1991 draft was judged to be more dictatorial than the 1978 'demi-democratic' Constitution, and could lead to a true parliamentary dictatorship. The main issues were the clauses which allowed an unelected Prime Minister and the extensive powers of an NPKC-appointed Senate. The CPD, as the "most active and vocal civic organization to challenge the constitutional drafting commission", soon criticized the draft constitution by writing letters and issuing press releases.[122] The CPD was thus involved in the legal aspects of democracy, and tried to make the constitution a topic of public discussion.[123] One prime example of this was the calling of a national convention to draft a people's version of the constitution. Many groups from Bangkok and the provinces came together to propose a democratic charter, which they presented to the National Assembly on 24 June 1991 — the anniversary of the day when absolute monarchy was changed to constitutional monarchy.

In the latter half of 1991 the SFT and CPD were again at the forefront of anti-NPKC activities when the new constitution with its dictatorial provisions

> led to widespread controversy. In protest against this abhorrent conduct, fifty one groups comprising of intellectuals, labour

> experts, pro-democracy groups, teachers, slum activists, etc.
> together with the main opposition parties (Democrats, Palang
> Dharma, New Aspiration and Solidarity) organized a confer-
> ence. It was agreed that the dictatorial constitution would be
> opposed.[124]

Again, the opposition to the constitution was not limited to these
urban groups. Non-governmental organizations utilized their rural
development networks to provide people in the provinces with
information about the constitution and organized many activities
on this subject with village leaders.[125]

The criticism of the undemocratic provisions of the constitution
culminated in a mass rally at Sanam Luang on 19 November
1991 which drew over 70,000 protesters and thus was the largest
public demonstration since October 1976.[126] In an effort to head
off this protest, Suchinda declared on 18 November that neither
he nor his ally ACM Kaset Rojananil would accept a nomination
to become Prime Minister, and agreed to reduce the number and
power of Senators.[127] Though many were still not satisfied, the
constitution was soon promulgated under pressure from the palace,
and the election was planned for 22 March 1992.

PollWatch. To make sure that the March election was clean and
fair Anand Panyarachun set up PollWatch in January 1992. The
thirty-three leaders who formed PollWatch came from non-governmental organizations and POs such as trade unions, academia,
and professional associations.[128] The CPD was key in organizing
PollWatch, for Gothom was appointed by Anand to lead it. In the
three months leading up to the March 1992 election PollWatch
recruited 20,000 volunteers from all over Thailand. PollWatch had
two tasks: curbing vote-buying and encouraging democratic consciousness. The first task was largely legal-technical and received
much media attention due to the popularity of vote-buying stories.
The second task of raising democratic consciousness has had a
much more lasting effect, for the 20,000 volunteers and those they
influenced saw democratic participation as more than casting a
ballot on election day. Democratic participation also means that
people can take part in policy debates, including drafting the
constitution.

Most importantly, PollWatch served as a meeting place for people of broad backgrounds and diverse experience. It expanded the networks of non-governmental organizations and POs, but also extended working relationship to other groups and people outside these networks. For example, through PollWatch the SFT — which is limited by government regulations to representing the seventeen public universities — was able to join with private universities and teachers' colleges, and thus work with over 200 institutions and thousands of students on democratic issues.[129] This networking was particularly important in the provinces where PollWatch gave the middle strata a political consciousness and organizing experience which they would use in future democratic movements:

> in the course of such struggles the networks of these social activists and those of political information, resources, and facilities, have been gradually transformed into what might be designated as popular sector's "socio-political infrastructure."[130]

Indeed, most of the provincial leaders in the anti-Suchinda protest had been involved in PollWatch for the March 1992 election. So over the course of the fourteen months between the February coup and when Suchinda became Prime Minister in April 1992 various groups of academics, workers, professionals, businesspeople, and students worked together in various activities against a dictatorial constitution and for a fair election. People formed friendships, build bonds, and made connections in a socio-political infrastructure that went beyond the official activities of non-governmental organizations as specific groups addressing specific issues to form the roots of a mass movement in a blurring of public and private, official and unofficial.[131]

Anti-Suchinda Demonstrations

When Suchinda became Prime Minister on 7 April 1992, he was working directly against the movement for a democratic constitution and a government from a clean election. It was not just that Suchinda broke his promise of 18 November 1991 not to become Prime Minister. Suchinda was seen as perpetuating the power of the NPKC, confirming the fears of the groups which had been organizing themselves over the previous year. Actually the initial reaction of the public and the activists was not very effective. The SFT held a demonstration in early April which was notoriously unsuccessful. Suchinda's military government was a new challenge and demanded different tactics from those used to deconstruct the constitution and organize PollWatch.

The building of public sentiment against the Suchinda military government can be traced to the hunger strike of Chalard Vorachart. The general secretary of the SFT recalls that before Chalard's fast the SFT figured it would need at least six months of campaigning to force Suchinda to resign. But the risk of Chalard dying made them use more immediate measures.[132] As soon as Chalard heard that Suchinda was appointed Prime Minister, he began a hunger strike in front of Parliament Building in Bangkok, demanding that Suchinda resign.[133] Chalard's hunger strike served as a focus of attention for nearly one month, and was only displaced when Chamlong declared his own "fast to the death" on 4 May. There have been numerous hunger strikes in Thai history,[134] but in 1992 non-violent action caught the Thai imagination and led to public discussion of both the legitimacy of the Suchinda regime and the use of non-violent action against "tyrants".

Chalard's fast was riveting because his self-deprivation was seen as a sincere sacrifice for democracy and national interest. "People believed that it was not just a tactic; Chalard fasted for so long that it was clear that he would really die for democracy."[135] Though Suchinda and the army-controlled media repeatedly tried to paint protesting politicians as "sore losers" in the March election, they were never able to brand Chalard as self-interested. All three of Chalard's fasts had taken place when the parliamentary system was not working, and thus other methods from Summy's third sphere of non-violent politics were necessary.[136] From that moral high ground Chalard was able to impress people, and make them want to know more about democracy and non-violent action. Actually Chalard's fast was not to pressure Suchinda to resign — Suchinda did not care if Chalard lived or died[137] — but more to pressure "lovers of democracy" to act for a more democratic government.

As the anti-Suchinda demonstration grew in April in response to the appointment to the Suchinda Cabinet of the same corrupt politicians who were ousted in the 1991 coup, Chalard's hunger strike in front of Parliament Building became a rallying point in the workings of the socio-political infrastructure.[138]

> All groups, academics, teachers, students, workers, poets, slum activists, businessmen, lawyers, musicians, monks, human rights activists, theologians, non-government organizations, politicians, etc made the effort to come and encourage Chalard as he continued to fast.... In sum, the events in front of parliament can be considered to be the longest democratic rally ever to have occurred in Thailand.[139]

After the first major rally on 20 April 1992 — in which forty-three people joined Chalard's fast — *The Manager Daily* carried a daily report on Chalard's hunger strike and had several commentaries on hunger strikes and *ahimsa*. The discussion of non-violent methods intensified once Chamlong started his fast on 4 May 1992. Pro-military commentators worked to discredit fasts as un-Buddhist and thus un-Thai.[140] Actually, most activists did not dwell on Chamlong's 'death-fast' since it was generally seen among non-violent activists as less than non-violent. Indeed, in an interview Chamlong was not interested in talking about his understanding of *ahimsa*, and told me to read his book, *Unite to Fight*.[141] Yet in the book the references to non-violence are scattered and unsophisticated. Still, for the general public the book had a riveting appeal, and led to further discussion of the meaning and use of *ahimsa*. This is evidenced by the many columns and articles that had a very sympathetic treatment of non-violent action. One series called "Ahimsa, Forgiveness and Tyrants" proclaimed that the non-violent demonstrations had transformed the streets in front of Parliament into a "political school".[142]

The rallies were successful because the non-violent action brought people together. The non-violent action of Chalard's hunger strike had common roots in the non-governmental organizations and POs that had been active in the struggle since 1991 as well. As soon as Suchinda was appointed, the CPD resolved that "[o]ur principle was to struggle in a non-violent way against Suchinda's appointment using symbolic and direct action".[143] Pro-democracy non-governmental organizations led by the CPD and the SFT were also active in organizing rallies and spreading information through their networks. The networking was crucial in providing alternative sources of information since the official electronic media were heavily biased in favour of the Suchinda government: "This 'socio-political infrastructure' also embodies modern information technology and telecommunication devices such as electronic mail, fax machines, mobile phones, and databases."[144] The broader non-governmental organization movement thus provided various groups of people with information so they could make their own decisions. In this way, the anti-Suchinda protests blossomed from non-governmental organization activists to being a truly broad-based movement which came out in force.

> In such an upsurge of the struggle they were joined by other POs and professional organizations as well as the masses, thus expanding the "socio-political infrastructure" for a wide-based, multi-class final confrontation with the military NPKC.[145]

Like previous movements, this one spread far beyond Bangkok, for people in the provinces organized their own demonstrations, especially after the army started shooting unarmed protesters on 18 May 1992. The activities in the provinces were organized by non-governmental organizations and PollWatch volunteers, not by political parties.[146] Here again, the networks funnelled information. At the 17 May demonstration mobile telephones linked stages in Bangkok, Korat, and Chiangmai. The provincial demonstration sites were also filled with diplays of pictures, faxes, clipped newspaper articles, and other sorts of media.

Confederation for Democracy. As the mass rally was growing, its large size was becoming unwieldy. So on 14 May 1992 twenty-six organizations that had been active in the rallies banded together in a confederation with representatives from key groups: Chamlong Srimuang (Palang Dharma Party), Sant Hattirat (academics), Somsak Kosaisuk (labour), Prateep Ungsongtham Hata (slum dwellers), Weng Tojirakan (October 14 Group), Prinya Thewanarumikul (SFT), and Jittravadee Vorachart (Chalard's daughter).

There was a need to form a united oppositional movement of academics, professionals, students, labour, non-governmental organizations, and slum dwellers since in the previous week conflicts between political parties and other groups had undermined the movement's strength.[147] In many ways the CFD signified a further development of the ties between the non-governmental organizations and POs in an oppositional alliance which did not include direct ties to political parties.

Actually, the creation of the CFD is still a controversial topic, and there is much debate over the roles of Chamlong and the CPD. It is important to note that though organizations directly committed to non-violent action had been involved in previous umbrella groups, the CPD and the Santiprachakorn Dhamma Institute were excluded from the CFD board because of previous disagreements over how to organize the demonstrations.[148] Regardless of the contradictions between the visions of the CPD and the CFD, a more effective unity was necessary in the second week of May because, as Gothom later commented, the diversity of the movement made it difficult to organize: "In May 1992, the organization of the protest was rather loose. We couldn't decide how to proceed to 'protest without violence'."[149] The mass rally of 17 May 1992 provided a particular challenge since it involved so many people, and since the government's hostility to the gathering was obvious. So it is noteworthy that non-violent action and participatory democracy were deliberate aspects of the planning, which in important ways challenges the mob discourse which characterizes this social formation: "On the 17th we planned ahead. We prepared for tear gas, [arranging] plastic bags, towels, and water for the people. We didn't plan for a massacre or for real shooting."[150] But unfortunately the military started shooting and began a crackdown which lasted for four days — the longest period of urban political violence in Thai history.

Spread of Non-violent Action. Actually, after the violence started on 17 May and Chamlong was arrested on 18 May, non-violent action became more focused with mass rallies spreading all over Thailand. After the military won the first round of struggle on

17–18 May at Rajdamnoen Avenue, the tactics of non-violence shifted from an offensive non-violent action — which was characterized by unarmed struggle — to defensive non-violent action at Ramkhamhaeng University on 19–20 May. Many people came to join the students, and the lesson that they learned from 17 May was that non-violent action involved more than unarmed struggle: the struggle needed defensive non-violent action which worked to prevent the factors that could cause violence.[151] So the activists at Ramkhamhaeng sealed off the area around the university and had guards at the gates to keep out agent provocateurs.[152] After night fell 50,000 people barricaded themselves at Ramkhamhaeng. The tactics of non-violent action adapted during the demonstration to meet the new circumstances as they developed.

Once the violence stopped, there was an outbreak of non-violent activity that was directed not just at Suchinda, but for building a more participatory society which many felt the military was impeding. On 25 May, the day after Suchinda resigned, the CFD, students, workers, and the Business Club for Democracy went to Parliament to demand amendments to the Constitution. As mentioned earlier in the chapter, on 1 June even large institutional private sector organizations such as the Board of Trade, the Federation of Thai Industries, and the Thai Bankers Association broke their tradition of non-involvement in politics to demand a dissolution of the House of Representatives when it looked like the NPKC-backed parliamentary dictatorship would continue beyond Suchinda.[153] Thus the business class through both leading organizations and progressive groups such as Business Management Systems (BMS) and the Business Club for Democracy followed the lead of other non-governmental organizations to act as POs co-operating with the CFD and the CPD after the events of May.

PollWatch came back under Gothom's leadership with the second Anand administration, and was even more effective, mobilizing 60,000 volunteers who further extended the socio-political infrastructure, especially to the middle class. Anand repeatedly confirmed that the main accomplishment of PollWatch was not necessarily in the specificities of the campaign and voting, but that people from all around the country had become active and involved in democratic politics.[154]

The protest also spread from constitutional amendments and elections to the political-economic power of the military.[155] Beyond the organized activity there were highly imaginative individual non-violent protests, including huge withdrawals from the army-controlled Thai Military Bank.[156] Another tactic in the non-violent arsenal was the boycott — a strategy that engaged in long-term struggle against the institutional position of the Thai military. Academics and non-governmental organizations gathered information about companies in the private sector which consistently supported the military so people could pressure them through consumer action: department stores, automobile companies, and other businesses which had military leaders on their boards were targeted for sanctions.

State enterprises were also criticized. Indeed, the army's control of the electronic media was not just for political reasons: in 1990 it earned Bt160 million from radio alone.[157] All the major state enterprises headed by military commanders — including Thai International Airlines,[158] the telephone company, the state railroad, the airport authority, the port authority, maritime navigation, and aeronautical radio — also came into question.[159] The social sanction of not associating with those who benefited from violence also became an important non-violent activity when the legal measures against those who ordered the killings were cut off by Suchinda's amnesty decree.

Non-idealized Non-violence and Cycles of Protest

Still, some feel that the non-violent mass demonstration was a failure because people were killed, and that when they gather together in the hundreds of thousands protesters necessarily become a mob. Summy provides a way out of these self-defeating fundamentalist formulations when he deconstructs his trinity of conventional/violent/non-violent politics into (another oppositional consciousness of) 'non-idealized non-violence' which accounts for overlapping spheres:

> In its non-idealized form a nonviolent campaign may extend into other political categories. Though remaining predominantly nonviolent, it may contain some actions that

are conducted in the conventional sphere, and perhaps may even lapse into the violent sphere. These actions may even be going on simultaneously. Conversely a particular action that begins with elements of violence may move into the nonviolent realm. And there are many issues or aspects of a campaign first raised in parliament, which, if ignored or rejected there, are then taken up in the nonviolent sphere.[160]

Summy thus helps us to explain non-violent movements that are not pure; he helps us to learn from them without having to declare non-violent action a total success or failure. The shifting of participants and tactics is an important characteristic of the mass demonstrations of May 1992, and Summy's figuration helps chart out the events in terms of shifts and overlaps among the three spheres, and thus order the 'chaos':

1. April 1992: the crisis started out as a constitutional problem in the first sphere of conventional politics;
2. 7 April: Parliament did not address the people's needs, so the struggle shifted to the third sphere of non-violent politics with hunger strikes and then peaceful mass demonstrations;
3. 8 May: the government threatened demonstrators with the second sphere of violent politics but the non-violent protests continued;
4. 11 May: the protesters disbanded after they had forced negotiation in the conventional politics sphere; the coalition parties promised to push for constitutional amendments through Parliament;
5. 17 May: Parliament did not act, and the struggle shifted back to the non-violent sphere with a mass demonstration, leading to a violent reaction from the second sphere;
6. 18–20 May: Parliament and all government offices were closed down with a curfew in Bangkok and the surrounding provinces; political parties were absent; protesters were violent on Rajdamnoen Avenue while motor-cyclists vandalized symbols of public authority; the non-violent protests continued in the provinces;
7. 19 May: the third sphere reasserted itself in Bangkok at Ramkhamhaeng University;

8. 20 May: the palace as third party appealed to Suchinda and Chamlong to stop the violence and negotiate a settlement;[161]
9. 25 May: non-violent action spread to social and economic arenas to sanction military leaders;
10. June-September: conventional politics reasserted itself with the passage of amendments, the appointment of Anand Panyarachun as interim Prime Minister, and the September 1992 election; the CPD and the CFD pushed for further constitutional amendments.

If we widen the focus to examine the non-violent struggle since the February 1991 military coup, we can see that Thai politics move in cycles of protest, which again shift among the three spheres with corresponding changes of tactics. In this way the events of May were not a defining moment, a revolution — a people's coup[162] — that would overturn Thai society in one fell swoop. Rather, the May events formed one more episode in a long-term struggle for what Lorde calls "genuine change". Mass demonstrations — both violent and non-violent — come in cycles where activity intensifies and dissipates.[163] The modern history of mass demonstrations in Thailand began in the 1970s and was first characterized by student movements and then the CPT armed struggle. In the 1980s the cycle shifted first to small-scale, self-reliant non-governmental organizations, then to networks of non-governmental organizations at the national and international levels. In the most recent cycle of struggle, which began with the February 1991 coup, we can see how the organization and tactics of the popular sector are becoming more sophisticated.

These cycles are not part of a linear history of unified struggle. Rather there is an uneven pattern of activity which often appears spontaneous. But with the history of non-governmental organizations and the strengthening of the socio-political infrastructure between non-governmental organizations and POs, we can see that demonstrations in Thailand work according to the principles of repetition and have a fluid nature of ebb and flow. This cycle of demonstrations started slowly with the coup in February 1991, peaked first with the anti-NPKC Constitution rally on 19 November 1991, and then waned until the second peak of PollWatch activities leading up to the 22 March general election. The April-May mass demonstrations made up the third peak, and the fourth peak occurred with PollWatch in the September 1992 election, which attracted 60,000 volunteers nation-wide. After each event the organization dispersed because of the oppositional consciousness pattern of organization. But because of the socio-political infrastructure the basis of the 'massing' remained, although dormant, until another crisis on which to focus oppositional consciousness erupted.[164] Thus struggle involves repetition. But this repetition is different from that in (social) science, where repetition is necessary for replication to verify the results of an experiment. While repetition in science is to reproduce identical results, in Thai struggles it is more like that of poetry where repetition often highlights *differences* and notes the changing context from phrase to phrase in the text and phase to phase on the streets. Rather than for reflection, repetition is for change.

The CPD is an exemplary case of this cyclical sort of organization. It was not founded in 1991, but revived from previous democratic and constitutional struggles. It first appeared in 1981 when the military wanted to extend certain undemocratic clauses in the 1978 Constitution, including allowing an unelected Prime Minister, that were due to expire in 1982. The main objective of the CPD is to build public awareness of the Constitution, using "educational campaigns about the constitution" which Gothom says "was a new tactic for non-governmental organizations". The important characteristic of the CPD is that once the campaign is won, the CPD dissolves. "You can't maintain the momentum of a campaign. You can't expect to keep having peaks."[165]

But though the CPD dissolves, it does not disappear. Two years later, in 1983, the Constitution became an issue again. The CPD organized a second time under the leadership of Prateep to protest provisional clauses to the 1978 Constitution. Army Commander General Arthit Kamlang-ek wanted to keep the clauses which allowed civil servants — including the military — to concurrently be political officials. The CPD activity overlapped with one of Chalard's fasts on this issue. Once this second task was achieved, the CPD again dissolved.

The CPD then formed again in 1991, and its strength is that it tries different tactics each time, depending on the issue. In 1991 the activists focused on the Constitution; in early 1992 they shifted to work with the government in PollWatch; then in May 1992 they focused on the unelected Prime Minister. After Suchinda resigned and a new election was called, they tried PollWatch again, and even though the September 1992 election put a 'pro-democratic' government in power they still pushed it on constitutional and environmental issues. Indeed, the election served to end parts of the configuration of oppositional consciousness, for non-governmental organizations and political parties have split up again, since the former allies have gone back to playing the state-power game.

The various narratives which explain the events in May 1992 have different beginnings and different endings. The events of May are always read as part of a larger story. The military story ended when the NPKC leaders were replaced in August 1992. The middle-class story ended when the Democrat Party won the September 1992 election. The non-governmental organizations' story continues with their pushing for more responsible government and policies that will benefit the popular sector. These different story lines can explain why, for example, non-governmental organizations after September 1992 were pitted against the Chuan government on environmental and constitutional issues even though the coalition was largely seen as pro-democratic. Indeed, many of the rural non-governmental organizations worked against Chuan and the Democrat Party in the July 1995 election because the pro-democracy government had not been attentive to their needs.[166] The CPD was still active after the political crisis of the coup since some groups still thought that it was more useful on political issues than NGO-CORD.

In Thai politics with each repetition — each new struggle — there is a new twist, and each new situation demands different tactics. The NPKC's mistake in May 1992 was that it was repeating the old tactics of anti-communist rhetoric and brutal crack-downs.[167] For the non-governmental organizations, on the other hand, political repetition is a learning experience since the struggles will never end. There is no telos; there will never be a total revolution, an end to (or a beginning of) history, class struggle, gender politics, or age struggle.

Conclusion: Non-governmental Organizations, Non-violence, and Democracy

The aim of this chapter has been to read the events of May in terms of their non-violent organization, instead of violently chaotic 'mobs'. To demonstrate this argument, I used strategies of feminist theory which appeal to decentred political action to formulate the struggle against the military in Thailand. Rather than using the violence of centralized bureaucracy to address the inadequacies of the Thai political system, as did both the NPKC and the CPT, the non-governmental organizations' non-violent struggle appeals to the popular tools of socio-political infrastructure and non-violent action to dismantle the master's house in a positive way. The strength of these discourses is that they are incomplete, and thus allow specific groups to determine the appropriate tactics according to context.

The narratives of non-governmental organizations and non-violence jam the discourse of Thai politics: this is both a danger and an opportunity. They do not fit neatly into the accepted political schema (and trends like 'civil society') which divides power between public and private, business and bureaucracy, and where violence is assumed to be a part of conflict resolution. This is a danger because the military does not see non-governmental organization movements as any different from past political intrigues. For example, in a common military figuration ACM Kaset Rojananil sees the May events as Chulachomklao Royal Military Academy Class 5 *versus* Class 7, and thus a continuation of the 1981 April Fool coup: "The 'April Fool' coup was meant to seize power. But there is another way of seizing power — through people power, if you know what I mean."[168]

In a way groups like the CPD and PollWatch oblige the military discourse by accepting the issues — of constitutions and elections — as they are presented by the junta. Political parties and demagogues also see non-governmental organizations and POs as an opportunity for mass mobilization — organized mobs — and this is perhaps even more dangerous. This is a problem that, for example, the CFD continues to face after the events of May since it seems to have made the mistake of many non-governmental organizations in the Philippines by allying itself with certain political parties and against others, rather than dealing with politics on an issue-by-issue basis. The third sector — non-governmental organizations and POs — is also often portrayed as a third hand which is manipulated by murky foreign forces. The reaction of the government to the protests in March 1993 against the Pak Mool Dam is a case in point. As one commentator wrote: "Many people ask, what are NGOs? Does it have anything to do with the PLO (Palestinian Liberation Organization)?"[169] The government agencies thus often treat non-governmental organizations like terrorist groups which need international publicity to ensure continued foreign funding. The army then is likely to keep dealing with new social movements in the same old violent ways.[170] Hence the challenge is not just to train non-governmental organizations and POs in non-violent action, but also to educate the military, bureaucrats, and politicians about non-violence, starting with simple things like non-violent demonstrations and crowd control.

The jamming of the discourse of Thai politics is an opportunity because it can lead to different understandings of democracy. Rather than letting the military order the discourse for them through conventional politics of constitutions and elections, many activists also saw these topics as opportunities to reorder and expand the Thai political discourse with participatory democracy which is fostered by participatory development programmes. The history of this social movement not only more fully explains the May events which were unique, but also highlights how these low-key movements (which had been active over the past decade) affect the possibilities for public opinion and participatory democracy in Thailand. In this way they can turn the anti-Suchinda demonstrations into meaningful pro-democracy movements.

NOTES

1. Audre Lorde, *Sister Outsider* (Freedom: Crossings Press, 1984), p. 112.
2. Again, "slit the chicken's throat to scare the monkeys", a Thai and Chinese idiom.
3. Prapoj Sithep, Interview, 1 September 1992.

4. For a discussion of Chamlong's role in the events of May see Duncan McCargo, *Chamlong Srimuang and the New Thai Politics* (London: Hurst & Company, 1997), pp. 239–74.

5. Chamlong Srimuang, Interview, 24 November 1992. This interview confirmed the stylistic message of Chamlong's book about the events of May which came out in June 1992. The narrative of the mass uprising is the narrative of Chamlong. The book begins with "Arresting Chamlong" because he sees this as the pivotal event. (Chamlong Srimuang, *Ruam Kan Su* [Unite to fight] [Bangkok: Khlet Thai, 1992].)

6. Khien Theeravit, *Wikritakankanmuang Thai: karani phrutsapha mahawipyok 2535* [Thai politics in crisis: the case of the May 1992 tragedy] (Bangkok: Matichon Publishing, 1993).

7. Unfortunately the response by the military and ultra-right wing forces was also multiple. During the May massacre there were soldiers shooting unarmed protesters and undercover police 'hunter-killer squads' shooting down motor-cyclists. After the May events ultra-right wing groups reorganized in a campaign of terror against pro-democracy activists.

8. Benedict Anderson, "Withdrawal Symptoms: Social and Cultural Aspects of the October 6 Coup", *Bulletin of Concerned Asia Scholars* 9, no. 3 (July–September 1977): 13–30.

9. The class nature, or at least the use of classes in understanding the period of open politics, is even more clear in *Political Conflict in Thailand: Reform, Reaction and Revolution* where David Morell and Chai-anan Samudavanija write a chapter each about students, labour, and farmers. (David Morell and Chai-Anan Samudavanija, *Political Conflict in Thailand: Reform, Reaction and Revolution* [Cambridge, Mass.: Oelgeschlager, Gunn & Hain Publishers, Inc., 1981].)

10. Prudhisan Jumbala, *Nation-Building and Democratization in Thailand: a Political History* (Bangkok: Chulalongkorn University Social Research Institute, 1992), p. 112; also see Suchit Bunbongkarn, *The Military in Thai Politics 1981–86* (Singapore: Institute of Southeast Asian Studies, 1987).

11. Anderson, op. cit., pp. 19–20.

12. Chai-Anan Samudavanija, "Thailand: A Stable Semi-democracy", in *Politics in Developing Countries: Comparing Experiences with Democracy*, edited by Larry Diamond, Juan J. Linz, and Seymour Martin Lipset (Boulder: Lynne Reiner Publishers, 1990), pp. 271–312. A recent book on this theme is by Likhit Dhiravegin, *Demi-Democracy: The Evolution of the Thai Political System* (Singapore: Times Academic Press, 1992).

13. Prudhisan, op. cit., p. 89.

14. Ibid., p. 90.

15. Saiyud Kerdphol, *The Struggle for Thailand: Counter-insurgency 1965–1985* (Bangkok: S. Research Centre, 1986), pp. 69–98.
16. Ernst Gohlert, *Power and Culture* (Bangkok: White Lotus, 1991), p. 28.
17. *Army News Announcement: Army Policy and Implementation*, Royal Thai Army briefing booklet in Thai and English (Bangkok: Royal Thai Army, 2 June 1993), p. 8. The Thai section of this booklet opens with a speech by King Bhumipol to the military academy's graduating class of 1993 outlining the military's post-Cold War national security mission in terms of rural development work. This speech is curiously missing from the English translation.
18. Prudhisan, op. cit., p. 113.
19. Prudhisan Jumbala, Correspondence, 27 October 1993.
20. Prudhisan, *Nation-Building*, p. 112.
21. Suchit, op. cit.; Pasuk Phongpaichit and Chris Baker, *Thailand: Economy and Politics* (Kuala Lumpur: Oxford University Press, 1995), pp. 328–30.
22. Surachart Bumrangsuk, Interview, 5 October 1993.
23. Prudhisan Jumbala, Interview, 5 October 1993.
24. Pasuk and Baker, op. cit., p. 335.
25. Anek Laothamatas, *Business Associations and the Political Economy of Thailand: From Bureaucratic Polity to Liberal Corporatism* (Singapore: Institute of Southeast Asian Studies and Boulder: Westview Press, 1992), p. 35.
26. Ibid., p. xi.
27. Ibid., p. 67.
28. Ibid., p. 71.
29. Ibid., p. 115.
30. Ibid., p. 85.
31. Ibid., p. 106.
32. Surin Maisrikrod and Duncan McCargo, "Electoral Politics: Commercialization and Exclusion", in *Politics in Thailand: Democracy and Participation*, edited by Kevin Hewison (London: Routledge, 1997), p. 15.
33. Kevin Hewison, "Political Oppositions and Regime Change in Thailand", in *Political Oppositions in Industrializing Asia*, edited by Garry Rodan (London: Routledge, 1996), p. 84.
34. "BMS decides to backtrack from politics", *Bangkok Post*, 15 July 1992, p. 15.
35. Pasuk and Baker, op. cit.; Kevin Hewison, "Of Regimes, State and Pluralities: Thai Politics Enters the 1990s", in *Southeast Asia in the 1990s: Authoritarianism, Democracy & Capitalism*, edited by Kevin Hewison, Richard Robison, and Garry Rodan (Sydney: Allen & Unwin, 1993), pp. 159–89; Pasuk Phongpaichit and Sungsidh Piriyarangsan,

Corruption and Democracy in Thailand (Bangkok: Political Economy Centre, Faculty of Economics, Chulalongkorn University, 1994); James Ockey, "Business Leaders, Gangsters and the Middle Class" (Ph.D. diss., Cornell University, 1992); William A. Callahan and Duncan McCargo, "Vote-buying in Thailand's Northeast: The July 1995 General Election", *Asian Survey* 36, no. 4 (April 1996): 376–92.

36. Anek, op. cit., p. 22.
37. *Directory of Non-governmental Development Organizations in Thailand 1987*, unabridged ed. (Bangkok: Thai Volunteer Service, 1987), p. 7; Pasuk and Baker, op. cit.
38. Suthy Prasartset, "The Rise of NGOs as a Critical Social Movement in Thailand", in *Thai NGOs: The Continuing Struggle for Democracy*, edited by Jaturong Boonyarattanasoontorn and Gawin Chutima (Bangkok: Thai NGO Support Project, 1995), p. 97.
39. Saneh Chamarik, *Democracy and Development: A Cultural Perspective* (Bangkok: Local Development Institute, 1993), p. 22.
40. See *Directory of Non-governmental Development Organizations in Thailand 1987* (Bangkok: Thai Volunteer Service, 1987), pp. 7–8.
41. Anek, op. cit., p. 4.
42. Of course military-oriented NGOs are called MONGOs and business-oriented NGOs are called BONGOs.
43. Surichai Wun' Gaeo, "The Non-Governmental Development Movement in Thailand", *Asian Exchange Arena* 6, nos. 2/3 (March 1989): 59–77.
44. Hewison states that there was an active civil society in the first half of the twentieth century. But these activities were located primarily in the city. (Kevin Hewison, "Political Oppositions and Regime Change in Thailand".)
45. Gohlert, op. cit., p. 99. Certainly the history of non-governmental organizations is much more complex than this. Amara Pongsapich and Nitaya Kataleeradabahn address some of this complexity when they write of the roots of Thai non-governmental organizations in Buddhist merit and Christian missions, as well as the self-help and mutual aid of Chinese secret societies. (Amara Pongsapich and Nitaya Kataleeradabahn, *Philanthropy, NGO Activities and Corporate Funding in Thailand* [Bangkok: Chulalongkorn University Social Research Institute, 1994], pp. 1–32.)
46. Wasant Techawongtham, "NGO movement: an angel or a devil?", *Bangkok Post*, 17 October 1993, pp. 20–21.
47. Suthy, op. cit., p. 99.
48. Gothom Arya, Interview, 19 November 1993.
49. Ibid.
50. Ibid.

51. Surichai, op. cit., p. 74.
52. Ibid.
53. Gloria Hull, Patricia Bell Scott, and Barbara Smith, eds., *All Women are White, All Blacks are Men, but Some of Us are Brave* (Old Westbury: Feminist Press, 1982).
54. Chandra Talpade Mohanty, "Introduction: Cartographies of Struggle, Third World Women and the Politics of Feminism", in *Third World Women and the Politics of Feminism*, edited by Chandra Talpade Mohanty, Ann Russo, and Lourdes Torres (Bloomington: Indiana University Press, 1991), p. 7.
55. Donna Haraway, "A Manifesto for Cyborgs: Science, Technology and Socialist Feminism in the 1980s", *Socialist Review* 15, no. 2 (1985): 68, 73–74.
56. One of the foremost peace researchers, Johan Galtung, uses this abbreviation. Johan Galtung, "II.14: On the Meaning of Nonviolence", in *Essays in Peace Research* (Copenhagen: Christian Ejlers, 1975), p. 341.
57. Haraway, op. cit., p. 74.
58. Poonsak Wanapong, who teaches at Ramkhamhaeng University, was notorious in late 1992 for writing a classified report for the army's National Defence College criticizing non-governmental organizations along these lines. In a political magazine he was quoted as saying: "Many NGOs teaching in up-country areas oppose the curriculum of the Ministry of Education. They are encouraging kids when they grow up to oppose social norms and oppose the state. This is a strategy of warfare to oppose government policy. What does this mean? Many NGOs contain ex-communists in disguise." (*Phujadkan Raisupda* [Manager Weekly] [Bangkok], 13–19 September 1993.) Chaiwat Satha-anand has a different explanation for the meaning of non-governmental organizations: "Why should they consider NGOs their enemies? To answer that, we have to ask what NGOs are doing. When we say development work, what we're saying is in fact mobilisation of the masses. The Thai state, like other states, doesn't like other people to mobilise the masses no matter how beneficial it may be. It likes to do the mobilising itself." (Chaiwat Satha-anand quoted in Wasant Techawongtham, "NGOs and the middle class: More cooperation needed", *Bangkok Post*, 17 October 1993, p. 20.)
59. This negative view of non-governmental organizations is expressed well in Norman Uphoff, "Grassroots Organizations and NGOs in Rural Development: Opportunities for Diminishing States and Expanding Markets", *World Development* 21, no. 4 (1993): 607.

60. According to Sørenson, the problem is that non-violence is often uncritically "treated as a lodestar... the brilliant solution to all our problems". He calls this Utopianism — an excessive emphasis on values to the detriment of data and theory — and fears this Utopianism "if left unchallenged, involve[s] the danger of bringing peace research into disrepute". (Georg Sørenson, "Utopianism in Peace Research: The Gandhian Heritage", *Journal of Peace Research* 29, no. 2 [1992]: 136, 141.)

61. Uphoff, op. cit., p. 608.

62. Gothom Arya quoted in Kanjana Spindler, "May 1992: When the tide finally turned", *Bangkok Post*, 19 May 1993, p. 5.

63. Dej Poomkacha, Interview, 24 November 1993.

64. Michel Foucault, "Revolutionary Action: 'Until Now'", in *Language, Counter-Memory, Practice*, edited by Donald F. Bouchard (Ithaca: Cornell University Press, 1977), pp. 232–33.

65. Ibid., p. 224.

66. Ibid.

67. Michel Foucault (with Gilles Deleuze), "Intellectuals and Power", in *Language, Counter-Memory, Practice*, edited by Donald F. Bouchard (Ithaca: Cornell University Press, 1977), p. 216.

68. Surichai, op. cit., p. 75.

69. Pibhop Dongchai quoted in Wasant Techawongtham, "NGOs and the middle class: More cooperation needed", *Bangkok Post*, 17 October 1993, p. 20.

70. Rosana Tositrakul quoted in Wasant Techawongtham, "NGOs and the middle class: More cooperation needed", *Bangkok Post*, 17 October 1993, p. 20.

71. *Directory of Non-governmental Development Organizations in Thailand 1987*; Suthy, op. cit., p. 102.

72. Gohlert, op. cit., p. 10; also see Claudia Pfirrmann and Dirk Kron, *Environment and NGOs in Thailand* (Bangkok: Thai NGO Support Project and Friedrich Naumann Foundation, 1992), p. 10.

73. While earlier efforts to fight poverty were welfare movements which David Korten would describe as being part of the first-generation non-governmental organization movement, the small-scale issue-oriented organizations signified a shift to the second-generation of non-governmental organizations which work at the micro level for a self-reliant strategy for sustainable local development. According to the popular three-generation theory, the third generation addresses the macro level for sustainable systems of development where non-governmental organizations work at the national and international levels to influence institutions and public policy changes for

decentralization. Korten stresses that an effective non-governmental organization will have all three generations. (David C. Korten, *Getting to the 21st Century: Voluntary Action and the Global Agenda* [West Hartford: Kumarian Press, 1990].)

74. Gawin Chutima, Interview, 24 November 1993. This was confirmed by many other activists.
75. Dej, Interview.
76. Gohlert, op. cit., p. 118.
77. Dej, Interview.
78. Suthy, op. cit., pp. 120–21.
79. Peter Oakley, *Involvement of People in Development Activities and the Role of Promotional NGOs in Asia* (Rome: Food and Agriculture Organization, 1989), p. 39.
80. Anderson, op. cit., p. 13.
81. Ibid., p. 13.
82. Ibid., p. 24.
83. Prudhisan, *Nation-Building*, p. 68.
84. Somchai Homla-or, Interview, 27 October 1993.
85. Prudhisan, *Nation-Building*, p. 76.
86. Ronald M. McCarthy, "The Techniques of Nonviolent Action: Some Principles of Its Nature, Use, and Effects", in *Arab Nonviolent Political Struggle in the Middle East*, edited by Ralph E. Crow, Philip Grant, and Saad E. Ibrahim (Boulder: Lynne Rienner Publishers, 1990), p. 118.
87. *Directory of Non-governmental Development Organizations in Thailand 1987*, p. 10.
88. Benedict Anderson argues that political violence has actually shifted to be the activity of bourgeois Members of Parliament (MPs): "We have had the extraordinary spectacle in the 1980s of MPs being assassinated, not by Communists or military dictators, but by other MPs or would-be MPs.... What all these killings suggest is that in the 1980s the institution of MP has achieved solid market value." (Benedict Anderson, "Murder and Progress in Modern Siam", *New Left Review*, no. 181 [May/June 1990], pp. 41, 46.)
89. Gothom Arya, Interview, 19 November 1993.
90. Somchai, Interview.
91. Actually many people criticize Chamlong for using military tactics with unarmed and untrained demonstrators.
92. Johan Galtung states that using a violent/non-violent opposition to categorize struggles is "one more false dichotomy; it can be both or neither". (Johan Galtung, *True Worlds: A Transnational Perspective* [New York: Free Press, 1980], p. 139.)
93. McCarthy, op. cit., p. 107.

94. Ralph Summy, "Democracy and Nonviolence", *Social Alternatives* 12, no. 2 (July 1992): 15–19.

95. Gene Sharp lists half a page of non-violent actions world-wide in "Nonviolent Action and Modern Political Relevance", mimeographed (Bangkok: Thammasat University, 3 November 1992), p. 6.

96. Chaiwat Satha-anand quoted in Wipawee Otaganonta, "The conflict between peace and democracy", *Bangkok Post*, 29 June 1992, p. 23.

97. Summy, op. cit., p. 16.

98. Interviews with Gothom Arya, Dej Poomkacha, Gawin Chutima, Prinya Thewanarumikul, Prateep Ungsongtham Hata, and Chalard Vorachart. Somsak Kosaisuk's main text starts with the February coup, as does Suthy, op. cit., and Gawin, Interview. (Somsak Kosaisuk, *Labour Against Dictatorship* [Bangkok: Friedrich Ebert Stiftung, Labour Museum Project, Arom Pongpangan Foundation, 1993], p. 83.)

99. For example, labour unions threaten to lead a general strike in case of a future coup, and the SFT published a pamphlet in June 1992 about how to resist a coup non-violently. Gene Sharp was invited to speak to the Thai Parliament in November 1992; see his "Notes for a Presentation to the House Affairs Committee of the Government of Thailand on Anti-Coup Legislation", mimeographed (Bangkok: Parliament of Thailand, 16 October 1992).

100. Prudhisan, *Nation-Building*, p. 119.

101. Sukhumbhand Paribatra writes that one of the factors that led to the coup in 1991 was "the failure of political parties to institutionalize themselves as true representatives of the people... and to promote, either in quantitative or qualitative terms, voluntary political participation". (Sukhumbhand Paribatra, "State and Society in Thailand: How Fragile the Democracy?", *Asian Survey* 33, no. 9 [September 1993]: 884.)

102. Gawin Chutima, Interview, 24 November 1993. Also see Amara Pongsapich, "Strengthening the Role of NGOs in Popular Participation", in *Thai NGOs: The Continuing Struggle for Democracy*, edited by Jaturong Boonyarattanasoontorn and Gawin Chutima (Bangkok: Thai NGO Support Project, 1995), pp. 9–50.

103. "Kaset blames coup, crackdown on 'fate of the nation'", *Bangkok Post*, 28 January 1993, p. 2. For a translation of the full interview from *The Manager Daily*, see "Kaset: No plans on politics yet", *Sunday Post*, 31 January 1994, p. 23. Prime Minister Chatichai Choonhavan reportedly planned to dismiss Supreme Commander General Sunthorn Kongsompong. So Kaset's men arrested Chatichai as he was boarding a plane to Chiang Mai to ask King Bhumipol to countersign the appointment of Sunthorn's rival, General Arthit Kamlang-ek, as

Deputy Defence Minister. After a thorough search of the plane, this order was never found.

The reason that this coup was successful while the coups of 1981 and 1985 were not is that for the first time since 1973, the military was united under Chulachomklao Royal Military Academy Class 5. For an analysis of the struggles among Class 5, the Democratic Soldiers, and Class 7 in relation to the 1991 coup see Hewison, "Of Regimes, State and Pluralities", pp. 164–67.

104. In December 1993 Major-General Manoon Rupkhachorn was acquitted of the royal assassination plot charges due to lack of evidence. In January 1994 Manoon sued the police for falsifying evidence in this case. Hence it would seem that the plot was actually against Manoon and the Chatichai government.

105. Anek Laothamatas, "Sleeping Giant Awakens: The Middle Class in Thai Politics", *Asian Review 1993* 7 (1993): 124–25.

106. Anek Laothamatas goes one step further and argues that the middle class more or less asked the military to come in and "clean up" the corrupt Chatichai government. (Ibid., pp. 100–1.)

107. The army maintains that coups are a normal means of transferring power in Thailand: "People go to discotheques when there is a coup." ACM Pisit Saligupta, the Armed Forces Chief of Staff, said the people had never protested a coup in the past. "They gave us bouquets of flowers to show their moral support to the military in staging coups." (*The Nation*, 25 April 1992, p. A2.)

108. The timing of the coup also down-played its significance on the global stage: in February 1991 the rest of the world was focusing on the Gulf War.

109. *Asian Business*, April 1991, p. 16.

110. Somsak, op. cit., p. 131.

111. Ibid., p. 86.

112. Prateep Ungsongtham Hata, Interview, 21 November 1992.

113. International non-governmental organizations did not participate, nor did official welfare-type organizations like the Red Cross Society or the various MONGOs and most BONGOs.

114. Paiboon Wattanasiritham, Interview, 3 December 1993.

115. Gothom, op. cit.

116. Anek's analysis, which allies rural politics with corruption and urban politics with coups, does not allow for groups to be against both (Anek, "Sleeping Giant Awakens").

117. Suthy, op. cit., pp. 132–33.

118. Somsak, op. cit., p. 96.

119. Hewison, "Of Regimes, State and Pluralities", p. 175.

120. Somsak, op. cit., p. 89.
121. Hewison, "Political Oppositions and Regime Change in Thailand", pp. 80–81.
122. Suthy, op. cit., p. 124.
123. Gothom, op. cit.
124. Somsak, op. cit., p. 90.
125. Dej, Interview.
126. Other groups, including members of the Democrat Party, also took credit for organizing the November 1991 demonstration behind the scenes.
127. Suchinda said: "To purify the new constitution and reassure you that the NPKC will not get involved with the formation of government after the election, let me state here that neither General Suchinda nor ACM Kaset will become prime minister. All politicians can relax now." (*The Nation*, 8 April 1992.)
128. Suthy, op. cit., p. 127.
129. Prinya Thewanarumikul, Interview, 17 January 1994.
130. Suthy, op. cit., p. 126.
131. Victor Karunan comments that there is an important difference between non-governmental organizations as organizations and non-governmental organizations as a social movement. However one must note that this blurring worked against certain activists whose personal lives and business were adversely affected. Chalard Vorachart nearly went bankrupt in mid-1992 because no one wanted to do business with him after the May events. Even though Prateep resigned as director of the Duang Prateep Foundation once she became active in the protest, it too lost much of its middle and upper class financial support.
132. Prinya, Interview.
133. Chalard ate again only after Suchinda stepped down on 24 May 1992. Chalard intended to fast after the 23 February coup, but the NPKC anticipated his action and arrested him. (Interview, 27 March 1993.)
134. Fasts were first used during the events of 14 October 1973. They were also part of the demonstrations on 6 October 1976 and 19 November 1991.
135. Prinya, Interview.
136. Chalard started a fast in 1979 over oil prices and corruption because as a Member of Parliament (MP) he had no influence. In 1983 Chalard fasted to oppose the constitutional changes that would enshrine military power. Again, at first he tried to talk in Parliament, but nobody listened to him. Chalard fasted during May–July 1994

to again push for a more democratic constitution, but he was rather unsuccessful in mobilizing a sustained mass audience. His fast was also 'criminalized' by the Chuan government. Likewise a semi-fast in 1995 was not popular, although the government did fall before Chalard resumed his normal diet on 25 May 1995.

137. Ubon Boonyachlothorn, the pro-military Sammakitham Party MP for Yasothon, sent Chalard a coffin and said she would host one night of funeral prayers too (*Bangkok Post*, 16 April 1992, p. 3). Though the sponsoring of funerals is a common practice in the patron-client relationship, in this context it was quite rude.

138. Though Chalard's fast was an individual statement, he had support from friends and colleagues with whom he had worked before. At one point in mid-April, when Chalard was sick and the movement seemed to be waning, Prateep fasted for half a day in spite of being pregnant. She did this both out of personal connections in the socio-political infrastructure — she had worked with Chalard on slum issues while he was in Parliament in the 1980s — and out of principle because she felt the cause was important. (Prateep, Interview.) This is an example of the informal workings of the socio-political infrastructure.

139. Somsak, op. cit., p. 95.

140. The line of reasoning was: "*Ahimsa* means not causing trouble to oneself and others", while "Chamlong has hurt himself by fasting, caused worries to his family members and the rally is making many people suffer" ("No dharma in the pro-Suchinda propaganda", *The Nation*, 11 May 1992, p. A6).

141. Chamlong, Interview.

142. Kamnoon Sittisaman, "Ahimsa, Forgiveness and Tyrants (part 1)", *The Manager Daily*, 7 May 1992, p. 8; "Ahimsa, Forgiveness and Tyrants (part 2)", *The Manager Daily*, 8 May 1992, p. 8. Next to the 7 May column was an op-ed article on non-violent action by Chaiwat Satha-anand of the Peace Information Centre, Thammasat University.

143. Victoria Combe, "Quiet Voice of Reason", *The Nation*, 4 June 1992, p. C1.

144. Suthy, op. cit., p. 126.

145. Ibid., p. 131.

146. Gawin, Interview.

147. Sant reports: "Formally it tried to be [a confederation with representatives from each organization], but because the conflicting ideas at that time were so great they just selected middle persons like me who had never been involved in conflicting positions or anything to

head this organization." (Interview, 18 November 1992.) Others question Sant's self-description of being neutral, and point to his later actions which show him to be a Chamlong loyalist.

148. The CFD also gave Chamlong official control since he was already exercising *de facto* control on the streets. McCargo analyses the dynamic between Chamlong and the CPD at length (McCargo, op. cit., pp. 255–57).

149. Gothom Arya, "Has anything changed since last May?", *Sunday Post* (Bangkok), 16 May 1993, p. 23.

150. Sant, Interview; Somsak's book also testifies to the various meetings and planning that took place for the demonstrations from 4 May 1992. One is struck by Somsak's outrage at the times when the collective decision-making processes did not work. (Somsak, op. cit., pp. 92, 105, 110, 112.) This is part of a general criticism directed at Chamlong for making decisions unilaterally.

151. Prinya, Interview.

152. One way to do this was to search people for weapons before they could enter the non-violent action zone. At times this got out of hand, for newspapers reported that the guards beat up an agent provocateur when they found weapons on him.

153. The text of this document is reproduced in "Private sector formula to restore Thai image", *The Nation*, 2 June 1992, p. B18.

154. "Anand praises ranks of volunteers", *Bangkok Post*, 8 September 1992, p. 1.

155. That the military is an economic corporation more than a security institution is attested to by what was censored in the 20 May issue of the *International Herald Tribune*: "Spoils of power: military risks loss of wealth under civilians". It described the army's involvement in Thai business as well as its connection to the drug and other smuggling activities of both the Burmese junta and the Khmer Rouge.

156. In response, the bank almost changed its name, and was only stopped by someone claiming to be the younger sister of the founder of the bank, Field Marshal Sarit Thanarat. ("TMB decided to retain name", *Bangkok Post*, 4 September 1992, p. 22.)

157. Academic and television political talk-show host Chermsak Pintong comments: "I don't know if it's fortunate or unfortunate, they [the army] don't really use the radio and the television effectively as mass media, but as a source of funds. They get money from selling time of the radio and the television, this money goes to the army or to the persons in the army, I'm not clear. They use it to make money, not for mass media." (Interview, 1 February 1993.)

158. Thai International was a very celebrated case since it was headed by Kaset, and was known for its factionalism and corruption. In many ways Thai serves as a case study for the overwhelming influence of the military on Thai society. It lost much business as a result of the May massacre because of the general drop off in tourism, but also because people in Thailand and abroad did not want to support an airline that was seen as the "piggy bank of mass murderers". For an analysis of Thai as a "miniature model of Thailand under military rule" see Pana Janviroj and Yingyord Manchuvisith, "Thai flying in political turbulence", *The Nation*, 23 June 1992, p. A6.
159. See "Focusing on men in green on state unit boards", *The Nation*, 28 May 1992, p. B1.
160. Summy, op. cit., p. 16.
161. One should not romanticize this intervention: "The negotiated settlement, belatedly brokered by the King, *does not* suggest an unambiguous victory for the democratic forces of the bourgeois revolution. Suchinda resigned, but was effectively pardoned of any responsibility for the massacre by the King. The constitution was changed, but by a parliament put in place by the NPKC. Class 5 has not been destroyed and, most importantly, the King's intervention represents another attempt to save military conservatism. With perhaps up to a hundred slaughtered, the King only intervened when it appeared that the military was about to turn on itself (see *Asian Wall Street Journal*, 21 May 1992). In preventing this he has ensured that the struggle between the military and civilian politicians will continue. This was clearly seen in the campaign for the September 1992 election, where the military continued to destabilize the political situation and threaten its critics." (Hewison, "Of Regimes, State and Pluralities", p. 184.) For the speech itself see "Royal Advice by His Majesty the King", 20 May 1992/2535 at 21:30 (Bangkok: Office of His Majesty's Principal Private Secretary, 1992).
162. Chamlong once described the success of the movement as a "people's coup" (*The Nation*, 12 May 1992, p. 1).
163. This holds true for China and the United States as well. For an analysis of this phenomenon in the German context see Ruud Koopmans, "The Dynamics of Protest Waves: West Germany, 1965 to 1989", *American Sociological Review* 58 (October 1993): 637–58.
164. "The role of this type of NGO such as the ones mobilising the May demonstrations becomes more prominent when there is a crisis. Their role, thus, ends automatically once the crisis is over. But the basis of each organization remains." (Kanjana Spindler, "May 1992: When the tide finally turned", *Bangkok Post*, 19 May 1993, p. 5.)

165. Gothom, Interview, 19 November 1993.

166. William A. Callahan and Duncan McCargo, "Vote-buying in Thailand's Northeast: The July 1995 General Election", *Asian Survey* 36, no. 4 (April 1996): 376–92.

167. See Tulsathit Taptim, "Same old rhetoric", *The Nation*, 10 May 1992, p. A10. After the September 1992 election conservative groups tried to use the same 'hunger strike in front of Parliament' tactics to keep Chamlong and Palang Dharma Party out of the government, specifically the Education Ministry. But this fast — which also used the same Cold War rhetoric — did not have any popular appeal and soon passed. ("Support Buddhism and the Monarchy" protest, Interview, 17 September 1992.)

168. "Kaset: No plans on politics yet", *Sunday Post*, 31 January 1994, p. 23.

169. Pravit Rojanaphruk, "NGOs: Chamber for the oppressed", *The Sunday Nation*, 13 March 1993, p. A10.

170. Chalard's hunger strike was seen as a "suicide threat". In 1994 students used a common non-violent direct action tactic of going limp so the police officers had to pick them up and carry them away from a demonstration for farmers. But this was reported in the newspapers as "resisting arrest".

chapter 4

MISSING MEMORIES

The bloody massacre in Bangladesh quickly covered over the memory of the Russian invasion of Czechoslovakia, the assassination of Allende drowned out the groans of Bangladesh, the war in the Sinai Desert made people forget Allende, the Cambodian massacre made people forget Sinai, and so on and so forth until ultimately everyone lets everything be forgotten....

Since we can no longer assume any single historical event, no matter how recent, to be common knowledge, I must treat events dating back only a few years as if they were a thousand years old.

– Milan Kundera[1]

We have to find a limited number of words to convey our limitless feeling.

– Nawarat Pongpaiboon[2]

Before we are forgotten we will be turned into kitsch. Kitsch is the stopover between being and oblivion.

– Milan Kundera[3]

Memories and Lessons

During the third anniversary of the massacre, attention was drawn to other political events: the pro-democratic government that was swept into power because of the May 1992 mass movement fell on 19 May 1995. Because of such things, Thais like to think that only

144

they are forgetful, but as Kundera writes in *The Book of Laughter and Forgetting*, this is a condition of modernity. Many other places share this habit, which has both its strengths and weaknesses. In this last chapter I would like to examine how memories of the May events were formed between 1992 and 1995. Rather than simple recovery of past experience, I would treat remembering as an active construction of images, which may or may not be true to each of our experiences. Or more to the point they may be both true and false at the same time. Authentic while misleading. Earnest, though ironic.

To examine this process, I divide memories into three types. The first section recalls an art exhibition, 'Ratchdamnoen Memory', held six months after the May events, which aided in the construction of the pro-democracy memory. The second section examines the institutional memory — the numbers — of the people who went 'missing' during the crack-down, and how they were produced. The third section considers the limits of such rational investigations through a literary analysis where emotion is a valuable knowledge practice. These sections do not fit together neatly, and the gaps and inconsistencies highlight the tension between the subjective and objective, the artistic and the statistic, the emotional and the rational memories.

Art, Politics, and the Middle Class

We create consciousness through literature and arts.[4]

In the first few months after May 1992 remembering the demonstration became a lucrative business. It spawned new industries — which bordered on the kitsch — to produce massacre videos, Music Television shows, and special magazines full of photos, chronologies, and commentaries[5] — not to mention the t-shirts, cassette tapes of popular 'democratic' songs, postcards, calendars, and Paan Faa Bridge razor wire commemorative paper weights.[6] Still, while fine art and politics usually do not mix in Thailand, the 'Ratchdamnoen Memory' exhibition, which was held during 23–30 November 1992 at the Imperial Queen's Park Hotel, graphically shows how art is used by a society to remember crucial political events.[7] It is not just that artists are getting political, but politicians and the middle class are getting artistic — then Prime Minister Chuan Leekpai, who is known for his drawings, was among the contributors to this project.

"Art is not new for the democratic movement in Thailand," reports Somchai Homla-or, the Secretary-General of the Campaign for Popular Democracy (CPD), who organized 'Ratchdamnoen Memory'.[8] Between 1973 and 1976 students created pictures and posters to resist the dictatorship. But the memory of this popular art quickly faded after the brutal right-wing crack-down of 6 October 1976. "Most of the pictures were lost."[9] But this exhibition of works by professional artists at a luxury hotel again shows how the 1990s are different from the 1970s. The switch from the popular culture of posters to the Fine Art of 'Ratchdamnoen Memory' reflects the shift from the students-led demonstrations of the 1970s to the obessions with 'middle-class movements' in the 1990s.

To put it another way, with the participation of the middle class, consciousness raising became linked to fund raising: the exhibition was not just for education, but to raise money for the CPD and the relatives of the victims. It shows that the business community is political not just by attending the demonstrations, but also adds to the economic side necessary to make this a sustainable development of democracy in Thailand. "Most of the buyers are former activists [from the 1970s]...many of whom are now executives in corporations and middle level government officials."[10]

Of course this commodification of democracy and consumerism of politics can be abused. Some art critics are cynical about such 'Black May Art', feeling that some of the artists were just jumping on the bandwagon to get attention. One should be careful to see that this "democracy business" does not get out of hand with excessive consumerism.[11]

'Ratchdamnoen Memory' Exhibition

But that was not a concern for the 'Ratchdamnoen Memory' exhibition which was dominated by dark browns, blacks, and bright blood-red. The 126 images assembled by the CPD included oil paintings, water colours, acrylics, line drawings, caricatures, batik, sculptures, and mixed-media collages. Many of the mixed-media and abstract pieces in particular spoke of the confusion, the terror of the military, and horrible pain of death. "Some of the pictures look horrible, and show feelings of suppression," says Somchai. By and large it was a sombre show which recalled the violence of the soldiers against unarmed demonstrators and the violence of the military against democracy.

But a few of the paintings went against this grain of what Thais now call "Black May". Napad Assawachaicharn[12] used bright water colours to paint smiling, non-violent, middle class (they had cellular phones) flowers who stood up to the military power. These images were also reproduced as postcards. But even more interesting were the four paintings from the Kleum Sup Thai (Following Thai Tradition) group which addressed contemporary issues and events through the mural painting style commonly found in temples. Issara Thayahathai's three paintings in particular ironically played with the events of May. Everyone seemed to be dancing his way through life in Thai-style temple paintings. This was reproduced with a political twist in Issara's "Incident at Paan Faa Bridge", and "Monument: Road to Democracy". In these images soldiers danced as they beat demonstrators who included the old and the young, students, motor-cyclists, and the middle class — who also mockingly danced their way through the massacre. The people are dancing because "they're not afraid to die," Issara says. "They are ready to fight regardless of whether they win or lose. They know the power is theirs."[13]

Reframing the Military Image

But even more important than this 'people power' message is the way the military is painted. This is where art and politics mix most directly because image is central to military power. "Leaders of the army are concerned with building their image... not with changing the military itself."[14] The artists and poets represented at the exhibition attack this question of representation by changing the 'saviour' image of the military to better mesh with its brutal actions. Rather than being the hero, the military in this exhibition is portrayed as the villain.

SEA Write Poet Laureate Angkan Kalyanapong uses historical memory:

> Soldiers always think that they are the masters of the people. They think like Buraengnong, Tabeangchaweti and Alongphraya — all of them are bandits who loot cities. If we separate the soldiers who shot at Ratchdamnoen Road one by one, they are like bandits. But when they gather themselves together they call themselves an army.[15]

These three bandit characters are the Burmese kings who attacked Siam in the Ayuthaya period and are commonly portrayed as Thailand's arch-enemies.[16]

In Issara's paintings the military is not just criminal, but is turned into a mythological and cosmological villain. In "Monument: Road to Democracy" the ogre Rahoo from Thai and Indic mythology is dressed in a military uniform as he consumes the sun. In "The Complete Picture of Black May" the giant monkey Hanuman from the Ramayana — also in Thai military garb — holds the Democracy Monument in his jaws. Hence the military is reframed both historically and mythologically — the two ways a society remembers — from being the defenders of the Thai nation to being the looters of Thai democracy.

This mix of art and politics is important because it addresses the events of May on a symbolic and cultural level. It is clear that Thais could not depend on the legal structures to bring them justice, so other avenues were needed to remember the dead, wounded, and missing and seek social justice for Thailand. But more importantly the military and its political parties gain their legitimacy, and hence much of their power, from the army's position as a defender of the nation and the monarchy. The images of this exhibition call this into question, and it is this question that empowers the democracy movement and the middle class in Thailand.

The Discourse of the Missing

The first section was quite subjective and artistic. The second deals with the rational management of the missing problem through statistics. While poets and painters were busy constructing memories through writing phrases and painting images, other groups were appealing to rational investigation to construct categories, and thus systematically search for the missing. This task was shared by two main clusters of groups, one organized by the Ministry of the Interior, while the other was largely organized by university student groups.

One of the first things that the Suchinda government did during the crack-down was to exert control over casualty information. Hospitals were instructed that they were forbidden to give out statistics of the dead and injured. Only the government was allowed to relay such information. Since the government media had already been discredited, students' unions quickly started gathering information about the missing. Because there were already rumours of the army carting the dead bodies away, the Chulalongkorn Student Information Centre and the Jira Boonmark Centre run by the National Institute of Development Administration (NIDA) Postgraduate students' union opened on the evening of 18 May 1992. Soon after the shootings stopped, six other centres were established: the Relief Centre for Pro-Democracy Victims run by the Children's Foundation, the Ramkhamhaeng University Information Centre, the Lawyer Council's Ad Hoc Relief Centre, Students' Federation of Thailand's Centre, the Relief Centre of the Law Faculty at Thammasat University, and the Mahidol University Hotline Centre. They arranged a meeting one week after the events, and on 6 June 1992 agreed to set up a co-ordinating centre at the Mahidol University Hotline Centre to cross-check information.[17]

There were also three government facilities: the Police Department (telephone 191);[18] Interior Ministry, Local Administration Department; and Interior Ministry, Social Welfare Department. At first the government was mostly interested in controlling information rather than finding the missing:

> While the cooperation among the eight centers runs smoothly and efficiently, the cooperation between the Eight Information-Gathering Centers and the Interior Ministry's agencies hardly exists. The state agencies seem to mistrust and fear to exchange their information.[19]

Thus the eight centres' numbers and the government numbers never matched: the government always had a lower number of missing people.

The government attitude towards the missing outlived the Suchinda administration. For example, when answering questions about the missing at the Foreign Correspondents' Club of Thailand, Anand Panyarachun replied: "I lived in New York City for 12 years, and never saw the New York Police Department's missing persons list get any shorter." Anand chuckled while he said this, and this little joke sparked quite a reaction.[20] Relatives of the dead, missing, and injured set up their own organization, Committee of the Relatives of May '92 Heroes, because they were disappointed with Anand.[21] The eight information-gathering centres sent an open letter to Anand "to protest the PM's indecent conduct and to request for a clear-cut measure to track down the missing".[22] The open letter resulted in more co-operation from the state agencies. For the first time the Mahidol University Hotline Centre was allowed access to Interior Ministry records and could co-ordinate information.

In July 1992 the Mahidol University Hotline Centre started a systematic gathering and study of the evidence of missing people. It tried to contact the relatives of each of the 651 people listed as missing at that time, and sent out questionnaires to evaluate the likelihood of the missing people being tied to the May events. Thus the eight centres gathered information to divide cases into three groups: most likely, likely, and unlikely. Each case was categorized based on the weight of clear evidence that (1) the individual was at the demonstration during 17–19 May; (2) there was frequent contact between the missing person and the person who reported him/her; and (3) there was no other plausible explanation for the missing person's failure to return home. This method was explained by Sidney Jones, the executive director of Asia Watch, who argued that the centres should set aside cases that did not meet these criteria: "Unless the effort is made, an unrealistically high figure of disappearances is going to enter the national consciousness and hamper attempts to get at the truth."[23]

Since the generals who were responsible for the massacre were still in power, co-operation from the military was non-existent. Anand transferred these officers in August 1992, and there was much fanfare about the new military leaders pledging co-operation. But this was misleading.[24] While the Mahidol Hotline was able to interview key informants from police, politicians, and activists, it was not allowed access to the active soldiers.[25] "[Supreme Commander] ACM Voranart publicly promised to aid us, but when we asked to interview truck drivers and key battlefield soldiers, he only sent the people who prepared the food."[26] The Defence Ministry's report on the May events, which was used to justify transferring Kaset, Issarapong, and Chainarong, was not released to the public. Interior Minister General Chavalit tried to interview the soldiers again in January–February 1993, but was unsuccessful.

In November 1992 the Mahidol Hotline was invited to join the Interior Ministry's committee headed by Aree Wongariya, who was then the Deputy Permanent Secretary of the Interior, and later became the Permanent Secretary of the Interior. Three subcommittees were set up: a police subcommittee for tracing the missing; a subcommittee to trace rumours of where the bodies were hidden; and a public relations subcommittee. Later a fourth subcommittee was formed to co-ordinate the social welfare support for families of the missing.

The Interior Ministry adopted the three-category method of classification, and moved at the end of November to cross off the names of people who did not have a family response. This dramatically lowered the number of official missing people:

> About a week ago the Interior Ministry listed the missing at 174. Within one week the figure had dropped to 117 and the Ministry declared that by the middle of [December 1992] the figure...which is to be the final one for the missing, will stand at between 40 and 60.[27]

This dramatic decline in the number of missing was the main issue of disagreement between the Mahidol Hotline and the Interior Ministry. The Interior Ministry was using the Asia Watch method to cross off many names as "unlikely". In December 1992 this amounted to discarding 81 cases where there was no family response, while the Mahidol Hotline "tried to keep the list open as long as possible".[28] These 81 cases have now been dropped by both the Mahidol Hotline and the Interior Ministry — there was no way to pursue cases without proper information. But beyond the particulars of these 81 names, the controversy at the end of 1992 served to raise issues about how the 'missing' were to be defined.

The politics of numbers is familiar in Thailand. It is often used in estimations of the numbers of prostitutes and child prostitutes in Thailand. The government always uses a much smaller number than independent groups. Government leaders such as Chuan Leekpai — usually without evidence — often criticized NGOs for "inflating" the numbers so they could get more money from foreign sources. Thus numbers get politicized not in terms of 'human rights' or 'public health', but in terms of 'national security' and 'foreign intervention'. Likewise, the debate over the missing built up discourses and counter-discourses of the missing, which both carry the same name. 'Missing' means different things to different groups.

The Missing Discourse

In other words, in the same month — November 1992 — that poets and artists were displaying their memories at the 'Ratchdamnoen Memory' exhibition, the Interior Ministry went to work painting its own image of the protesters, and thus the missing. Simply put, the Interior Ministry took the three criteria from Asia Watch and the Mahidol Hotline — participation, family/friend contact, and home — and strictly used them to bring down the official numbers in creative ways. The Interior Ministry took advantage of the gaps in knowledge to go beyond the evidence to paint certain people out of the demonstration picture.

Criterion 1. The Interior Ministry seemed to pounce on the first criterion of the method outlined by Asia Watch and the Mahidol Hotline: proof that the missing person was at the demonstration during 17–19 May. This was used to build up a sociological profile of a demonstrator, which served more to exclude people than to find them. As the following editorial from June 1992 shows, early on the government was using a criminalized notion of demonstrators to categorize the missing:

> [The] propaganda the authorities...tried to fool us into believing that the demonstrators were just a rabble of leftist students and motorbike-riding hooligans bent on destroying the institutions of this country.
>
> Is this the proper description of a 14-year-old boy, the youngest of those believed missing, or a 70-year-old man, the oldest. Or the 133 women on the list?[29]

Hence when the Interior Ministry started shrinking the official number of missing in late November, there was understandable suspicion:

> At first glance, the steady decline in the number of people officially listed as missing from the May incidents might be viewed as an encouraging development. ... But the real reasons contributing to this sharp drop are most disturbing. The Interior Ministry and Police Department investigators have reportedly established a set of tough criteria whereby those who were earlier pronounced as missing were taken and would be taken out of the list unless their relatives could prove that they were *directly* connected with the May protests. The reasoning behind the establishment of such criteria is difficult to understand as the anti-dictatorship protests at Sanam Luang and Ratchdamnoen Avenue in May attracted a wide spectrum of people from various professions, many of whom joined the rallies because they were fed up with the one-sided propaganda and distortion emanating from the government controlled media at the time.[30]

More than controlling the media, the bureaucracy was trying to control the memory of the protest and its participants — even though on-the-spot reports confirmed a broad-based and spontaneous gathering: "The demonstrations in Bangkok and provincial towns drew support from a wide spectrum of society: workers, students, farmers, and business people. Observers noted a large proportion of middle-aged women."[31]

This method of cutting the numbers was even more suspect because the Interior Ministry's committee announced, without explanation,[32] "that the final number of missing people will probably be 38 when the subcommittee" finalized its report.[33]

> More serious institutional memories are being written by the Interior Ministry. The police department is erasing the memories of the violence as it erases names from the list of missing. The police are not crossing off the names because the missing have been found, but because there is no "proof" that these people were at the protest. What makes this bureaucratic forgetting even more suspect is Interior Ministry's prediction that the final number for the missing will be between 40 and 60 people, by the time the final report is written later this month. How can they know, unless they have already decided on a "suitable" number — and thus a suitable memory?[34]

Another fascinating aspect of the clash of categorizations concerns not whether the people were at the demonstrations, but whether the search was for live or dead bodies. Many of the activists were concerned with finding missing bodies of people who were killed at the May events; there were constant rumours of the army trucking the bodies away and dumping them.[35] There is still no hard evidence to confirm this, but the Interior Ministry's explanation is even more unconvincing. Then Deputy Permanent Secretary Aree repeatedly suggested that the missing were not dead, but actually just hiding.[36] Without presenting any evidence or argument, Aree assumed that these missing people must be afraid that they would get into trouble if they returned.

Here Aree and others were reading the May events in terms of the previous Bangkok massacre on 6 October 1976. At the Rio Conference in June 1992 Princess Chulabhorn explained the 'missing' issue by telling foreign correspondents that many of the people who went missing after the 6 October 1976 massacre and coup were actually in the jungles. Aree seemed to be using the same logic of the missing as "communist insurgents" who would eventually come back to the towns. Such explanations did not convince many people: there is no insurgency, and most of the jungles have now been cut down.

Still, this image of the missing guided official searches for the missing: "Police went into this job with an assumption that there were no missing persons. Their mission was to find the persons on the list. They are not interested in investigating to see if these people were really missing."[37] There seemed to be an assumption among the police that they were dealing with trouble-makers and criminals. Thus they looked in different places. This actually was successful in resolving a few missing cases. The police used their methods to find out that some of the missing had criminal records. They ended up not missing but in jail.[38] Still, such assumptions also led the investigators away from evidence that would indicate army-led violence.[39]

Criterion 2. To be missing from the May events, according to both the government and the non-government centres, you need two other important factors: (1) to get on the list, you have to have someone report you; and (2) to stay on the list you have to have a family who will verify that you exist and are missing. Those who did not have friends/family members to report them[40] and/or were transient do not show up on the list. By these factors most people in Bangkok do not exist, or would qualify as the missing missing.

Criterion 3. When talking of the missing-absent, there must already be a notion of what it means to be present. Recall that the third criterion for a strong case is that "there is no other plausible explanation for the missing person's failure to return home".[41] Thus to be missing you have to have a home. But — again — this is a difficult measure to use. Bangkok society is very fluid, and thus it is quite difficult to trace the whereabouts of people in the best of circumstances. There are large numbers of seasonal migrants who have no official residence, and come and go without informing family or friends — let alone the state. Even many middle class residents often maintain more than one home, and the official housing registration system is thus unreliable. For example, there is one case of a missing man which arose out of a conflict with his wife. The man ran off with a minor wife, so the first wife reported him missing.[42] You need to have a stable place — a home — to be missing, and such stability is ephemeral in Thailand.

Even though Kritaya states that "Interior Ministry people who were collecting data were quite good" and that many of the police officers were sincere and hardworking,[43] you could argue that they were still looking in the wrong places. Such unwarranted and often unworkable assumptions about home and family can easily produce a misleading sense about the missing people.[44] These twists in the three criteria can cause us, in turn, to twist around Jones' statement quoted above: "Unless the effort is made, an unrealistically *low* figure of disappearances is going to enter the national consciousness and hamper attempts to get at the truth."

Horror and Thai Politics

The secretary-general of the Students' Federation of Thailand condemned the government's search for the missing as "just a stage play because they have been looking for people who are still alive".[45] Yet sometimes politics makes more sense if you read it like a story. With this in mind, the questions that arise in reading the tragic events of May and their aftermath become: what kind of story is now being told?, how is it being written?, and by whom?

The official investigations of the events in May 1992 by parliamentary committees, the Defence and Interior Ministries, and the Mahidol Hotline were involved in writing a mystery story to get to the bottom of the problems of the system. Their proceedings had all the elements. The detectives conducted careful investigations so that rational courses of action could be charted to set things straight in an increasingly humane world.[46] But as the investigations proceeded, things were not being clarified so much as confused.[47] At the parliamentary committee meetings some prominent witnesses lied, for the record, while others did not show up at all. Indeed, the investigations' noble mission broke down around certain crucial points — never mind who ordered the shooting, where were all the missing protesters?

The investigations have raised questions, and the shadowy power relations behind these uncertainties no longer make sense when read as a mystery story where a solution is just around the corner. Actually, if it was a murder mystery, then the mystery has been solved. In June 1992 Supreme Commander ACM Kaset Rojananil and the Army Commander General Issarapong Noonpackdee took responsibility for executing Operation *Paireepinart* (Destroy the Enemy). When it was confirmed in August 1992 in the Defence Ministry's report that they had used excessive force, they were transferred to less important posts.

But that did not solve the mystery. It is not just the answers that are still missing. Even years later, people are still missing. Just what kind of story is being told in Bangkok? In a classic murder mystery story you have the dead body and need to find the murderer. Yet with the tragic events of May this story is inverted. We already know who killed the people. But where are the bodies? What started out as the investigation of a mystery has now become something else. When you have the murderers but no dead bodies, you no longer have a mystery caper, but a horror story complete with its monsters, evil spirits, and uncertainties which breed fear and deadly silence about the brutal murders. There is evidence, but the rational workings of the committees are useless in the face of the horror of the situation. Something powerful shut up the chairperson of one of the investigating committees, Dr Pradit Charoenthaithawee, when he reported that he knew where the bodies were buried.[48]

The crux of this story then is not solving the mystery of the whereabouts and motives of certain military leaders, but confronting the horror of the missing bodies. The first horror was the massacre and it is over; the second horror is the uncertainty and it is nagging. The horror is that although we know who killed them, we are still uncertain about the event: no one even knows just how many are missing. Estimates range from dozens to hundreds of names: ghostly names that haunt Thailand and call out for justice, or at least recognition — certainly not jokes.

Thais can't bury the dead, even in their imaginations, because the horror story is not over yet. "...after all," Somerset Maugham tells us, "one of the conventions of the detective story is that the mystery should in the end be solved and the criminal brought to justice."[49] Horror stories, on the other hand, terrify because their villains endure. The ghouls are not subject to normal justice or morality. And even after they are vanquished they always return

— though sometimes in a different form, always with the same vengeance. Terrifying horror films feed on this need. They afford more sequels than any other genre: *Friday the Thirteenth* had over a baker's dozen. In *Nightmare on Elm Street*, Freddie just keeps coming back. The horror movie *Thai Coup* now numbers seventeen parts (with only ten commercial successes); and their sister film *Bangkok Massacre* is in its third run. Massacre video sales flourished for months outside the Royal Hotel.

The Thai press' labelling of the pro-military political parties as "devilish" fits right in with the horror movie motif. Like a black cat, these people have many political lives. Meechai Ruchuphan, the Deputy Prime Minister under the disgraced Suchinda government, was elected President of the Senate within one month of the massacre. Through this position he was nominally in control of judging the General Amnesty in October 1992 — the law that he reportedly drafted in May 1992. Chainarong Noonpackdee, who was in charge of the First Army Region in 1992, was promoted to full general and given the post of deputy chief of staff in 1995. Though the Sammakhitam Party disintegrated in July 1992, the "demonic politicians" reorganized under different names and logos, but unfortunately with the same aims and tactics to succeed in the July 1995 elections. They used the plot line of a horror story all too well. The ultra-conservative paramilitary organizations that executed students in horrifying ways in 1976 reorganized in May 1992 to intimidate activists.[50]

Conclusion

Sometimes the same memories that liberate can also enslave. There is a dangerous tendency to read everything that happened in May 1992 in terms of the October events of 1973 and 1976. The art exhibition would be better titled 'Ratchdamnoen Memories' rather than 'Ratchdamnoen Memory'. Nawarat says: "I saw the events on Ratchdamnoen three times already: October 14, October 6, and May 18."[51] The sense of *deja vu* at the exhibition is overwhelming: many of the paintings contained images of 1973 and 1976 — not 1992[52] — and "Most of the buyers are former activists."[53]

My concern here is not merely with historical accuracy; after all these are artistic works, not documentary evidence. What is important is the larger story of which this 'Ratchdamnoen Memory' exhibition is a part, and the dangerous narrative rut it dances along. Issara's paintings give a clue. Even though the people are the heroes, the struggle in his paintings is still framed by the camouflage ribbon of the army — the generals are still in control of the story. This all-too-common blurring of the memories of 1992 with those of the 1970s has important consequences. It catches Thailand in a narrative of democracy and destruction, the cycle of violence, which can only end with another crack-down like that which occurred on 6 October 1976.

There were many memories of May along Rajdamnoen Avenue. For almost one year, there was a sign hanging from the ruins of the Public Relations Building which read "Who burnt this?" Pro-military party leaders and Members of Parliament (MPs) declared that they did not care about the people who were killed in May. "I don't think they were heroes," said one, while another remembered them as "city burners".[54] Even with seemingly innocent statistics, the Interior Ministry recalled images of those missing from the 1970s. The stage was being set to justify a *deja vu*, not of the 1973 student movement, but of the 1976 military coup. By 1995, this sense seemed to have passed — but no one can ever be quite sure.

The only way to get out of the recurring nightmare of horror stories and the cycle of Thai political violence is to refuse to participate in this tale. Remember that while the demonstrators were telling a non-violent story with their protests, they were in charge. Once someone (whoever it was) added violence to the demonstration, the army took control of the tale and turned it into a horror story full of death and deceit.

The crux of the democratic story then lies with the people, not just those living, but those who have died. Umberto Eco, the master of the irrational mystery, suggests a way out of the horror plot when he switches from asking "Who speaks?" (in this case who gives the orders to shoot, who shows up at investigating committee meetings, who remembers, who forgets) to focus on the central question of "Who dies?"[55] As the problems faced by the Mahidol Hotline show, this is a difficult question to answer even for those with the best of intentions. As Sidney Jones points out, "Winnowing out the strongest cases is a difficult undertaking, logistically and ethically."[56] This is not just a technical question, but a moral one.

So the events of May are not a mystery story of a single trail leading to a smoking gun, but a horror story of mazes in the circular nature of Thai politics. But even in this horror story there is hope: but it lies in more than just shedding light on the situation as do investigating committees and fact-finding missions. Democracy means that you take part in writing your own story, rather than listening to the tales that military officers, national politicians, and government bureaucrats spin. It is fascinating to see how the management of information and the distrust of the public were not limited to the military, but were also a bureaucratic practice in three governments. But there are ways of getting around this control of the imagination. As Tepsiri Suksopa tells us:

> I heard about the May incident when I was at Children's Village (Chiang Mai). I was writing a tale. I serve children. I try to think of how to tell my grandchild about this incident. How to convey the incident. I never succeed in telling the story of democracy, so [the crack-down] happened again. I'm thinking how we can paint pictures to make the young people understand democracy.[57]

NOTES

1. Milan Kundera, *The Book of Laughter and Forgetting* (New York: Knopf, 1981), pp. 7–8.
2. "Perspectives of artists toward May incident", *The Nation*, 17 October 1992, p. C1; also see Pongpet Mekloy, "The events of May through artists' eyes", *Bangkok Post*, 21 October 1992, p. 23.
3. Milan Kundera, *The Unbearable Lightness of Being* (Boston: Faber and Faber, 1984), p. 278.
4. Kowit Kaymananta in *'Ratchdamnoen Memory'* — *An Exhibition Featuring: Paintings, Sculptures, Caricatures, and Poems of the May Incident*, 23–30 November 1992, The Imperial Queen's Park, Sukhumvit 22, Bangkok. There are no page numbers in this catalogue.

5. Nearly every newspaper and magazine published its own special publication about the events of May. The presentation of the events ranged from a massive tome from the Reporters' Association of Thailand, a collection of political cartoons, to the 1–15 June issue of the teen magazine, *Star Family*. Others in my collection include books from the The Nation Publishing Group, *Sukang*, The Manager Group, the *Bangkok Post*, the Foreign Correspondents' Club of Thailand, *Thai Financial Daily*, *Kao Thai*, *Interest News*, and *Siam Rath*. I also have twelve special publications that are not tied to any specific media group; they are often supporters of Chamlong.

6. The paper weight consists of a piece of plexiglass bent into a horseshoe shape. The razor wire is glued to the inside of the bend, and on the front is written, in red: "For the Museum of Democracy. The razor wire from the May events 1992" (in Thai) and "In memory of May 1992" (in English). On the back is a short poem in Thai: "Neither razor wire nor thick walls can obstruct brave people."

7. At the time of the exhibition, this new hotel was owned by a new Member of Parliament (MP) who was seen as exemplary of the hope for a new breed of responsible businessmen-politicians. Ironically this new concept of responsibility motivated this MP to resign when he was marginally involved in a stock scandal. He then sold the hotel.

8. Somchai Homla-or, Interview, 2 December 1992.

9. Somchai, Interview. The poster memory returned for the 'Second Anniversary of the May Bloodshed: Walking to Nowhere' (1994) exhibition held at Thammasat University which recalled the rough style of posters. For a review see Khetsirin Knithichan, "The politics of art", *The Nation*, 16 May 1994, p. C8.

10. Somchai, Interview.

11. At the end of the exhibition, Somchai estimated that Bt600,000 would be raised. Actually, the Campaign for Popular Democracy (CPD) lost money on this project, because middle class people did not want to buy such macabre images for living-room display. The CPD also lost money on the exhibition catalogue: 3,000 copies were printed while only 1,000 copies were sold. (Naruemon Thabchumpon, Interview, 20 April 1995.)

12. Napad used to be called Suchinda, but she changed her name in 1992.

13. Issara Thayahathai, Interview, 2 December 1992.

14. Somchai, Interview.

15. '*Ratchdamnoen Memory*'. Chamlong also uses the Burmese imagery in a different way. In a speech during the May events, which Chamlong

quotes in his book, Chamlong says to Suchinda: "Why are you (my brother) still standing under the tree? Please come out and let's fight together on elephant-back." Chamlong uses this famous speech where King Naresuan challenges a Burmese prince to do battle. Chamlong is challenging his brother from the military academy, Suchinda, to stand in an election. Thanks to Kittiporn Chaiboon for this reference.

16. Angkan also compares the soldiers to "animals" for shooting unarmed people.
17. Kritaya Archavanitkul et al., "Political Disharmony in Thai Society: A Lesson from the May 1992 Incident", *Asian Review 1995* 9 (1995): 44; Kritaya Archavanitkul, Interview, 24 April 1995.
18. In Thailand 191 is the emergency number, like 911 in the United States or 999 in the United Kingdom.
19. Kritaya et al., op. cit., p. 44.
20. "Anand should be serious about the missing" (Editorial), *The Nation*, 8 July 1992, p. A6.
21. *Bangkok Post,* 6 July 1992.
22. Kritaya et al., op. cit., p. 45.
23. Sidney Jones, "A new method to trace the missing", *The Nation*, 8 July 1992, p. A6.
24. Information suggests that the army kept some of the hard-core activists in camps for as long as six months (Kritaya, Interview).
25. "Junior soldiers who took part in the brutal suppression have been confined to barracks, out of reach of government and parliamentary investigators as well as the media." (*The Nation*, 5 August 1992.)
26. Kritaya, Interview.
27. *Bangkok Post*, 4 December 1992.
28. Kritaya, Interview.
29. "We cannot ignore the fate of the 'missing'" (Editorial), *Bangkok Post*, 5 June 1992, p. 4. Notice that in the *Bangkok Post*'s own reading of the "demonstrator", women are not allowed to be hooligans.
30. "Number games won't locate May 'missing'" (Editorial), *Bangkok Post*, 1 December 1992, p. 4. The last sentence is rather self-serving. The issues went far beyond media censorship.
31. Asia Watch, "Uncontrolled use of lethal force", *The Nation*, 22 May 1992, p. A6.
32. "Relatives of the missing, students and members of the Mahidol Hotline centre claim the Interior Ministry is trying to push down the figure by arbitrarily removing from the list the names of those who could not be said for certain to have attended the rally. They said hundreds of thousands of people from all walks of life joined the protest at its height so it was difficult to say who among the missing were there."

("Families of May missing claim Govt insincere", *Bangkok Post*, 19 January 1993.) Also see *The Nation*, 18 January 1993.

33. *Bangkok Post*, 3 January 1993.
34. "Remembering the events of May" (Editorial), *The Nation*, 6 December 1992, p. A10.
35. Though there were many rumours, and unconfirmed reports coming from university rectors and politicians, after three years there was still no hard evidence of bodies being carted away and dumped by the army.
36. Wasant Techawongtham, "Saga of missing persons", *Bangkok Post*, 13 December 1992, p. 24; "May missing have to be accepted as national trauma" (Editorial), *The Nation*, 14 May 1993, A6; *Bangkok Post*, 16 May 1993.
37. Kritaya, quoted in Wasant Techawongtham, "Saga of missing persons", *Bangkok Post*, 13 December 1992, p. 24.
38. Kritaya, Interview.
39. The Relatives' Committee charged that the pro-democracy government was more concerned with protecting military secrets than solving the missing issue. ("May victims kin mount renewed pressure on Govt", *Bangkok Post*, 14 January 1993.)
40. Reports from friends were not always reliable. Some reports came from people who had just met each other, and exchanged only first names, nicknames, etc. Likewise, family members — even spouses — were found to be not always reliable.
41. Jones, op. cit.
42. Kritaya, Interview.
43. Ibid.
44. As one investigator commented: "There is one thing I've learned from this research: Don't trust the government. Don't trust the people."
45. *Bangkok Post*, 18 January 1993.
46. Even the artists follow this rational plan. Pipop: "To remember the missing people who are almost forgotten now, we must help remember them so that there will be an investigation so there will be an attempt to find the missing, the wrong doers and punish them." ('*Ratchdamnoen Memory*'.)
47. One thing that the statistics did clarify was that the demonstration was not middle class for the dead, injured, and missing.
48. This is not to say that Pradit actually solved the mystery. He never produced any evidence. But the response of right-wing hate groups, which threatened violence against Pradit and his family, raises suspicions about the army's actions. In other words, what does it mean when the right-wing groups believe the army buried the bodies?

49. W. Somerset Maugham, *Collected Short Stories*, vol. 3 (London: Pan Books, 1976), p. 63. He says that in a mystery story "proving the murderer's guilt is by the discovery of his motives". Not evidence.
50. Major-General Sudsai Hasdin, the organizer of the Red Gaur (1970s), maintains that the Apirak Chakri Group (1990s) was much more militant than he was (Pravit Rojanaphruk, "Right-wing causes a flap", *The Nation*, 1 August 1992, p. C1).
51. *'Ratchdamnoen Memory'*.
52. "I have 2 things to say. One is the thought that continues to happen, the other is the feeling that happened once and is gone." (Kowit in *'Ratchdamnoen Memory'*.)
53. Somchai, Interview.
54. The sign was put up by Prachakorn Thai leader Samak Sundaravej. He also said: "I am a politician and don't care about those 40 people who were killed. I don't think they were heroes." Recall that Samak was well rewarded for his loyalty to the military in 1976: he became the Interior Minister after the 6 October coup. Chat Thai MP Chaowarin Latthasaksiri said: "Why did the PM have to attend a religious ceremony for those who burned the city. Why doesn't he take care of the soldiers who died at the border?" (*The Nation*, 26 November 1992, p. A2).
55. Umberto Eco, quoted in Teresa de Lauretis, *Technologies of Gender: Essays on Film, Theory and Fiction* (Bloomington: Indiana University Press, 1987), p. 65. Eco's point here is to switch from the élite discourse to practices that concern common people.
56. Jones, op. cit.
57. *'Ratchdamnoen Memory'*.

MILITARY TESTIMONY

Ministry of Defence No. 100/1109[1]

> The Capital Peacekeeping Force
> Suan Miksakawan
> Rajdamnoen Road
> Dusit, Bangkok 10300

15 June 1992

Subject: To testify to the facts

To: The chairman of the ad hoc committee with reference to the Parliamentary Letter (Most Urgent No. 361/2535, 12 June 1992) regarding permission of military officers to attend the ad hoc committee meeting

Accompanying documents:

1. Document No. 1: Proclamation of the Minister of Defence about granting military officers to do civil servants' work
2. Document No. 2: Directorate of Internal Peacekeeping Force's Order (specific) No. 4/2535, 7 May 1992 concerning the appointment of the officers (additional)
3. Document No. 3: Directorate of Internal Peacekeeping Force's Order (specific) No. 10/2526, 16 April 1983 concerning the appointment of officers

4. Document No. 4: Directorate of Internal Peacekeeping Force's Order (specific) No. 4/2527, 18 September 1984 about authorizing the capital peacekeeping commander in maintaining law and order

5. Document No. 5: Directorate of Internal Peacekeeping Force's Order (specific) No. 5/2535, 7 May 1992 about appointing officers

6. Document No. 6: The chronology of events, unrest, and disorder in Bangkok and the neighbouring provinces during May 1992

Responding to the ad hoc committee's asking me to testify to the facts of the political crisis during 17–20 May 1992 I would like to inform you in detail as follows:

I, General Issarapong Noonpackdee, was appointed as Army Commander in Chief by a Royal Command on 7 April 1992 and became involved in those incidents. (Document No. 1.) Facts and details of my involvement are as follows:

Position and Authority
As director of the Army's Internal Peacekeeping Force, I am empowered to mobilize army, navy, and air force troops and civil servants — who are based in areas under the army's jurisdiction (except for Satthahip District of Chonburi province, Rayong province, and Trat province) — to perform necessary duties. The army's command areas consist of Regional and Provincial Army areas. (Document No. 2., Point 4.2.1.)

As Director of the Capital Security Command, I am authorized to order army, navy, air force as well as civil servants to use force in maintaining law and order in Bangkok and the neighbouring provinces (Samut Prakan, Prakarm, Nontaburi, Patum Thani, and Samut Sakorn). (Document No. 2, Point 4.2 and Document No. 3, Point 4.2.)

As the Capital Peacekeeping Commander, I can order army, navy, air force as well as civil servants to use force in maintaining law and order and pursuing duties assigned by the director in Bangkok and the neighbouring provinces.

Plan and Orders

The Capital Peacekeeping Force adopted Operation Paireepinart/ 22 with the aim of maintaining peace and preventing and suppressing any type of public unrest in Bangkok and neighbouring areas. The plan also involved protecting important places and providing security to important national figures.[2]

The plan consisted of four stages as follows:

1. Preparation stage
1.1 Intelligence management by planning and extending the intelligence network with co-ordinating among units closely and continuously
1.2 Provide peacekeeping units for preventing all types of unrest and prepare forces, arms, transport, communications equipment, and other necessary equipment
1.3 Prepare to mobilize units to perform duties and cope with potential problems
1.4 Use all forms of mass operations, public relations, and psychological operations to reach the people closely and continuously through all kinds of media
1.5 Prepare a special strategy to face and suppress all types of unrest, protect important places, and provide security to important figures in the command area

2. Prevention stage
2.1 Perform public relations and psychological operations to both people and the opposite side in order to inform them of the facts of situation
2.2 Use the forces to encircle unrest areas, disperse mobs, protect important places, and provide security to important figures
2.3 Use our mass force to support the operation to prevent all types of unrest in command areas

3. Suppression stage
Use force to suppress the people who instigate all kinds of unrest in command areas

4. Transferring all responsibility to the state stage
    The Capital Peacekeeping Force will step back from its operation as soon as the situation is normal. Then it will hand over responsibility to the state.

On 6 May 1992 the Capital Security Commander sought permission to launch Operation Paireepinart/33 because intelligence reports and other signs showed that unrest would take place in Bangkok and might escalate to neighbouring areas. Peaceful demonstrations were turning violent and threatening to greatly affect the overall economy and society. This plan was allowed by the Internal Peacekeeping Commander on 7 May 1992.

On 17 May 1992, the Capital Peacekeeping Command ordered strategy 1/25 to launch Operation Paireepinart/33 because the gathering of the people was in a position necessitating officers to maintain peace and order. The mission aimed at protecting the nation, religion, and monarchy of the Chakri royal family by restoring peace as rapidly as possible, and providing security to important places and national figures. The operating officers must abide by the following rules:

1. Capital Peacekeeping Command used police troops as the key force to protect and suppress the unrest in command areas under the state's jurisdiction.
2. In case the situation deteriorated beyond control, Capital Peacekeeping Command would sacrifice their lives to protect the nation, religion, and monarchy of the Chakri dynasty in order to restore normalcy as rapidly as possible. Forces involved in the operation, however, would refrain from clashes which might cause great losses, by starting from light to heavy measures in accordance with the circumstances.

Recommendations for co-ordinating among each unit:

1. We must sacrifice our lives to protect the Chitraladda Palace
2. Every unit should co-ordinate with each other closely and continuously
3. Every unit should closely co-operate, particularly in the use of automatic weapons in areas where units border each other

4. When we need to encounter rioters,[3] the performance should be as follows:

4.1 Use negotiation and psychological operations

4.2 Use barricades to counter the rioters and try to disperse the crowd

4.3 Use equipment to suppress these rioters progressively from light to heavy weapons

4.4 Realizing that the rioters are our Thai compatriots, we should if possible avoid using force and arms, and prevent clashes that would cause great losses.

The strategic order 1/35 would be sent to involved units as a major order to be carried out in accordance with Operation Paireepinart/33.

The Gathering, the Situation, and the Riot

From the beginning of the gathering, the Capital Peacekeeping Force, which has the task of keeping peace and order in Bangkok and neighbouring provinces which include Patum Thani, Nontaburi, Samut Prakan, and Samut Sakorn, very closely followed the situation which had the tendency to result in turmoil in the command area. At first, it employed lenient action by observing the circumstances from a distance. Until it was necessary to mobilize the armed forces, only police troops were authorized in keeping the peace. When the situation worsened into riots, which were beyond the police capability to control, the Capital Peacekeeping Force was obliged to deploy soldiers to create peace and order in the command area according to authorized power. Every operation of units of the Capital Peacekeeping Force was logically followed and was strictly in accordance with each particular situation, and strictly followed orders from the chain of command. Every operation had been approved by or was reported through the chain of command up to the highest rank of Supreme Commander who was the director of the Internal Peacekeeping Force, and was also reported to the government for permission and/or acknowledgment. All details of the situation and all operations appear in the chronology (Document No. 6).

I can stress that the overall mission was entirely based on the legal authority and orders of the relevant superiors. Everybody, including myself, did not want to see loss of lives as well as damage to public and private property. The authorities decided to implement Operation Paireepinart/33 because intelligence evaluations and what had actually happened made it clear that without such measures, the loss of lives, damage to public and private property — including damage to the economy and national stability, including the country's main institution, particularly the monarchy — might have been damaged beyond all estimate. <u>The escalation of the rallies into riots had been planned systematically in advance.</u>[4] I can guarantee careful judgment throughout the operation. All authorities concerned were asked to ensure peace and unity while trying their best to avoid losses on either side and keeping in mind that everybody was Thai. The operation had to start with the lightest necessary measures. It was obvious that all officers exercised extreme restraint though they were hurt mentally and physically. They were scolded and insulted. Sometimes they had to yield to pressure by the protesters, knowing that further confrontation would lead to much greater violence. They were forced to retreat and refrain from arresting arsonists — just to reduce pressure which might have made events deteriorate beyond control. The dispersal of mobs, arrest of protesters, warning gunfire, or shooting the tires and engines of buses and oil trucks were all done only after careful judgment in accordance to the circumstance. Therefore, all the losses suffered by the public and private sectors were unavoidable. I, together with all officers, realized the plight, suffering, and grief of every party concerned. If there is anything I can do within the scope of my authority to relieve the result of what happened, I and all officers are willing to do our best to achieve that. We sincerely hope that such a tragic incident will not happen again in our society.

I am testifying in this written statement to the ad hoc committee because I believe that even if I testify in person, the content will not be any different. Besides, this report will make it easier for the ad hoc committee to consider. If there is anything the committee would like to know from me, please let me know so that I can comply. And if there is the need to have officers in the Capital Peacekeeping Force testify because of their direct involvement, I will be willing to co-operate.

Yours faithfully,
General Issarapong Noonpackdee
Army Commander in Chief
Director of the Capital Security Command
Commander of the Capital Peacekeeping Force

Document No. 6
The Capital Peacekeeping Force's chronology:

7 April 1992: A royal command appointed General Suchinda Kraprayoon as prime minister, which was recognized by the international community. The appointment followed political conflicts that soon affected the military establishment.

After the 22 March general election, five political parties which commanded the parliamentary majority could not find a suitable man to be prime minister. After Samakkitham Party leader Narong Wongwan failed to become prime minister due to problems [concerning drug trafficking], Supreme Commander and Army Commander in Chief Suchinda was asked to accept the top executive post.

Although there was opposition from several senior military officers, General Suchinda resigned from all military positions and was appointed prime minister for the sake of national security and in accordance with the democratic system and the Thai Constitution.

General Suchinda's appointment reduced political tension. The general public indicated that they would give the new Cabinet a chance.

9 April 1992: Former MP Chalard Vorachart started a hunger strike, but received little public attention.

Later, however, there were problems concerning the formation of the new Cabinet. People questioned the honesty of certain new

Cabinet members, creating a negative image of the coalition parties. The situation generated a major impact on the public faith in the government and the prime minister.

The Students' Federation of Thailand, the Campaign for Popular Democracy, and other allies exploited public confusion, sending their members to join Chalard in the hunger strike. They hoped that if something happened to any of the protesters, it could be used as a pretext to extend their campaign.

20 April 1992: The Opposition proposed constitutional amendments. About 30,000 people joined a rally at the Royal Plaza. The movement, which had earlier only criticized the prime minister for not having participated in the March poll, went further by demanding his resignation.

4–5 May 1992: Anti-government moves were renewed to pave the way for a major protest on 6 May, when the administration was set to declare its policy in Parliament. The new protests were well planned and joined by a large number of people.

Major-General Chamlong Srimuang's vow to fast to death raised the number of protesters, who were soon infiltrated by certain groups bent on violent acts such as throwing stones at police.

6 May 1992: The violent trends of the campaign became more obvious. The number of protesters rose to 50,000. They were joined by Opposition MPs in front of Parliament House. When the parliamentary meeting ended, the demonstrators tried to push their way into the compound and threw missiles at security forces.

The situation indicated that riots could break out at any time.

7–9 May 1992: Demonstrators who had gathered since 4 May in front of Parliament moved to Sanam Luang on the night of 7 May with the number swelling to about 70,000. Chamlong still continued his fast.

On the night of 8 May Chamlong moved about 30,000 people from Sanam Luang to the Rajdamnoen Avenue and nobody knew his destination. The masses were blocked at Paan Faa Bridge and tension nearly erupted into violence.

Chamlong ended his fast on the morning of 9 May.

11–16 May 1992: The coalition parties pledged urgent steps to amend the Constitution. The protesters insisted that the prime minister must resign and scheduled 17 May as D-Day for another major rally.

There were endless demands from the protesters.

The government parties felt that constitutional amendments must be in accordance with the democratic system, which required them to seek prior consent from party members. But the Opposition accused them of breaking their promise and alleged that the military was behind the delay.

Rumours discrediting the military were widespread. The government was accused of trying to break up peaceful demonstrations.

17 May 1992: About 70,000 people joined a rally at Sanam Luang. Chamlong decided to move the masses toward the Paan Faa Bridge at around 9:20 p.m.

About 200 people who were obviously aggressive planned to break through police barricades at the bridge. They threw objects at police, and tried to demolish the barbed wire blockade. Police turned water cannons on the people in a bid to stop the crowd.

Some protesters seized a fire engine at around 22:00 p.m. and tried to break up the barricades. Police resisted. Seven or eight officers were injured.

Crowd violence continued late into the night. The Phukhao Thong fire brigade station was besieged. Five fire engines were burned down. Policemen were assaulted.

18 May 1992: The government declared a state of emergency before 1:00 a.m. But the protesters failed to perceive the government's good intention to restore peace.

The mobs broke through the police barriers at the Paan Faa Bridge and finally were confronted with army troops who formed the second line of resistance. They kept provoking the soldiers, who were armed with unloaded rifles. The troops, in a bid to avoid violent clashes, sought permission to retreat from the bridge to the Makkawarn Bridge.

After the soldiers retreated, the mobs went on a rampage, destroying private properties such as cars and motorcycles.

The mobs set fire to the Nanglerng Police Station as well as the Youth and Children's Welfare Division at around 2:30 a.m. Prisoners were released. Over 50 police and private vehicles in the area were set ablaze.

At around 4:00 a.m. security forces laid a siege to the crowds. Careful measures were applied. People were allowed to pass through checkpoints. Some of those who wanted to go home were provided with transportation.

Lines of troops marched toward the bulk of troublemakers in a bid to disperse them. But they met with intense bombardment of molotov cocktails and stones. The soldiers applied the next measure, firing into the air. But the throwing of missiles was continued.

Some soldiers instinctively ducked for cover when molotov cocktails fell near them. This accidentally caused some rifle barrels to lower and apparently harmed a few people. Four people were injured and were immediately taken by the security forces to a hospital.

No arrests could be made because the troublemakers dissolved into the main crowd. Most protesters were still concentrated on Rajdamnoen Avenue.

After that there was no violent incident. The situation improved with many protesters returning home.

At 3:20 p.m. troops detained Chamlong and about 600–700 demonstrators in a bid to prevent highly possible riots. The operation caused no losses, though there were sounds of sniper fire from high places.

The violence-prone side spread rumours that hundreds or thousands of people were killed by soldiers. That is absolutely untrue.

At 4:00 p.m. three officers were injured by sniper shots, which also killed a foreigner.

Troops seemed to gain control of Rajdamnoen Avenue. But at 7:00 p.m. the worst riot broke out, with people who were instigated and who were out of their minds burning all objects on the street, including two air force cars. Soldiers still refrained from using force.

The situation worsened at 8:00 p.m. when rioters seized five or six buses and forced the passengers to join the protest. The buses were used to put pressure on troops and obstruct their work.

All-out riots continued at 10:30 p.m., apparently because of soldiers' lenience. Nine buses and oil trucks were used to pressure troops. One oil truck was set ablaze. The Government Lottery Bureau was also on fire. Rioters torched the Public Relations Department building.

An unimaginable incident took place when rioters drove buses and oil trucks toward the soldiers. The troops fired warning shots but finally were forced to shoot at the vehicles' tires and later the engines. This use of weapons might have caused losses due to stray bullets.

This was the worst incident. The authorities deeply and sadly regretted it. All security forces only wanted to protect important places and stop the rioting with no intention to hurt any of their Thai brothers.

Violence spread out of Rajdamnoen Avenue at 11:30 p.m. Motorcycle gangs roamed streets and destroyed government properties, including police kiosks, public telephone booths, and traffic lights. The Revenue Department building was also burnt. Arsonists also attempted to torch the Treasury Department building. There was widespread robbery.

19 May 1992: Rioting continued in front of the Department of Public Relations. At 5:00 a.m. the government decided to have the Capital Peacekeeping Force disperse the rioters in front of the department building and the Royal Hotel.

About 700 rioters were arrested, including nine motorcycle gangsters.

There were no casualties on either side, nor was there any violence, specifically inside the Royal Hotel.

None of the rumours was true. It is not true that troops fired into the hotel, killing many people. It is not true that thousands of protesters' bodies were taken on trucks to dumping sites. Bloodstains inside the hotel came from the injured people treated by doctors there.

No body was found in the hotel. Its manager can confirm this.

At 4:15 p.m. some protesters threatened to set fire to the Chanasongkram Police Station in an attempt to force police to release prisoners there. Police tried to use soft measures to disperse the mob, only to face gunfire.

The situation improved to a certain level at night. But there were attempts to prolong the violence. Public properties were destroyed. A gunshop was robbed, resulting in a clash between rioters and the authorities. Both sides suffered injuries.

Protesters regrouped at Ramkhamheang University.

20 May 1992: Scattered violence dragged on. It seemed the unrest would become drawn out.

At 8:30 p.m. General Suchinda and Chamlong were granted an audience with His Majesty the King who told them to jointly work out a peaceful solution to the crisis.

The facts mentioned above can be concluded as follows:

1. The unrest was planned step-by-step. Instigators appealed to the mass by staging hunger protests. When the crowds grew in number, some groups with malicious intentions tried to turn the demonstration into a violent uprising by using abusive language and threatening authorities' safety.

    The peaceful rally turned violent when the masses were moved to confront authorities. Rumours were spread to make the demonstrators hate the government. This made the situation deteriorate beyond the rally leaders' control, leading to riots which caused the damage of government property and the loss of lives.

    It should be noted that the 4–11 May rallies were peaceful. But rioters during 17–20 May acted very differently. They apparently wanted to create situations which could develop into urban terrorism. The number of rioters was estimated at 500 and they tried to infiltrate the peaceful rallies. They would mingle with the demonstrators every time the authorities tried to arrest them. The demonstrators would not co-operate with the authorities when they tried to arrest the rioters.

2. The authorities tried to be as lenient as possible while quelling the unrest. They always kept in mind that the rioters were fellow Thai citizens. They tried not to use weapons and tried their best to avoid bloodshed.

   The authorities applied lenient measures before implementing harsher ones. They tried to block the crowds from moving to areas that would put key places, such as Government House, Parliament, and the Royal Palace, in danger.

   The troops did not retaliate when attacked with missiles, including molotov cocktails. They tried to avoid confrontation until convinced that the crowds had gone crazy.

   While the authorities tried to avoid confrontation, the crowds resorted to more violence, setting fire to government buildings and cars and looting government property.

   The government was forced to turn to tougher measures. Security forces only fired into the sky to drive away rioters. The soldiers tried to negotiate with the crowds to go back to Sanam Luang, but to no avail. As a result, they had to separate the crowds from their leaders to restore law and order.

3. Security forces returned to their barracks after His Majesty the King's intervention and carried out their routine duty by helping out villagers affected by prolonged drought.

4. The government tried its best to help the people affected by the violence. Centres were set up for relatives of the killed protesters. The Prime Minister's Office set up a committee to investigate the incident, so did Parliament.

NOTES

1. Since the Thai in this report is very poorly written — even by military standards — this translation has at times cut out many of the repetitions. We have left some of the army's twisted grammar in place to give a better sense of its reasoning.

2. "Important national figures" refers to the royal family as well as the Prime Minister.
3. A literal translation is "people who create disorder/unrest", but it is also commonly translated as "rioters".
4. This is the only sentence that is underlined in the report.

BIBLIOGRAPHY

Abhisit Vejajiva. Presentation at the Foreign Correspondents' Club of Thailand, 17 October 1993.

Amara Pongsapich. "Strengthening the Role of NGOs in Popular Participation". In *Thai NGOs: The Continuing Struggle for Democracy*, edited by Jaturong Boonyarattanasoontorn and Gawin Chutima, pp. 9–50. Bangkok: Thai NGO Support Project, 1995.

Amara Pongsapich and Nitaya Kataleeradabahn. *Philanthropy, NGO Activities and Corporate Funding in Thailand*. Bangkok: Chulalongkorn University Social Research Institute, 1994.

Ammar Siamwalla. "Thai Junta Does All the Wrong Things". *Asian Wall Street Journal*, 15–16 May 1992, p. 10.

Anderson, Benedict. "Withdrawal Symptoms: Social and Cultural Aspects of the October 6 Coup". *Bulletin of Concerned Asia Scholars* 9, no. 3 (July–September 1977): 13–30.

———. "Studies of the Thai State: the State of Thai Studies". In *The Study of Thailand: Analyses of Knowledge, Approaches, and Prospects in Anthropology, Art History, Economics, History and Political Science*, edited by Eliezer B. Ayal. Athens: Ohio University Center for International Studies, Southeast Asia Program, 1978.

———. "Murder and Progress in Modern Siam". *New Left Review*, no. 181 (May/June 1990), pp. 33–48.

———. *Imagined Communities: Reflections on the Origin and Spread of Nationalism*. Rev. ed. New York: Verso, 1991.

Anek Laothamatas. *Business Associations and the Political Economy of Thailand: From Bureaucratic Polity to Liberal Corporatism*. Boulder: Westview Press and Singapore: Institute of Southeast Asian Studies, 1992.

———. "Sleeping Giant Awakens: The Middle Class in Thai Politics". *Asian Review 1993* 7 (1993): 78–125.

————. *Mohp Mue Tua: Chonchunklang lae nakthurakit kap phattanakan phrachathipatai* [Mobile phone mob: The middle class and business people with democratic development]. Bangkok: Matichon Press, 1993.

"Answers by Chiang Mai University's Academics for Democracy to Questions Posed by the Public Regarding a Non-Elected Prime Minister". Mimeographed. 1992.

Apichart Tongyou. "Village: Autonomous Society". In *Back to the Roots: Village and Self-Reliance in a Thai Context*, edited by Seri Phongphit. Bangkok: Rural Development Documentation Centre, 1986.

Applegate, Colonel Rex (U.S.A. – Ret.). *Riot Control — Materiel and Techniques*. 2nd ed. London: Arms and Armour Press, 1981.

Asia Watch. "Uncontrolled use of lethal force". *The Nation*, 22 May 1992, p. A6.

Asian Business, April 1991, p. 16.

Asian Wall Street Journal, 21 May 1992, 18 May 1993, 19 May 1993.

Bangkok Post, various issues.

Bangkok Post. *Catalyst for Change: Uprising in May*. Bangkok: Post Publishing, July 1992.

Barmé, Scot. *Luang Wichit Wathakan and the Creation of a Thai Identity*. Singapore: Institute of Southeast Asian Studies, 1993.

Barthes, Roland. *Image-Music-Text*. New York: Hill and Wang, 1978.

Berghahn, Volker R. *Militarism: The History of an International Debate 1961–1979*. New York: Cambridge University Press, 1981.

Bourdieu, Pierre. *Outline of a Theory of Practice*. New York: Cambridge University Press, 1977.

Callahan, William A. "Gender, Ideology, Nation: *Ju Dou* in the Cultural Politics of China". *East-West Film Journal* 7, no. 1 (January 1993): 52–80.

————. "The Ideology of Miss Thailand in National, Commercial and Transnational Space". *Alternatives*. Forthcoming, 1998.

————. "Rescripting East/West Relations, Rethinking Asian Democracy". *Pacifica Review* 8, no. 1 (1996): 1–25.

————. *PollWatch, Elections and Civil Society*. Aldershot: Ashgate Publishing, 1998.

Callahan, William A. and Duncan McCargo. "Vote-buying in Thailand's Northeast: The July 1995 General Election". *Asian Survey* 36, no. 4 (April 1996): 376–92.

Chai-Anan Samudavanija. *The Thai Young Turks*. Singapore: Institute of Southeast Asian Studies, 1982.

————. "Thailand: A Stable Semi-democracy". In *Politics in Developing Countries: Comparing Experiences with Democracy*, edited by Larry Diamond, Juan J. Linz, and Seymour Martin Lipset. Boulder: Lynne Reiner Publishers, 1990.

Chai-Anan Samudavanija, Kusuma Snitwongse, and Suchit Bunbongkarn. *From Armed Suppression to Political Offensive: Attitudinal Changes of Thai Military Officers since 1976*. Bangkok: Institute of Security and International Studies, Chulalongkorn University, 1990.

Chalidaporn Songsamphan. "Supernatural Prophesy in Thai Politics: The Role of a Spiritual Cultural Element in Coup Decisions". Ph.D. dissertation, The Clairemont Graduate School, 1991.

Chamlong Srimuang. *Ruam Kan Su* [Unite to fight]. Bangkok: Khlet Thai, 1992.

Clarke, Gerard. "Participation and Protest: Non-Governmental Organisations and Philippine Politics". Ph.D. dissertation, School of Oriental and African Studies, University of London, 1995.

Combe, Victoria. "Quiet Voice of Reason". *The Nation*, 4 June 1992, p. C1.

Cook, Nerida M. "Thai Identity in the Astrological Tradition". In *National Identity and Its Defenders: Thailand, 1939–89*, edited by Craig J. Reynolds. Clayton: Monash Papers on Southeast Asia, no. 25, 1991.

Creative Media Foundation. *Langbang* [Cleanse the village]. Bangkok: Ongkan Glom, 1992.

Crisis in Democracy: Report of an International Fact-Finding Mission to Thailand on the Events of 17th–20th May 1992 in Bangkok. Hong Kong, November 1992.

de Lauretis, Teresa. *Technologies of Gender: Essays on Film, Theory and Fiction*. Bloomington: Indiana University Press, 1987.

Directory of Non-governmental Development Organizations in Thailand 1987. Unabridged ed. Bangkok: Thai Volunteer Service, 1987.

Dirlik, Arif, ed. *What Is in a Rim? Critical Perspectives on the Pacific Rim Idea*. Boulder: Westview Press, 1993.

Donaldson, Scott. "On the wrong side of Ratchadamnoen Ave". *The Nation*, 24 May 1992, p. B5.

Doner, Richard F. and Ansil Ramsay. "Postimperialism and Development in Thailand". *World Development* 21, no. 5 (1993): 691–704.

Eco, Umberto. "Towards a Semiological Guerilla War". In *Travels in Hyper Reality: Essays*. San Diego: Harcourt Brace Jovanovich, 1983.

Esherick, Joseph W. and Jeffrey N. Wasserstrom. "Acting out Democracy: Political Theater in Modern China". In *Popular Protest and Political Culture in Modern China*, edited by Jeffrey N. Wasserstrom and Elizabeth J. Perry. Boulder: Westview Press, 1992.

Far Eastern Economic Review, 21 May 1992; 10 December 1992, p. 29.

Foucault, Michel. "Revolutionary Action: 'Until Now'". In *Language, Counter-Memory, Practice*, edited by Donald F. Bouchard. Ithaca: Cornell University Press, 1977.

Foucault, Michel (with Gilles Deleuze). "Intellectuals and Power". In *Language, Counter-Memory, Practice*, edited by Donald F. Bouchard. Ithaca: Cornell University Press, 1977.

Galtung, Johan. "II.14: On the Meaning of Nonviolence". In *Essays in Peace Research*. Copenhagen: Christian Ejlers, 1975.

————. *True Worlds: A Transnational Perspective*. New York: Free Press, 1980.

Ganley, Gladys D. *The Exploding Political Power of Personal Media*. Norwood: Ablex Publishing Corp., 1992.

García Márquez, Gabriel. *No One Writes to the Colonel and Other Stories*. New York: Harper and Row Publishers, 1968.

Gawin Chutima. "Thai NGOs and Civil Society". In *Civil Society in the Asia-Pacific Region*, edited by Isagani R. Serrano. Washington, D.C.: Civicus, 1994.

"The General System of Phonetic Transcription of Thai Characters into Roman".

Girling, John L.S. *Thailand: Society and Politics*. Ithaca: Cornell University Press, 1981.

Gohlert, Ernst. *Power and Culture*. Bangkok: White Lotus, 1991.

Gothom Arya. "Has anything changed since last May?". *Sunday Post* (Bangkok), 16 May 1993, p. 23.

Haraway, Donna. "A Manifesto for Cyborgs: Science, Technology and Socialist Feminism in the 1980s". *Socialist Review* 15, no. 2 (1985): 65–107.

Hewison, Kevin. *Power and Politics in Thailand*. Manila: Journal of Contemporary Asia Publishers, 1989.

————. "Of Regimes, State and Pluralities: Thai Politics Enters the 1990s". In *Southeast Asia in the 1990s: Authoritarianism, Democracy & Capitalism*, edited by Kevin Hewison, Richard Robison, and Garry Rodan. Sydney: Allen & Unwin, 1993.

————. "Political Oppositions and Regime Change in Thailand". In *Political Oppositions in Industrializing Asia*, edited by Garry Rodan. London: Routledge, 1996.

Holloway, Richard. *Doing Development: Government, NGOs and the Rural Poor in Asia*. London: Earthscan/CUSO, 1989.

Hong Lysa. "*Warasan setthasat kanmu'ang*: critical scholarship in post-1976 Thailand". In *Thai Constructions of Knowledge*, edited by Manas Chitakasem and Andrew Turton. London: School of Oriental and African Studies, University of London, 1991.

Hull, Gloria, Patricia Bell Scott, and Barbara Smith, eds. *All Women are White, All Blacks are Men, But Some of Us are Brave*. Old Westbury: Feminist Press, 1982.

Iacopino, Vincent and Sidney Jones. *Thailand — Bloody May: Excessive Use of Lethal Force in Bangkok: The Events of May 17–20, 1992*. A report by physicians for Human Rights and Asia Watch. New York: Human Rights Watch, October 1992.

International Herald Tribune, 20 May 1992.

Issarapong Noonpackdee. "The Soldiers' Story". *The Nation*, 21 June 1992, p. A8.

Jaturong Boonyarattanasoontorn and Gawin Chutima, eds. *Thai NGOs: The Continuing Struggle for Democracy*. Bangkok: Thai NGO Support Project, 1995.

Jones, Sidney. "A new method to trace the missing". *The Nation*, 8 July 1992, p. A6.

Kafka, Franz. "Jackals and Arabs". In *The Penal Colony*. New York: Schoken Books, 1976.

Kamnoon Sittisaman. "*Mohp Rotkeng*" [Sedan mob]. *The Manager Daily*, 22 April 1992, p. 8.

————. "Ahimsa, Forgiveness and Tyrants". Pts. 1 and 2. *The Manager Daily*, 7 and 8 May 1992, p. 8.

Kanjana Spindler. "May 1992: When the tide finally turned". *Bangkok Post*, 19 May 1993, p. 5.

Khetsirin Knithichan. "The politics of art". *The Nation*, 16 May 1994, p. C8.

Khien Theeravit. *Wikritakankanmuang Thai: karani phrutsapha mahawipyok 2535* [Thai politics in crisis: the case of the May 1992 tragedy]. Bangkok: Matichon Publishing, 1993.

King, Daniel E. "The Thai Parliamentary Elections of 1992: Return to Democracy in an Atypical Year". *Asian Survey* 32, no. 12 (December 1992): 1109–23.

Klein, Bradley S. "The Textual Strategies of the Military: Or Have You Read Any Good Defense Manuals Lately". In *International/ Intertextual Relations: Postmodern Readings of World Politics*, edited by James Der Derian and Michael J. Shapiro, pp. 97–112. Lexington: Lexington Books, 1989.

Koopmans, Ruud. "The Dynamics of Protest Waves: West Germany, 1965 to 1989". *American Sociological Review*, 58 (October 1993): 637–58.

Korten, David C. *Getting to the 21st Century: Voluntary Action and the Global Agenda*: West Hartford: Kumarian Press, 1990.

Kritaya Archavanitkul, Anuchat Poungsomlee, Suporn Chunva- vuttiyanont, and Varaporn Chamsanit. "Political Disharmony in Thai Society: A Lesson from the May 1992 Incident". *Asia Review 1995* 9 (1995): 39–56.

Kundera, Milan. *The Book of Laughter and Forgetting*. New York: Knopf, 1981.

————. *The Unbearable Lightness of Being*. Boston: Faber and Faber, 1984.

The LaRouche Organisation. Bruxelles: International Confederation of Free Trade Unions, 1987.

Likhit Dhiravegin. *Demi-Democracy: The Evolution of the Thai Political System*. Singapore: Times Academic Press, 1992.

Longman Dictionary of Contemporary English. New ed. London: Longman, 1987.

Lopez, Barry Holstun. *Of Wolves and Men*. New York: Charles Scribner's Sons, 1978.

Lorde, Audre. *Sister Outsider*. Freedom: Crossings Press, 1984.

Luke, Timothy W. "'What's Wrong with Deterrence?' A Semiotic Interpretation of National Security Policy". In *International/Intertextual Relations: Postmodern Readings of World Politics*, edited by James Der Derian and Michael J. Shapiro, pp. 207–30. Lexington: Lexington Books, 1989.

Macdonald, Laura. "Globalising Civil Society: Interpreting International NGOs in Central America". *Millenium: Journal of International Studies* 23, no. 2 (1994): 267–85.

The Manager Daily, various issues.

Matichon, 9 April 1992, 22 April 1992.

Maugham, Somerset W. *Collected Short Stories*. Vol. 3. London: Pan Books, 1976.

McCargo, Duncan. "Thailand's democracy: the long vacation". *Politics* 12, no. 2 (1992): 3–8.

———. "Towards Chamlong Srimuang's Political Philosophy". *Asian Review 1993* 7 (1993): 171–208.

———. *Chamlong Srimuang and the New Thai Politics*. London: Hurst & Company, 1997.

McCarthy, Ronald M. "The Techniques of Nonviolent Action: Some Principles of Its Nature, Use, and Effects". In *Arab Nonviolent Political Struggle in the Middle East*, edited by Ralph E. Crow, Philip Grant, and Saad E. Ibrahim, pp. 107–20. Boulder: Lynne Rienner Publishers, 1990.

Mehmed Ali, Kathy E. Ferguson, and Phyllis Turnbull (with Joelle Mulford). "Gender, Land and Power: Reading the Military in Hawai'i". Paper presented at the Fifteenth World Congress of the International Political Science Association, 21–25 July 1991, in Buenos Aires.

Mohanty, Chandra Talpade. "Introduction: Cartographies of Struggle, Third World Women and the Politics of Feminism". In *Third World Women and the Politics of Feminism*, edited by Chandra

Talpade Mohanty, Ann Russo, and Lourdes Torres. Bloomington: Indiana University Press, 1991.

Morell, David and Chai-Anan Samudavanija. *Political Conflict in Thailand: Reform, Reaction and Revolution*. Cambridge, Mass.: Oelgeschlager, Gunn & Hain Publishers, Inc., 1981.

Mukdawan Sakboon. "When the troops fired". *The Nation*, 7 June 1992, p. A8.

The Nation, various issues.

Neher, Clark D. "Political Succession in Thailand". *Asian Survey 32*, no. 7 (July 1992): 585–605.

Newsweek, 1 June 1992, p. 34.

Oakley, Peter. *Involvement of People in Development Activities and the Role of Promotional NGOs in Asia*. Rome: Food and Agriculture Organization, 1989.

Ockey, James. "Business Leaders, Gangsters and the Middle Class". Ph.D. dissertation, Cornell University, 1992.

Pana Janviroj and Yingyord Manchuvisith. "Thai flying in political turbulence". *The Nation*, 23 June 1992, p. A6.

Pasuk Phongpaichit and Chris Baker. *Thailand: Economy and Politics*. Kuala Lumpur: Oxford University Press, 1995.

Pasuk Phongpaichit and Sungsidh Piriyarangsan. *Corruption and Democracy in Thailand*. Bangkok: Political Economy Centre, Faculty of Economics, Chulalongkorn University, 1994.

Pfirrmann, Claudia and Dirk Kron. *Environment and NGOs in Thailand*. Bangkok: Thai NGO Support Project and Friedrich Naumann Foundation, 1992.

PollWatch. "Using 2000 year old Khmer magic to get rid of devils who obstruct democracy". Press release, 10 September 1992.

Pongpet Mekloy. "Curse in a dead man's eye". *Bangkok Post*, 11 June 1992, p. 31.

———. "The events of May through artists' eyes". *Bangkok Post*, 21 October 1992, p. 23.

Pongsan Puntularp. "Political Stability: The Role of Political Culture in Thailand". Paper delivered at the Fifth International Conference on Thai Studies, 1993, in London.

Pratumporn Vajarasathira. "Quote, unquote". *Bangkok Post*, 24 May 1992, p. 31.

Pravit Rojanaphruk. "Right-wing causes a flap". *The Nation*, 1 August 1992, p. C1.

————. "NGOs: Chamber for the oppressed". *The Sunday Nation*, 13 March 1993, p. A10.

Price, Vincent. *Communication Concepts 4: Public Opinion*. London: Sage, 1992.

Prinya Thewanarumikul, discussion leader. "*Ruang Mohp*" [Discourse on mob]. *Newsletter of the Campaign for Popular Democracy* (Bangkok) 1, no. 6 (April 1993): 6–17.

Prudhisan Jumbala. *Nation-Building and Democratization in Thailand: a Political History*. Bangkok: Chulalongkorn University Social Research Institute, 1992.

Pura, Raphael and Cynthia Owens. "King's low profile reflects reluctance to meddle". *Asian Wall Street Journal*, 22–23 May 1992, p. 1.

'*Ratchdamnoen Memory*' — *An Exhibition Featuring: Paintings, Sculptures, Caricatures, and Poems of the May Incident*. 23–30 November 1992, The Imperial Queen's Park, Sukhumvit 22, Bangkok.

Regan, Donald T. *For the Record*. London: Arrow Books, 1988.

Reynolds, Craig J. "The Plot of Thai History". In *Historical Documents and Literary Evidence*, pp. 1–29. Bangkok: Thai Studies Programme, Chulalongkorn University, 1984.

————. *Radical Thai Discourse: The Real Face of Thai Feudalism Today*. Ithaca: Cornell University Press, 1987.

————. "Introduction". In *National Identity and Its Defenders: Thailand, 1939–89*, edited by Craig J. Reynolds. Clayton: Monash Papers on Southeast Asia, no. 25, 1991.

Riggs, Fred. *Thailand: The Modernization of a Bureaucratic Polity*. Honolulu: East-West Center Press, 1966.

Robison, Richard, Kevin Hewison, and Garry Rodan. "Political Power in Industrialising Capitalist Societies: Theoretical Approaches". In *Southeast Asia in the 1990s: Authoritarianism, Democracy & Capitalism*, edited by Kevin Hewison, Richard Robison, and Garry Rodan. Sydney: Allen & Unwin, 1993.

"Royal Advice by His Majesty the King", 20 May 1992/2535 at 21:30. Bangkok: Office of His Majesty's Principal Private Secretary, 1992.

Royal Thai Army, Directorate of Civil Affairs. *Army News Announcement: Army Policy and Implementation*. Bangkok, 2 June 1993.

Said, Edward. *Orientalism*. New York: Pantheon, 1978.

Saiyud Kerdphol. *The Struggle for Thailand: Counter-insurgency 1965–1985*. Bangkok: S. Research Centre, 1986.

Saneh Chamarik. *Democracy and Development: A Cultural Perspective*. Bangkok: Local Development Institute, 1993.

Saowarop Panyacheewin. "Seeking answers among the stars". *Bangkok Post*, 16 June 1992, p. 31.

Seiter, Ellen. "Semiotics and Television". In *Channels of Discourse*, edited by Robert C. Allen. Chapel Hill: University of North Carolina Press, 1987.

Serrano, Isagani R., ed. *Civil Society in the Asia-Pacific Region*. Washington, D.C.: Civicus, 1994.

Sharp, Gene. *The Politics of Nonviolent Action, Part Two: The Methods of Nonviolent Action*. Boston: Porter Sargent Publishers, 1973.

————. "Notes for a Presentation to the House Affairs Committee of the Government of Thailand on Anti-Coup Legislation". Mimeographed. Bangkok: Parliament of Thailand, 16 October 1992.

————. "Nonviolent Action and Modern Political Relevance". Mimeographed. Bangkok: Thammasat University, 3 November 1992.

Sirin Palasri. "Why were they anti-Suchinda?". *The Nation*, 23 May 1992, p. A6.

Somsak Kosaisuk. *Labour Against Dictatorship*. Bangkok: Friedrich Ebert Stiftung, Labour Museum Project, Arom Pongpangan Foundation, 1993.

Sophon Rattanakorn. "A Report on the Investigation of the Illegal Use of Power and Survey of Disaster According to the People's Demonstration during 17–20 May 1992 submitted to Prime Minister Anand Panyarachun on 5 August 1992".

Sopon Onkgara. "Soft landing for Kaset & Co?". *The Nation*, 19 July 1992, p. A9.

Sørenson, Georg. "Utopianism in Peace Research: The Gandhian Heritage". *Journal of Peace Research* 29, no. 2 (1992): 135–44.

Sorrayuth Suthassanachinda and Krittia Porasame. "Women behind the strongmen take opposing views on politics". *The Nation*, 18 May 1992, p. A4.

Students' Federation of Thailand. Anti-coup handbook, 1992.

Suchit Bunbongkarn. *The Military in Thai Politics 1981–86*. Singapore: Institute of Southeast Asian Studies, 1987.

————. "Thailand in 1991: Coping with Military Guardianship". *Asian Survey* 32, no. 2 (February 1992): 131–39.

————. "Thailand in 1992: In Search of a Democratic Order". *Asian Survey* 33, no. 2 (February 1993): 218–23.

Sukanya Bumroongsook. "Chulachomklao Royal Military Academy: The Modernization of Military Education in Thailand (1887–1948)". Ph.D. dissertation, Northern Illinois University, 1991.

Sukhumbhand Paribatra. "State and Society in Thailand: How Fragile the Democracy?". *Asian Survey* 33, no. 9 (September 1993): 879–93.

Sulak Sivaraksa. *Siamese Resurgence*. Bangkok: Asian Cultural Forum for Development, 1985, pp. 298–311.

————. *Seeds of Peace*. Bangkok: International Network of Engaged Buddhists, 1992.

Sumalee Bumroongsook. "Mate Selection and Youth in Twentieth Century Central Thailand". Paper presented at the conference on Youth in the Asia-Pacific Region, 30 June–4 July 1992, in Bangkok.

Summy, Ralph. "Democracy and Nonviolence". *Social Alternatives* 12, no. 2 (July 1992): 15–19.

Sunday Post (Bangkok), 16 May 1993, 31 January 1994.

Sungsidh Piriyarangsan and Pasuk Phongpaichit, eds. *Chonchanklang bonkrasae phrachathipatai* [The middle class and Thai democracy]. Bangkok: Chulalongkorn University and Friedrich Ebert Stiftung, 1993.

Sungsidh Piriyarangsan and Pasuk Phongpaichit. "Introduction: The Middle Class and Democracy in Thailand". In *Chonchanklang bonkrasae phrachathipatai* [The middle class and Thai democracy], edited by Sungsidh Piriyarangsan and Pasuk Phongpaichit. Bangkok: Chulalongkorn University and Friedrich Ebert Stiftung, 1993.

Surachart Bamrungsuk. *United States Foreign Policy and Thai Military Rule 1947–1977*. Bangkok: Editions Duang Kamol, 1988.

———. "The Military-Initiated Transition in Thailand: Causes, Conditions, and Costs". Mimeographed. Bangkok: Faculty of Political Science, Chulalongkorn University, 29 July 1991.

Surichai Wun' Gaeo. "The Non-Governmental Development Movement in Thailand". *Asian Exchange Arena* (Hong Kong) 6, nos. 2/3 (March 1989): 59–77.

Surin Maisrikrod. *Thailand's Two General Elections in 1992: Democracy Sustained*. Singapore: Institute of Southeast Asian Studies, 1992.

Surin Maisrikrod and Duncan McCargo. "Electoral Politics: Commercialization and Exclusion". In *Politics in Thailand: Democracy and Participation*, edited by Kevin Hewison. London: Routledge, 1997.

Suthy Prasartset. "Preface". In Somsak Kosaisuk, *Labour Against Dictatorship*. Bangkok: Friedrich Ebert Stiftung, Labour Museum Project, Arom Pongpangan Foundation, 1993.

———. "The Rise of NGOs as a Critical Social Movement in Thailand". In *Thai NGOs: The Continuing Struggle for Democracy*, edited by Jaturong Boonyarattanasoontorn and Gawin Chutima. Bangkok: Thai NGO Support Project, 1995.

Teeranat Karnjana-uksorn. "*Thahan kap thurakit*" [The military and business]. In *Chonchanklang bonkrasae phrachathipatai* [The middle class and Thai democracy], edited by Sungsidh Piriyarangsan and Pasuk Phongpaichit. Bangkok: Chulalongkorn University and Friedrich Ebert Stiftung, 1993.

Thai Development Support Committee. "Special Issue: 47-Day Crisis of the Mass Media under Suchinda's Rule". *TDSC Information Sheets*, no. 4, June 1992.

Thai Volunteer Service. *Directory of Non-governmental Development Organizations in Thailand 1987*. Bangkok: Thai Volunteer Service, 1987.

Thak Chaloemtiarana, ed. *Thai Politics 1932–1957*. Bangkok: Social Science Association, 1978.

Thak Chaloemtiarana. *Thailand: The Politics of Despotic Paternalism*. Bangkok: Thammasat University Press, 1979.

Thongchai Winichakul. *Siam Mapped: A History of the Geo-Body of a Nation.* Honolulu: University of Hawaii Press, 1994.

Tulsathit Taptim. "Same old rhetoric". *The Nation*, 10 May 1992, p. A10.

Uphoff, Norman. "Grassroots Organizations and NGOs in Rural Development: Opportunities with Diminishing States and Expanding Markets". *World Development* 21, no. 4 (1993): 607–22.

Vella, Walter F. *Chaiyo! King Vajiravudh and the Development of Thai Nationalism.* Honolulu: University of Hawaii Press, 1978.

Virilio, Paul. *Speed and Politics: an Essay on Dromology.* New York: Semiotext(e) Foreign Agents Series, 1986.

———. *Popular Defense and Ecological Struggles.* New York: Semiotext(e) Foreign Agents Series, 1990.

Vitit Muntarbhorn and Charles Taylor. *Roads to Democracy: Human Rights and Democratic Development in Thailand.* Montreal: International Centre for Human Rights and Democratic Development, 1994.

Vitoon Panyakul. "Postscript". In *Crisis in Democracy: Report of an International Fact-Finding Mission to Thailand on the Events of 17th–20th May 1992 in Bangkok.* Hong Kong, November 1992.

Wasant Techawongtham. "Saga of missing persons". *Bangkok Post*, 13 December 1992, p. 24.

———. "NGO movement: an angel or a devil?". *Bangkok Post*, 17 October 1993, pp. 20–21.

———. "NGOs and the middle class: More cooperation needed". *Bangkok Post*, 17 October 1993, p. 20.

White, Hayden. *Metahistory: The Historical Imagination in Nineteenth-Century Europe.* Baltimore: Johns Hopkins University Press, 1973.

Wilson, David. *Politics in Thailand.* Ithaca: Cornell University Press, 1962.

Wipawee Otaganonta. "A yuppie mob". *Bangkok Post*, 13 May 1992, p. 28–29.

———. "The conflict between peace and democracy". *Bangkok Post*, 29 June 1992, p. 23.

———. "Anti-red tirades mark ISOC democracy talks". *Bangkok Post*, 31 August 1992, pp. 1–2.

Withoon Ungpraphan. "A Study of Autopsy Reports from the Dead Occurring Because of the May 1992 Incident". Mimeographed. Bangkok, July 1992.

Young, Ernest P. "Imagining the Ancien Regime in the Deng Era". In *Popular Protest and Political Culture in Modern China*, edited by Jeffrey N. Wasserstrom and Elizabeth J. Perry. Boulder: Westview Press, 1992.

INTERVIEWS

Chaisiri Samudavanija, 18 September 1992, in Bangkok.

Chalard Vorachart, 27 March 1993, in Thonburi.

Chalidaporn Songsamphan, 4 July 1992, in Bangkok.

Chamlong Srimuang, 24 November 1992, in Bangkok.

Chermsak Pintong, 1 February 1993, in Bangkok.

Dej Poomkacha, 24 November 1993, in Bangkok.

Gawin Chutima, 24 November 1993, in Bangkok.

Gothom Arya, 4 September 1992, in Bangkok; 19 November 1993, in Bangkok.

Issara Thayahathai, 2 December 1992, in Bangkok.

Karunan, Victor, 18 January 1994, in Patumtani.

Khien Theeravit, 8 April 1993, in Bangkok.

Kritaya Archavanitkul, 24 April 1995, in Thonburi.

Naruemon Thabchumpon, 20 April 1995, in Patumtani.

Nidhi Aeusrivongse, 17 January 1993, Correspondence.

Osolmick, John, 8 June 1992, in Bangkok.

Paiboon Wattanasiritham, 3 December 1993, in Bangkok.

Paisal Wisalo, 12 April 1994, in Laos.

Prapoj Sithep, 1 September 1992, in Phisanoluk.

Prateep Ungsongtham Hata, 21 November 1992, in Bangkok.

Prinya Thewanarumikul, 17 January 1994, in Patumtani.

Prudhisan Jumbala, 5 October 1993, in Bangkok; 27 October 1993, Correspondence.

Ratchai Sasiwat, 28 August 1992, in Sukhothai.

Saiyud Kerdphol, 15 February 1993, in Bangkok.

Sant Hattirat, 18 November 1992, in Bangkok.

Somchai Homla-or, 2 December 1992, in Bangkok; 27 October 1993, in Bangkok.

Suchinda Kraprayoon, 1 March 1994, Testimony at Criminal Court in Bangkok.

Sulak Sivaraksa, 20 January 1993, in Bangkok.

"Support Buddhism and the Monarchy" protest, 17 September 1992, in Bangkok.

Surachart Bumrangsuk, 5 October 1993, in Bangkok.

INDEX

ABOUT THE AUTHOR

WILLIAM A. CALLAHAN is a Lecturer in the Department of Politics at the University of Durham, Great Britian. Formerly the Head of the Philosophy, Politics and Economics Programme at Rangsit University in Thailand, Dr. Callahan has also lectured at the University of Hawaii, and been a visiting professor at Seoul National University. He is the author of *Pollwatching, Elections and Civil Society in Southeast Asia* (1998), and his current research considers the identity politics in Greater China and the discourse of Asian Democracy.